FRAGMENTS OF A LIFE

Bryan Ellery, *Moelwyn Merchant* (bronze); coll. Eton College

FRAGMENTS
OF A
LIFE

Moelwyn Merchant

First Impression—June 1990

ISBN 0 86383 647 X

PRINTED BY
J. D. LEWIS AND SONS LTD., GOMER PRESS, LLANDYSUL, DYFED, WALES

CONTENTS

LIST OF ILLUSTRATIONS

List of Illustrations—Continued

List of Illustrations—Continued

List of Illustrations—Continued

x

List of Illustrations—Continued

ACKNOWLEDGEMENTS

The author's thanks are due

To the aritists who have generously assisted in selecting the works to be illustrated;

To Sarah and Alan Bowness for their assistance with the Barbara Hepworth material;

To Princess Mary de Rackewiltz for her generosity with the material of her father, Ezra Pound;

To Elisabeth Frink for the photographs of her work and to the photographers, Alex Csaky and Jorge Lewinski for permission to reproduce 'Judas', 'Tribute Head' and 'Walking Madonna';

To Mildred Eldridge (Mrs R. S. Thomas) for the landscape painting, 'Hill Sheep';

To Nick Tawney for the photographs of the Bryan Ellery bronze (frontispiece) and 'Confrontation of Angels';

To Eluned Brown for her generous interest throughout and for the photographs of the pictures and sculptures in her collection;

To the community of Eton College and especially the Head Master (Eric Anderson), the School Librarian (Michael Meredith) and Howard Moseley, for their warm interest in the production; and to Cameron Rose for his loan of the slides of John Piper's windows in Eton College Chapel;

To my wife for her patience and for assistance with the proofs of the book;

To both artists and writers for their readiness in allowing letters, poems and articles to be quoted; many of their letters to me are now deposited, with my manuscripts and sculptures in the School Library at Eton College;

And finally my most warm thanks to Huw Lewis and his colleagues at the Gomer Press for their scrupulous care throughout the production.

PREFACE

It has been a great privilege to be in the wings when important matters are performed on stage—and sometimes even to be accorded a small speaking part. To have been rather more than an admiring spectator of Ezra Pound's final months of incarceration in Washington; to have been on the studio floor as Barbara Hepworth, Josef Herman and John Piper created their finest work and to have wandered his beloved Snowdonia with Kyffin Williams, these were high days. It was necessarily only a 'speaking part' for me as some of Alun Hoddinott's largest works were in hand, but there were moments with Christopher Fry and Ted Hughes when words seemed potent—as they did at Yale and Chicago when, with Cleanth Brooks and Nathan Scott, university scholarship was richly significant. All this is what some of my forbears would have called 'uncovenanted grace.'

It is perhaps an arrogant man who essays to write an autobiography and so—with the arrogance of course lurking in the background—I performed evasive tricks: the book was to be called *Troops of Friends* but 'that play' has always been deemed unfortunate and the doomed Macbeth was saying precisely that he couldn't claim such troops. Then it became *Spots of Time* but this seemed impertinently to challenge Wordsworth.

And so *Fragments of a Life*. My many friends are indeed here—I hope more prominently than I—and their words and works constitute the bulk of the book.

This is the reason that 'Agenda' dominate these pages. For this is the record of working men, of poets, quarrymen, painters, dramatists, foundrymen, composers, sculptors, priests and teachers. It is a record of people who demanded that art should be related to the joys and travails of living people, that worship should reverberate into the market-place.

The book is therefore a kind of collage in which artists and writers, craftsmen, academics and priests speak for themselves but with the 'connecting paint', necessary for all collages, of my own narrative, not wholly chronological but moving from topic to topic as my friends direct me.

1

EARLY DAYS

Almost the first experience to remain in detailed freshness in my mind must have occurred in my seventh or eighth year. My maternal grandfather was a tin-worker, a silent, gentle and modest man and I had for a long time been awed by the contrast between those glimpses of him as he returned, exhausted and begrimed from work at the shearing-bench and the scrupulous freshness of his appearance at meal-time or Sunday worship.

I had begged him to allow me to go with him to a day shift to see him at his work and at last he agreed. We walked to the Port Talbot Tin Works and even as a child I realised the change in him, his confident poise, heavy tongs balanced in his hand as he waited for the cherry-red sheet-metal to come out of the searing heat. The sheet was gripped in the pincer jaws, curved into a fold as it was checked in its fall to the ground, and his steel-shod right boot came down with precision, completing the fold in the sheet.

Throughout this initial movement I was kept at some distance, a workmate's arm about my shoulder and I can even now feel the gritty scrunch of cinder dust and metal fragments as I shuffled back from the sudden blasts of hot air. I was deafened and fearful as the huge arm of the shearing blade rose and fell without pause on to the cutting surface. My grandfather again gripped the folded sheet of tinned metal, swung it on to the cutting bench, with double precision—to the exact point where the cut was to be made, fractionally in from the folded edge and, with a more daring precision, to reach this shearing point as the cutting blade swept in its highest arc before descending to the cut itself. Smiling, my grandfather gripped the two sheets which resulted from the cut, held them a moment for my admiration before swinging them on to the heap of sheets at his right side.

His smile told me, even as a child, a great deal about him. Here was his expertise; here in so many ways, was his fulfilment. 'Davy Davies the Shearer' was admired by all his mates as the finally

1

skilled craftsman—and I understood why his fore-arms showed fewer of those scars, heat-burns and dangerous gashes from the blade or the sheet edges than the arms of his fellows in the tin-works.

At a prayer-meeting or Seiat, if asked "to say a few words", he would always refuse, sometimes with no more than a deprecating gesture of his hand; but at the shearing-bench he expressed all the secure certainty of a craftsman's skill achieved over many dangerous years—even he had the scars to prove it.

It was to be nearly half a century before I realised the full import of that child's experience. Now a sculptor and in large part dependent on the skill of other craftsmen, at the bronze foundry, the sheet-metal works, the 'fine-finishers' or the quarryman, I realised that articulacy was not merely persuasive words in the right order; that articulacy could be a gesture; it could reveal itself not on the tongue alone but in the delicate deftness of a craftsman's fingers. And I have known, standing on the foundry floor with Paul Waters, at the finishing-lathe with Jim Olner, at the grinding wheel with Michael Owen, that a questioning glance from the craftsman requires no more than a gesture or nod of the head by the sculptor to establish the stage which the sand-mould or the abrading edge has reached, before the sculptor again takes over. This wordless accord, which I first learnt as a child from 'Davy Davies, Shearer', is one of the ancient and most precious mysteries.

*

Of his wife, my grandmother, Mary Davies, it is much more difficult to write. She was a formidable woman, as handsome in her ninety-fifth year as her wedding photograph shows her to have been in her eighteenth. She had been orphaned at the age of eight and left her immediate Anglican family to be passed from aunt to aunt, becoming successively Independent, re-baptised by total immersion at the age of fourteen, Methodist (the 'Calvinistic Methodism' of Howell Harris and Daniel Rowlands) at sixteen and so, at eighteen, married the equally handsome countryman from Cardiganshire, who had come to try his fortune in the growing industry of Port Talbot.

My mother was the eldest of seven children and, I'm afraid, took from an early age, more than her share of the up-bringing of the other six. My grandmother, largely self-educated, had a keen, quick and dangerously articulate mind—as successive ministers found to their cost when their sermons were subjected to her barrister's scrutiny—and as my brother David and I suffered every Saturday morning as we listened, until we were word-perfect, to her reminiscences of childhood. Some of these gave us invigorating glimpses of a life beyond the reach of Methodism—of my great-uncle Thomas whose macaronic Welsh-English was the valley's delight ("There was the first car, the very *cyntaf*, dashing down the street. 'Stop: *gan bwyll*' said the policeman, but come she went!"); or my scape-grace uncle Will, a truly accomplished poacher who always got away from the keeper by his speed and his ability—beyond the keeper's—to leap the boundary-brook. "Naid go dda, Jenkins" ("A pretty good jump, Jenkins") was his friendly taunt from the other bank.

But these stories suffered under repetition and we were glad when we ceased to have the Saturday errands to perform. My brother and I were also aware of the tensions as Granny Davies used her extraordinary powers to control all the children's marriages except those of my parents. Then came our university and professional days and close contacts became rarer.

There was no doubt that she looked forward to being a hundred years old; (she was never simply 'ninety' but 'in her ninety-first year'). But as she approached her ninety-seventh birthday I was called to her bedside and there heard her last words, phrases she had not used for a life-time: "Duw, trugarha wrthyf" ("Lord, have mercy", "Kyrie eleison"). It was an absolution as the words faded.

*

My paternal grandfather was a quite different personality from my mother's father. Very handsome, trimly bearded and with a broad forehead, his smile was rare but gentle. He had been a coal-miner, working a ten-hour shift after a long climb over the hills to the pit. He told me gravely that for many months in the year he never saw the sun. By his mid-forties his health had broken and he

3

left coal-mining for a clerical job, I believe in insurance. Wholly without aggression, he was the acknowledged intellectual leader of the Methodist community in which I grew up; what Evan Merchant said was almost law and he came into his own as he expounded a theological principle from the Gospels or teased out a knot in a Pauline argument. Our congregation had preserved a debating tradition very like a mediaeval disputation and one of these remains vividly in my memory. The congregation sat in the body of the chapel (strangely named Dyffryn Ajalon) while the two disputants, my grandfather and Richard Llewelyn, a tin-worker, sat above and before us in the 'gallery'. The question in dispute was 'the primacy of prevenient Grace over sacramental Grace' and the exposition and argument went on for over an hour, as we listened spellbound, the weight of rhetoric shifting subtly from side to side. I should be happily prepared to match these two, a tin-worker and a coal-miner, against any two theological-college principals of to-day!

My youth was the day of the great preachers who modelled their rhetoric on the Edwardian actors. The theatre was forbidden to the laity (as novels were also suspect, my mother for many years avoiding them, for they were 'fiction', 'feigning') but the ministers spent some of their holidays in the London theatre, noting the professional skills of Irving or Beerbohm Tree—presumably on grounds analogous to the taking of brandy 'for medicinal purposes'. During these years I listened intently to Brynsiencyn, Cynddylan and Philip Jones of Porth-cawl; but for all their oratory—and I could repeat for you now the outlines of several of their sermons—my grandfather was still for me the standard of exposition.

*

Since my father quite early joined my grandfather in leading the worship and was therefore seated in the dignity of the great pew ('y set-fawr') below the pulpit, my mother and I, and my brother David when he was old enough, joined my grandmother in the family pew. Where my grandfather was a slightly remote figure of dignity, Granny was gentle, silent and generous. The pleated black silk dress, into which I leaned during the sermons, smelt faintly of camphor and more strongly of the peppermint sweets which would be secretly slipped into my mouth if the sermon became tedious.

The same mischievous generosity applied in her garden: their house in Tanygroes Street was near the shop of 'Morgans the Baker'. There I was sent to buy my father's favourite bread, Hovis, which was kept carefully apart from the other bread; for Mrs Morgans deemed it contagious, since she hadn't quite got the significance of wheat-*germ*. When the days were warm I was taken by my grandmother to the bottom of the garden where the gooseberries were ripening to bursting. "These are for eating," she said and they crushed delectably on my palate.

*

My stock, then, seems impeccably Welsh, the coal-mine and the tin-works as the back-drop and the cultivated theology of the worshipping community as the stimulus to social betterment, a schooling and a university career beyond the reach but not the dreams of grandparents.

Still there were family questions to be asked: what was the origin of my grandmother's maiden name, Hardee (kept by my brilliant preacher-uncle, Evan Hardee Merchant)? Her demure sense of fun was more blatantly apparent in her brother, 'Uncle Tom Hardee', whose clear tenor voice and vitality made him welcome in any gathering—especially at the grave-side, when the hymn, 'O fryniau Caersalem'—'From Sion's heights'—was sustained on the clarity of his upper register. In my early teens I was quite unable to assess the tone in which he said to my father one day, as he mourned his increasing deafness: "Oh Willy, there's no pleasure in going to a funeral nowadays, now that I can't hear the singing!"

A greater mystery lurked further back in the family history: where, in this staunchly Welsh family, had we found the name Merchant? There were many theories: a solitary Breton giving us a slightly exotic Celtic strain; a Channel-Islander, whose name, Marquand, had been Anglicised for readier adoption. But the favourite story—carefully left unresearched lest it should be found wanting—was that of a sailor—of course called Marchand—who had been wrecked on the South Wales coast and had settled and married my great-great-grandmother. Gradually a body of domestic legend grew about him, for he was sufficiently distant to make a certain buccaneer quality very desirable, if only to distance us just a little from our dismayingly respectable Methodist contemporaries!

The legends reached my son, Paul, to his great pleasure and in 1981, on our press here in our Leamington house (the Windmill Hill Press), he produced his little sequence of poems, *Clearing Nettles*, exploring his ancestry, with two drawings by our friend Kyffin Williams R.A. The first poem, 'Ancestor', with the frontispiece, gives us exactly the inheritance we dreamed of.

*

I was not even adolescent, a boy of perhaps ten or eleven years, driven at a leisurely pace in my grandmother's primitive Standard through the crooked country roads near Kenfig Pool. We turned a corner at a ruined wall and there was a straight run of perhaps a hundred yards, but alongside a gypsy encampment. It was as well to be wary of children and ambling puppies.

Romanies were a fearful mystery—there had been tales, warnings in rhyme:

> My mother said I never should
> Play with the gypsies in the wood—

and I looked with curiosity at the handful of older men and women at their caravan steps. And then, at the end of the encampment, at the downward slope of empty shafts, she stood, in dark skirt, white blouse and a scarf with careless grace over her black hair.

But it was her eyes, the smile. I suppose only a certain kind of russet apple has that delicate flush beneath the rough light-brown of the skin. It was there; her eyes seemed black but the smile had the frank invitation of an extended hand.

We must have passed her in about five or six seconds but she moved me to a memory that has been vivid over the sixty intervening years. It was of course another country, even though Kenfig was on our doorstep.

*

ANCESTOR

1

Red-bearded pirate
scourge of merchantmen
Guillaume Marchant

Wintering in a Welsh haven
where they turned a blind eye
decided to burn his boat

And made a garden for leeks and potatoes
clearing the nettles
with a rusty cutlass

Carved tiny figures of bone and driftwood
bartered them for penny whistles
with the travelling tinkers

2

A fisherman taught him
where to draw up crabs
with a whelk on a string

He liked to challenge them eye to eye
as they clung to the prize
in the face of death

Then throw them back
enjoying this late flowering
of his milder nature

Kyffin Williams/Paul Merchant, *Clearing Nettles*

7

Childhood, to my adult memory, was a long series of bronchitis and asthma illnesses which kept me in bed for the greater part of every winter. One of the severest illnesses was during the influenza epidemic of 1918-19. In the previous summer I had been taken up the valley which led to Pistyll Cwm-Gwinau ('The Vale of the Wine-like Spring') past the celluloid works which had become a German Prisoner of War camp. My young aunt Blodwen was my guide that day and she wore a German regimental badge as a brooch, which her brother had sent her after the battle of Mametz Woods. Down in the valley at the edge of the stream a German prisoner waved to us and I was fearfully certain that it was a gesture of anger at his recognising the regimental badge as his own. My aunt had difficulty in reassuring me that even a German was unlikely to identify it at the distance of half a mile.

Soon after this I was gravely ill with the influenza which killed so many people stronger than I. Then at dawn one day, as I was recovering a little strength, I heard a fearful rhythmic beat outside the house and my mother ran in to take me to the window to see the German P.O.W.s being marched away to the railway station and to repatriation. A fearful interlude was over.

My bronchial troubles were by no means wholly disadvantageous. I was sent very little to school and I also learned quite early from our family doctor what urbane scholarship could be. For Dr Hubert Phillips was the son of the Dean of St Davids and spent a wholly inexcusable proportion of his visiting time chatting at the edge of my bed. He was a very handsome man with a rich voice and—to my ear—an exaggerated 'English accent', though I knew his Welsh was impeccable. He understood from his own Pembrokeshire boyhood the intellectual richness and confusion of a bilingual upbringing; he knew that the language of our hearth was strictly Welsh but from the age of three I was taught to read English and my parents very early gave me a subscription to Arthur Mee's *Childrens' Encyclopaedia*, then appearing in fortnightly parts. This gave me ample time to read each part before the next appeared and I devoured everything, from Geology (with which I believe I remember it opened) through literature, world history and geography, explorations in science and the wonders of astronomy—a child's university which Dr Phillips shared with me in learned discussion and argument. It was a proud pleasure for me, many years later and just a little while after my ordination, to preach at the handsome parish church of St Theodore where Dr Phillips was church-warden and to have his grave commendation of my sermon as we walked together down the length of the church after the service. More than twenty years had been stripped away.

My weekly treat from the age of about eight was to be given sixpence each Saturday morning to visit Woolworth's to buy one of the classic novels in their hard red and gold covers; I had most of the nineteenth-century novels in this format (*Les Miserables* was in two parts and cost a fortnight's purchasing) but because we had a handsome complete edition of Dickens—with all the plates—I bought none at Woolworth's. I had read all the novels of Dickens before I was ten, with one exception: I cannot remember why *Edwin Drood* was spurned but I can remember that a severe attack of bronchitis in about my eighth year enabled me to read *The Pickwick Papers* in three days. Many of these days in bed were spent in a dream-like isolation in a Crusoe island, created by drawing a linen sheet completely over me, reading in the diffused light which filtered through.

If Hubert Phillips added discrimination and a degree of sophistication to all this reading, my father's telescope gave it literally another dimension, teaching me early and instinctively the quality of awe. On a still and cloudless autumn or winter evening, he would wrap me up carefully and take me to the garden lawn where the telescope stand he had made was already set up, with the telescope strapped into its movable holder. So that the focussing should not be greatly disturbed, I was given a stool to bring me up to my father's height, after he had identified the object he wished me to see.

The Childrens' Encyclopaedia had taught me something of the stars and planets but this was wandering in the heavens themselves. Earlier in the evening we would have consulted the astronomical atlas and the large, linen-mounted star-maps. The mystery of constellations, the wonder of identifying North from the geometry of the Plough, the delicate shift in the pattern of the constellations and the variable brilliance of the stars in Pleiades or the Scorpion, the marvel that their relative distance made the sun and the moon, so vastly different in size, appear of such identical diameter that 'total eclipse' was possible—of all these things my father spoke with a kind of loving possessiveness, as if the ancient knowledge were private to us.

I remember my first eclipse—the grey stillness, the cold and the mystery of the sun's halo of flame; it was fearful and I was glad of its passing, as my earliest forbears would have greeted with relief the lengthening of days after winter. But of one mystery I would never tire. When the moon had waxed or waned to a modest third of its area, the telescope was focussed there. Two marvels now revealed themselves: the 'invisible' area of the quarter or half moon, completing the globe outside the crescent brightness, was now a mysterious greyness; it was *there* but diffidently withdrawn. The still greater marvel was to watch closely the interior of the larger craters on the moon's surface, as the shadows lengthened or withdrew, and my father explained that this was 'sunrise on the moon'. I was transported to a world of unbelievable mystery. It was I believe akin to Wordsworth's sense in the Lakeland that he could feel the world swinging beneath his feet and through space. All this was of course very different from our present astronomy, its mathematics and physics beyond—far beyond!—my intelligence but the early landings on the moon and the racing articulacy of 'The Sky at Night' have lost none of the wonder with which, as a child, I explored the nearer heavens with my father.

*

There is curiously little I can say about my schooling. Our home, 9 York Place, overlooked the Secondary School where my uncle's friend, Philip Burton taught and where, as an undergraduate home from Cardiff, I saw Richard Burton's first substantial performance, in Shakespeare's *King Henry V.*

I did rather well in the 'Eleven-plus', largely because of a 'Life-Story of a Pit Pony' in the English paper. (I dictated it to my father immediately on my return from the examination and I cherish his typewritten copy—the opening words, "It befell me in my old age" reveal very clearly that English was still not my first spoken language.) I went to the Port Talbot County School which was some distance from my home, along the main shopping road of the town and my health improved marginally, probably because of the walking, but I was still—to my pleasure I'm ashamed to say —able to take little part in sport. I did once take a wicket in a House cricket match, the ball bouncing *twice* before sneaking under the extended bat—I suppose a kind of exaggerated 'yorker'; and I did once score a try. I was passed the ball, to my horror, on the half-way line, with an apparently open field before me. I ran in fear for the corner, hearing, it seemed to me, far more than fifteen pairs of boots pounding behind me; sheer terror took me to the corner to cries of derisive delight, especially from those who piled on top of me as I grounded the ball. For the rest of my schooling I succeeded in avoiding any pass that threatened to come my way.

Two debts to my time at 'the County' would be difficult to repay. We were a mixed school and those of us who wished to pursue an arts degree course at the university were denied the superior masculinity of the laboratories and were taught by a majority of women. One, the shy and diffident Miss Lee taught me Botany (Latin and Botany were, strangely, our alternative to the more robust Physics and Chemistry). I have never regretted this and it is still a happiness to recognise a member of the natural order Ranunculaceae, Rosaceae or Scrophulariacae—and some twelve others—and to know such mysteries as osmosis, entered into some sixty years ago. The other and even greater debt was to the Welsh teacher, Miss Thomas, who disciplined my demotic Welsh to the quite exacting standard of the old Higher School Certificate and University entrance. I was the only pupil taking 'Higher' in Welsh and the tutorials I received in the classical metres and the complex rhythms, alliteration and assonances of early bardic *cynghanedd* enabled me to enter a literary world very different from the English classics which were already mine. She introduced me to Middle Welsh and I hope that my translation later for the B.B.C. Third Programme of *Chwedleu Seith Doethon*, (*Tales of the Seven Sages of Rome*) repaid her in part for the care with which she taught me. It was a grounding in the rich structure of the language which served me well when I returned from academic life in England to become vicar of the well-nigh monoglot Welsh parish of Llanddewibrefi.

*

The hinterland of University College, Cardiff in the 'thirties was the South Wales coalfield and the steel industry, with the terrible and growing certainty of the 'depression'. Teaching posts were difficult to get and my parents decided with me that it was prudent to read for two honours degrees as well as for the University Teaching Diploma. It is perhaps worth mentioning, in view of the plight of some graduates today that, though I had honours degrees in English and History and had been President of the Union and Secretary of the National Union of Students, my first interview for a post in a grammar school came after I had applied for eighty-three. Then, when I was appointed two years later (in 1937) to the post of English lecturer in Caerleon Training College, 78% of the students had unemployed fathers and all of them applied to be teachers in Birmingham or London, for there was little hope for them in Wales.

In 1938 I decided to prepare for the priesthood in the Church in Wales. My bishop was the saintly scholar, Dr Joyce, Archbishop of Wales and the Chancellor of the University. He decided that I should not interrupt my teaching career to study at a theological college but to take four years instead of the customary two over the General Ordination Examination, my theological studies to be directed during vacations by Canon Frederic Hood, Principal of Pusey House, Oxford and my pastoral studies to be directed by Father Pridham of the Society of St John the Evangelist—the Cowley Fathers. Each was an astringent experience and I treated the examination as a strictly post-graduate discipline, which the thirteen papers of the General Ordination Examination merited, certainly in those days. I was ordained at St Mary's Church, Monmouth on St Thomas's Day, 1940 and became honorary curate of Caerleon, with care of the adjacent rural parish of Llanhenog.

*

In the year of my ordination I had also been appointed to a lectureship in my old department in University College. The war years were therefore spent in travel between Caerleon and Cardiff, fire-watching at both places and delivering some nine honours lectures each week, apart from tutorials and seminars, with at least three sermons each Sunday at Llanhenog, St Cadoc's, Caerleon and the Caerleon Mental Hospital; it was all very invigorating!

In many ways this was the richest teaching period in my life. The Senior Common Room in Cardiff had three colleagues, Leslie Bethell, Aubrey Johnson and Saunders Lewis, who would have enhanced the academic brilliance of any university. Leslie Bethell, a passionate High Anglican, took warily the influence of Leavis and *Scrutiny* on his literary criticism; a gripping teacher, with a pawky and eccentric wit, he quickly undertook to discipline my critical thinking and extending my sense of liturgy and church history. We firewatched in the University College one night each week and we arranged that our team consisted of about ten of our own undergraduates. So, from ten o'clock until about two we conducted a seminar, usually Shakespeare, the Metaphysicals or modern critical theory, to which piquancy was added by the not infrequent air-raids on Cardiff.

One of these raids caused a tragedy in another of these departmental teams. Our gentle, most unwarlike Heywood Thomas, Professor of French, was at a look-out post at the back of the main building, with one of his undergraduates; it was, I believe, a fragmentation bomb which landed some yards away and the undergraduate fell with a wound in the arm. Professor Thomas was binding this wound when the young man died—the superficial wound had concealed the fact that a larger fragment of shrapnel had fatally entered his side.

*

Bethell's writings, especially *Shakespeare and the Popular Dramatic Tradition* and his full-length study of *A Winter's Tale*, were very influential in his teaching and are still valuable and I was fortunate to be commissioned with him to produce the *Winchester Shakespeare*; we did most of this work and though it was never published, my handling of the illustrations for all the plays, with notes, formed the basis of *Shakespeare and the Artist* a few years later.

Tragically our academic collaboration was all too brief. Bethell died of cancer in his forties and it was my sombre privilege to see him each day of his dying and to wonder at his growth in stature in those last weeks.

Aubrey Johnson, our Professor of Hebrew, was a very different man. Urbane and of scrupulous scholarship, from his deftly-held Baptist beliefs he found our Anglo-Catholicism intriguing and, I believe, slightly amusing! To talk over a point of theology in the light of Old Testament scholarship was an astringent pleasure and I owe a great deal of my wonder at the mystery of 'Trinity in Unity' to his seminal work, 'The One and the Many in Hebrew Thought' which, though much briefer than his other works and especially the important *Sacral Kingship*, established a major tradition in the study of Hebrew thought.

*

And Saunders Lewis—here was a man of wholly different stature again. This elfin, quick-silver personality re-entered academic life into our Department of Welsh, already a Cymric legend. He had taken part in burning the buildings of the newly begun bombing school at Penyberth on the Llŷn peninsula. The pamphlet shared by him and Lewis Valentine, *Why we Burnt the Bombing School*, published by Plaid Cymru in 1936, price three pence, is an important document, deserving a wide circulation. In the first half of the pamphlet, Saunders Lewis, in his six-thousand word statement at the opening of the trial at Caernarfon on 13 October 1936, establishes a remarkable defence:

> The fact that we set fire to the buildings and building materials at the Penrhos Bombing Range is not in dispute. We ourselves were the first to give the Authorities warning of the fire, and we proclaimed to them our responsibility. Yet we hold the conviction that our action was in no wise criminal, and that it was an act forced upon us, that it was done in obedience to conscience and to the moral law, and the responsibility for any loss due to our act is the responsibility of the English Government.

He goes on to declare his willingness to put at risk, for himself and his family, the honourable security of his profession:

I profess the literature of Wales in the University College of Wales at Swansea. That is my professional duty. It is also my pride and my delight. Welsh literature is one of the great literatures of Europe. It is the direct heir in the British Isles of the literary discipline of classical Greece and Rome.

And it is a living, growing literature, and draws its sustenance from a living language and a traditional social life. It was my sense of the inestimable value of this tremendous heirloom of the Welsh Nation that first led me from purely literary work to public affairs, and to the establishment of the Welsh Nationalist Party. For in the University lecture rooms I have not professed a dead literature of antiquarian interest. I have professed the living literature of this Nation. So that this literature has claims on me as a man as well as a teacher. I hold that my action at Penrhos aerodrome on September 8th saves the honour of the University of Wales, for the language and literature of Wales are the very raison d'etre of this University.

Saunders Lewis had already attained distinction in public life, was on the Advisory Committee for Welsh broadcasting and was the originator of the Welsh National Industrial Development Council. And this was no merely 'academic' concern; very movingly he declares his social concern at that time of dire poverty:

In South Wales I have been in constant touch with my un-employed fellow-countrymen and have successfully founded a Club, the membership of which is growing and spreading over Wales, whereby on Thursday of every week a man whose position in life is comfortable gives up his dinner and sends the price of it to provide a three-course dinner for an unemployed fellow-Welshman whose larder on Thursday is empty.

The air ministry had already destroyed Penyberth House, a centre of Welsh literary life in North Wales from the early Renaissance and "a resting place for the Welsh pilgrims to the Isle of Saints, Ynys Enlli, in the Middle Ages. It had associations with Owen Glyndwr. It belonged to the story of Welsh literature. It was a thing of hallowed and secular majesty. It was taken down and utterly destroyed a week before we burnt in its fields the timbers of the vandals who destroyed it."

The anger turns to a bitter irony as he records the refusal of the Air Ministry to consider the Welsh protests, the refusal of the Prime Minister even to receive a delegation of leading churchmen and politicians, and the contrasting action of Government and Ministry at the English protests against establishing similar bombing ranges in Abbotsbury in Dorset, Holy Island in Northumberland and Friskney on the Wash. In every instance the Air Ministry withdrew their proposals:

> Will you try to understand our feelings when we saw the foremost scholars and literary men of England talking of the "sacredness" of duck and swans, and succeeding on that argument in compelling the Air Ministry to withdraw its bombing range, while here in Wales, at the very same time, we were organising a nation-wide protest on behalf of the truly sacred things in Creation—a Nation, its language, its literature, its separate traditions and immemorial ways of Christian life— and we could not get the Government even to receive a deputation to discuss the matter with us? The irony of the contrast is the irony of blasphemy.

The pamphlet grounds its plea on Natural Law and its demands over against the state.

> The moral law recognises the family and the nation to be Moral Persons. They have the qualities and the natural rights of Persons. And by the law of God the essential rights of the family and of the nation, and especially their right to live, are prior to the rights of any State. It is part also of the moral law that no State has the right to use any other national entity merely as means to its own profit, and no State has a right to seek national advantages which would mean genuine harm to any other nation. All that is universal Christian tradition.
>
> It is also Christian tradition that men should obey the moral law rather than the law of a State whenever the two should clash. It is universal Christian tradition that it is the duty of members

16

of a family and of a nation to defend the essential rights of the family and of the nation, and especially it is a duty to preserve the life of a nation, or to defend it from any mortal blow, by all means possible short of taking human life unjustly or breaking the moral law.

Richard Hooker would have agreed warmly with the nature of this plea, as he wrote in *The Laws of Ecclesiastical Polity*:

See we not clearly that obedience of creatures to the Law of Nature is the stay of the whole world.

The verdict at that Caernarfonshire Assize? Guilty—and imprisonment; but there was a more shameful 'verdict': the University of Wales, after the trial, did itself deep dishonour in dismissing Saunders Lewis from his post in University College, Swansea. We in Cardiff, however, were soon the beneficiaries, as Professor Griffith John Williams appointed him to our Department of Welsh, to the enrichment of all our lives. He had already written a novel, much poetry and the finest Welsh plays of his generation and when I returned to Wales I had the very great pleasure of seeing his grand-daughter perform in my favourite of all his plays, *Siwan*.

Yet as he returned to academic life, so ironically he seemed to lose some of his power in Welsh political life. In the pamphlet at his trial he had spoken of the 'aristocratic' quality of Welsh culture and the occasional complaint that the Nationalist Party he had to so great an extent created was "too academic and highbrow". He was also opposed to violent and destructive measures for the attainment of political ends and, perhaps most telling of all, his political views were based on catholic theology. To think in a Christian and 'aristocratic' manner, this was to deny the current exaltation of 'Y Werin' ('the People') as opposed to 'Y Bonedd' ('the Gentry') who had for centuries been the natural patrons of bards and musicians, the springs of classical Welsh culture.

It was therefore difficult for so many of his contemporaries to understand the delicate sophistication and the historical vitality of his kind of Welshness. Yet the wit and the forthrightness were always there. One day I walked into the S.C.R. after giving a lecture

and, quite without thinking greeted him in English. The response
was astringent—and in Welsh:

> "Moelwyn, I'm quite willing to speak with you in French, Italian
> or German—or in Welsh—but never in English."
> "Why, Saunders?"
> "Not one of them is a danger to our language, but the sheer
> power of English, just there over Offa's Dyke, threatens to
> annihilate our Welsh."

It was then that I realised how osmosis can be more than a botanical
or bio-chemical force; that the language of a powerful culture like
English, can, perhaps without the least intention, draw out the very
life of a less powerful culture on its border. The irony here, as I
knew, was that Saunders Lewis was born into the self-conscious
pocket of Welshry in Liverpool and had read his initial degree in
English. He moved with the same easy grace through English
literature as he did in the major European languages—and indeed
with the same sophistication that he savoured their vintages. I was
telling him one day with enthusiasm the pleasure I had had the
previous evening in a bottle of Moulin à Vent and said that I thought
it a good wine.

> "No, not a *good* wine, a *great* wine—and by the way, where did
> you get it?"

When we came to live in Penarth, which was also his home, he
sometimes drove me there, since I had no car in those days. It was
a rare and chastening experience. His vivid conversation never
ceased in the densest traffic, to which he seemed to give a tithe of
his attention. There was a lithe grace about his actions, especially
in gear-changing, that had something balletic in its movements, a
quality I tried to express in a poem I sent him:

> Even to change gear is a ritual gesture;
> the small, intense face, brooding eyes
> wide open for the movement of traffic,
> never a moment's pause in conversation

as ideas run to the swift impulse
of a caustic wit. But gears
are another matter; to change from second
to third involves a small ceremony,
the meshing completed with a graceful
upward flicker of the hand,
wholly unnecessary, wholly gratuitous,
a gracious blessing of technology
or absolution for its very existence.

I was disconcerted to receive a note from him in reply, saying that he was dismayed to realise that I thought him a poseur. I wrote back that the poem had been written in pure affection and I know he believed me.

Many years later, when he was a tragic old man in his nineties, whom Wales had set aside, I telephoned to greet him on his birthday. He barely remembered me but when he understood who I was, with great bitterness he deplored his long life. That such delicacy of insight, such radiant creative vision should have reached that end is, I fear, an indictment of his people.

*

It was the happy custom of University College, Cardiff to send the President of the Union to Europe in the summer vacation before his presidential year, to the annual conferences of International Student Service and the World Student Christian Federation. In the academic year 1933-4, in which I read an honours degree in History, following English honours in the previous year, I was Secretary of the Union and had begun to take an active part in the social work that was being pursued in the devastated coal-mining areas of South Wales, and especially in the Rhondda and Cynon valleys. In particular I was very moved by the work of the Quakers in the valleys and the truly re-creative work of the Maes-yr-haf Settlement. All this interest was to culminate for me the following Easter vacation in a conference I set up in the University College on 'The Problems of a Depressed Industrial Area', attended by senior and junior members of many British universities who now, some of

19

them for the first time, saw for themselves what the mining valleys were suffering.

It is interesting to go back to the publication in 1936 of *Young Minds for Old*, edited by Lincoln Ralphs (then President of the National Union of Students and later a distinguished and influential educationist); it was a series of essays by fourteen members of British universities who had held undergraduate office. The first essay, 'The Socialist Solution' was by R.D. Smith who later became the liveliest of B.B.C. poetry and drama directors and the generous friend of young writers. It was a great pity that his tenure of a chair in Coleraine was so brief. To him, the Socialist creed which he maintained to the end of his life was a living, organic thing:

> Tradition is not a thing anyone can escape. But it is not a fixed, static order: it is a continual development, which preserves what is best in the past and incorporates what is necessary for the present.

and characteristic of Reggie Smith was the ironic disclaimer towards the end of his essay:

> The young Socialists . . . make no extravagant claims about discovering Utopias, and they offer no divinely inspired prophets to point out with the assurance of water-diviners or Boy Scouts the way to a promised land . . . They seek the objectification of ideals which all people, reformist and revolutionary and tory alike, confess to.

When Reggie and his wife, the novelist Olivia Manning, returned from the Balkans and the Middle East, where he taught for the British Council, I saw a good deal of him as we lectured in Stratford and Westham House, Barford. I never saw him ruffled or aggressive, though his views and attitudes were clear and stated without compromise. His theatre direction had the direct clarity of his lecturing and his production of Marlowe's *Edward II* in Canterbury was a valuable and rare experience. We grieved at his death.

Equally brilliant and equally temperate in projecting his deeply-felt views was the second contributor, John Cornford. There was a complete absence of rhetoric in his 'Communism in the University'. It ends with a vision of society which he was tragically not to live to see:

> The changes that are going on now, often imperceptibly, but none the less steadily, will perhaps later assume a national importance that very few of the actors in the present small-scale events realise. But when the next crisis that will strike the whole system explodes, whether it is war crisis, economic crisis, or political crisis, the relatively quiet and petty developments of these pre-war, pre-crisis years, will emerge in their real significance.

My own essay, 'The Undergraduate and the Crisis' came out of my early experiences in Port Talbot, my family background and from my practical experience in the 'unemployed valleys'. I had realised that the University of Wales, founded in the last two decades of the nineteenth century on 'the pennies of the poor' had grown in numbers and status by the determination of desperately poor parents to sacrifice all they could for the education of their children. It was notable therefore that there were few theorists of left or right among my fellows but a fixed determination to see the betterment of society and the alleviation of immediate despair:

> The problem of the University in a Depressed Area is no mere intellectual exercise. It is in fact a crucial test of many of our superficially accepted social axioms whereby it is assumed that education erects almost insurmountable barriers between classes . . . Paradoxically enough the University has been the first partially to abandon the rigidly intellectual position and to be prepared to accept the issue in its human terms without sentimentality, but with no desire to be deflected from its concern by plausible theorising. Where a University is in the closest daily contact with the needs and problems of a community, academic segregation becomes an impossibility.

It was natural therefore that when in the summer of 1934, I went to Paris and on to Bouffémont for the conference of International

Student Service, I was alert to immediate domestic needs and the purely economic problems of other countries, but naively unprepared for the even greater crisis which faced young academics in other countries, in Europe, Africa and the Far East. As a member of the British Standing Committee of I.S.S. I learned the desperate salvage efforts needed to cope with collapsing economies and industrial structures. In Bouffémont these considerations were of course important but marginal; discussion there was violent, breathless, under the impact of Hitler and Mussolini—for the previous year, 1933, was to those young men and women, the passing of a divide. Day after day we heard the appeals of students from Germany, Italy and Eastern Europe that we should heed their plight as the march of totalitarian power seemed inexorable and as they grievously marvelled at our inability, especially in Britain and France, to see the erosion of all moral and intellectual values as Fascism spread.

It seemed to some sections of the conference that this apparent hysteria would repel sympathy; gradually, as the week went on, everyone saw that it was no hysteria but a real grief at the dulled vision of those who seemed to be outsiders. Gradually their appeal prevailed and by the end of the week the whole body of the conference appeared to be welded together, with great emotional power.

Two things made these experiences indelible for me. My background in South Wales had of course made me more receptive to these matters than many of my fellows from Britain, from more affluent parts of the country. But now for the first time I met a movement, *Jocism*, which crystallised and clarified ideas that had been merely embryonic. Jocism (Jeunesse Ouvrière Chrétienne) had begun in Brussels and flourished later in France. Its ideals were manifestly more relevant than ever in the light of our thinking at Bouffémont: an attempt to relate classical moral principles in the Christian tradition to the changing, the revolutionary structure of contemporary industry. Those of us who discussed these ideals with the students who held to Jocism felt that we had been given a clue to the maze of economic and political thought around us. It was three years later, as I studied moral theology formally, that I read—and was startled by—the encyclical of Pope Leo XIII, *Rerum*

Novarum which had inspired early Jocism—and Bouffémont flooded back.

The second clarifying factor for me in the conference was the good fortune that the British delegation had the guidance of the greatly experienced churchman, Canon Tissington Tatlow of St Paul's. 'T' gently—almost austerely—guided discussion among us when it threatened collapse, for behind the austerity there was wit and a cheerful sanctity. For many of us, his ability to relate the grief of the German students at the death of their ideals to the quite different but equally tragic plight of the British unemployed, prepared us, at least in part, for the traumatic wakening to holocaust for Europe in 1938-9. The catastrophe of Czechoslovakia and of the Rhineland now became comprehensible if no less horrifying. 'T' and the I.S.S. Conference were for many of us our second and profoundly important university.

*

Some of us went on from Paris to Geneva to our second congress, that of the World Student Christian Federation. There was a sense in which the W.S.C.F., though very different from the I.S.S. in tone and ideas, had another facet of the same tragic pattern to show us. For here was the Christian exploration of the dilemmas of Europe, the troubled birth-pangs of a new Africa and the turmoil of Asia. As at Bouffémont, senior members of the Congress made our paths clearer if more painful. In my memory, two personalities tower above the rest: Visser t'Hooft, who combined uniquely a clarity in belief and worship with the diplomat's skill of the 'international churchman', and Karl Barth. Karl Barth! and at the height of his powers and influence and we were to hear him each morning expound, clearly and patiently a passage from the *Epistle to the Romans*. It is an experience which remains with me over the years and was a leading influence in my taking Holy Orders. In Barth's slow, so alien Swiss-German, I heard theology that was intellectually exciting and spiritually intense. When, in a year or two afterwards, I acquired the English translation of *Romans* and then his books on Dogmatics, they failed to shake my instinctive Thomism but remained always an outcrop of rock with which my course had always to reckon.

23

For Barth in those critical years was a central figure in European theology and hence, as tragic happenings unfolded, in European politics. Though Swiss by birth he had received a great deal of his university education in Germany and, with the coming of Hitler to major power in 1933, Barth became the intellectual leader of the German church. In the year, 1934, in which we were privileged to hear him, he had shaped the 'Barmen Declaration' at the first synod of the 'Confessing Church', in opposition to the 'German Christians' who compromised with National-Socialism. The Declaration asserted the primacy of Grace, with Christ as the sole foundation of the Church as revealed by the Word. We heard Barth in Geneva, though his smile was still and his seminars quietly unassertive, as a prophetic-figure, an answer to the despairing pleas heard from the German students in Bouffémont.

Very soon, when I had committed myself to intensive study for ordination, Barth's exposition of Reformation theology, his clear definition of the 'primacy of the Word', his astringent debates with Brunner, whom I also found immensely attractive, all these things gave me that necessary tension of thought which I could not find in the faith and worship of my home environment. At the same time it went into a similar tension with the Catholic tradition I found so satisfying, at Pusey House and with the Cowley Fathers.

From the perspective of Geneva, the return to a presidential year at Cardiff was an exciting prospect. There was much work to be done, for I was training for my Teachers' Diploma—admirable opportunities for teaching at the Cardiff High School, whose headmaster, Mr Diamond gave me a remarkably free hand even when I taught in the sixth form. And I was not to lose touch with student affairs in other universities, for I had been elected secretary of the National Union of Students, which involved meetings in London on alternate weekends, catching the 'Milk Train' from Paddington, arriving between 4 and 5 a.m. at Cardiff. Fortunately my brother David had now begun reading for a degree at Cardiff and shared my lodgings. When I had had about three hours' sleep, he woke me and got me to the High School in time for my first lesson at nine o'clock.

*

In the years before the war the National Union of Students allowed graduates of no more than two years' standing to participate in the holiday tours which they offered to undergraduates. You could trek in Iceland, take the Golden Road to Samarkand, cross Europe to Asia and the Great Wall of China. My fiancée and I decided, since we planned to get married in the summer of 1938, that we would take our last chance, in 1937, of the N.U.S. scheme. I had begun teaching in the Queen Elizabeth Grammar School in Carmarthen, had moved after a year to the Newport High School and after just another year had been appointed English lecturer in Caerleon Training College. It was therefore a propitious moment and we decided on a three-week tour which took us through Holland, down the Rhine, on to Innsbruck, to Vienna, down the Danube to Budapesth and then to Lake Balaton, across the Tatras to Prague, a journey by train to Nüremberg and so home again via Holland.

It was now exactly three years since my visits to Paris and Geneva and Europe had moved nearer the abyss. With the alertness of I.S.S. and W.S.C.F. behind me and especially having pursued Karl Barth's prophetic warnings, the route we proposed taking posed grave matters for meditation. We could cope with the natural phenomena which greeted us at Innsbruck, the most vigorous thunder-storm I had ever known seeming to knit the surrounding peaks in a lightning-skein. But this did nothing to prepare us for the bullet holes in Vienna's buildings, the political tensions which faced her in the *Anschluss*. Grinzing was as happily refreshing as ever but the Austrian students had sombre forebodings which the next years fully realised.

Still stranger was our stay at Budapesth. It had its delightful Magyar moments and unforgettable was the result of our wish to go to Mass at the cathedral on the Sunday morning. We entered as the *Kyrie* was about to be sung and were astonished to hear the soloists, the full chorus and the orchestra of the State Opera perform a Haydn Mass to accompany the celebration. It was my first experience of baroque worship at its finest.

But these pleasures were overlaid, often stifled, by the rumbling unease of the political parties who feared equally threats from the east and the north-west. We knew that the very fabric of their political existence was threatened and we became accustomed to the cries and the posters of 'Nem, Nem, Soha!'—'No, No, Never!' It was the same as we went on to Prague. The river, the bridges, the Hradcany were as beautiful as I had expected and Dvořák still echoed from the landscape but over all was the certainty that Hitler was on the move. Czech and Sudeten-Deutsch consciousness was the material for what one sensed to be inevitable conflict and tragedy, and again one knew from student conversation that they felt hopelessly defenceless and sceptical of the goodwill of the rest of Europe. It was the world, the very air of Capek and Kafka.

It had been planned that the tour should come to its climax in Nüremberg. What the tour participants had not realised was the impact on us of arriving in the city just three days before the opening of the Nazi Party Rally. Before the bombing and the turmoil of the war, this was the loveliest of mediaeval German cities, and was it not the home both of Hans Sachs and of my ironic German tutor, Franz Schoberth? Sights and memories had not prepared me for the stilted ugliness and swagger of the uniformed louts by whom the city was infested. We went to one of the preliminary open-air rallies, addressed by a minor and meaner version of Hitler and I found myself astonished that a sensitive and cultivated people could be seduced by such reverberant idiocy.

The ugliest moment came that evening and made us thankful to be leaving the next day. It was a modest inn and a seemly meal and we were I think the only non-German guests. The door was flung open and a young Nazi officer stood in the door, his cold survey of the dining-room a palpable threat; after about half a minute of scrutiny, he flung his arm in salute and barked, 'Heil Hitler.' The response was a muttered raggedness and a few raised arms. We kept our eyes on our meal but were glad when he went.

Just twenty-seven months later we heard that we were at war with Germany.

*

During the academic year 1934-5 my brother David, four years my junior, joined me in my lodgings in Richmond Road and began his degree course. He had different skills from mine; to my love of

26

music he added great ability in his violin playing and spoke with greater insight than I could achieve, of the techniques of performance. He was a fine linguist and though, like me, he read an honours degree in English, he added to it an honours degree in French, and after four years in Cardiff, read for his teachers' diploma in the London Institute of Education.

This all took him to the summer of 1939 and the outbreak of war before he could apply for a teaching post.

I have to confess that I frequently envied him the hardships and dangers of the next five years. We were both committed pacifists but I was already an ordinand, while he entered one of the first training camps of the Friends Ambulance Unit, where he joined many like himself, contact with whom shaped much of his life after the war. There were Stephen Verney, Freddie Temple (now bishops) and Robert Bruce (later a colleague of mine, when he joined our music department at Cardiff). They were all subjected to great moral and emotional strains as they debated among and with themselves the status and actions of pacifists in time of war.

When the Middle East became a major theatre of war, the F.A.U. was sent to Egypt and the desert and my old school friend, Jack Harris, also in the first camps of the F.A.U. and himself of Quaker stock, was sent to Abyssinia.

From David and from Jack Harris there came a constant flow of Airgraphs, those splendid miniaturised letters which could hold so much news. I learnt a great deal about Egypt and the desert and of course much that was newer about Abyssinia; it was David's vivid descriptions of Palestine, which was the Unit's nearest approach to restful relief from desert warfare, that gave me my first immediate and personal insights into the austere beauty of the wilderness of Judah, the brilliance of flowers after rain and the piercing beauty of stars in a desert night.

All this naturally passed the censors but David spoke little of the battlefield, partly for obvious official reasons but I believe even more from reticence which came from their engagement in a delicate moral poise—non-combatants at the heart of the fighting. The consequences were interesting, David and Freddie Temple taking Orders as soon as they were able after the war, Robert Bruce moving to the R.A.F. and winning a D.F.C. and Jack Harris

27

Josef Herman, *Ystradgynlais* (oil), coll. Eluned Brown, Edinburgh

becoming an Adult Education lecturer in the University of Manchester.

On only one occasion after his return to this country was I able to break down, with great difficulty, the reticence that David maintained about the desert campaign. He spoke of Rommel's brilliance in manoeuvre which (I think it was the notorious 'Knightsbridge Box') succeeded in surrounding a tank detachment with the F.A.U. at the centre of the box. The firing on them was therefore from all sides and the F.A.U., engaged in transfusions for the wounded, ran out of blood. Their only remaining resource was their own blood which at least saved some lives until Rommel's stranglehold was broken and they survived.

After ordination, one of David's early positions as a priest was to be a Minor Canon at St Asaph Cathedral, where his musical ability had an outlet and, I believe, some of the mental and spiritual wounds of North Africa were healed.

2

IKON MAKERS

JOSEF HERMAN

"Beauty and I were in long-lasting conflict but not until 1951 did I get the better of it."

"To get to know what is permanent in our feelings is a pretty slow affair."

"The simple tale of human bondage."

"The pride of human labour . . . the fortitude . . . the calm force."

"I hate self-pity. The most tragic things I see as part of being human."

It is tempting to quote extensively from the wise, wry, half-deprecating, asides of Josef Herman as he chronicles his course from Warsaw, through Brussels, Glasgow, Ystradgynlais and Suffolk to the studio in London where his work comes to fruition. His autobiography, *Related Twilights* is a complex account of the first half of his creative life—complex, in that it states, without the artifice of paradox, the tragic and the comic irony in so much of his life. And this tension is without any suggestion of fragility, of snapping under the strain. Hence it happens that Herman's vision of man's tragic destiny, unlike that of Munch (whom he admires) does not issue in a scream of despairing rage. Labouring man is recorded faithfully, compassionately, and without histrionics. His Warsaw childhood is remembered as 'Years of the sun'; but there were clouds. A painting survives from the period, of his father, a cobbler (yet not always so, but brought to his craft by the defaulting of a business partner). It is a still picture, a hammer held above the boot on the last, poised as if in indecision, the face in profile,

29

Josef Herman, *Ystradgynlais* (drawing); coll. the author

Josef Herman, "Memory of Memories"
1. At Home

patient almost to the point of vacancy. This is no visionary recollection but a first step towards Herman's rendering of the "terrible patience of the poor."

Just a week ago as I write this, Paul and I were questioning him about anti-semitism in Poland. "It would be strange if it were not

31

(2) The Story Teller

there. Every child when it reaches the age when suckling should
stop, is told by its mother: 'The Jews have taken away my breasts.'"
This was said in an even, neutral tone, without surface rancour and
we were reminded of an incident from his adolescence. He had
been asked by a painter, Professor S., to pose as Young Orpheus in
an allegorical painting.

'That morning before coming to model I had read in a leading
newspaper an anti-Semitic call to restrict the entry of Jews to
learning. It was signed by some of the better-known anti-Semites
and by Professor S. Now, standing before his picture I remarked:
'With that silver leaf covering my sex nobody will ever guess that

(3) The Old Man

yours is the first circumcised Orpheus in the history of art!' That
was the end of my career as a model.'

*

The menace of Nazism sent him from Poland and the first stage of
his journey was to Belgium, to the world of Permeke, Servaes and

33

(4) After a Pogrom

van den Berghe but the war drove him further, until, in 1940, he reached Glasgow. There the home and studio of Benno Schotz kept for him a tenuous hold on Poland and his Yiddish identity; and this enabled him to produce the astonishing sequence of drawings which he later called his 'Memory of Memories'. I was in his London studio a year or two ago, very soon after the portfolio had come to light again after some forty years. For me it was a vivid insight into a pre-Holocaust Poland I had never expected to see; for Josef, as he turned over the sheets of drawings in almost complete silence, it was a renewed revelation, of tragedy and exaltation.

In November 1984 a very large selection of the drawings was shown in the Ben Uri Gallery in London (it was characteristic of Josef Herman's generosity that he invited me to show a number of my sculptures in the same exhibition) and the following year his 'Memory of Memories' was splendidly shown at the Third Eye

Gallery in Glasgow—they had returned full circle. Agi Katz, the director of the Ben Uri Gallery, describes their range:

> He poured himself into these memories, capturing the fabric of his distant life. This was a time when Herman painted solely Jewish themes. He drew his family, his memory of street musicians, the personalities of the street where he lived in Warsaw. He recorded, in drawings, the singing voices. He illustrated from memory—for he had no books—stories by Peretz and Sholem Aleichem—

and we should add, the rhetoric of the Yiddish theatre ("that theatre, more than anything, was my strongest influence"), a rhetoric of gesture seen very rarely in his later work.

Josef Herman himself, in a foreword to the Glasgow catalogue describes very precisely the mood of these drawings:

> 'I was drawn to depict all I could remember as faithfully as a chronicler, though always in colours and scenes that also expressed my own nostalgia for a vanishing past and a deep sense of sympathy for the millions of Jews who had remained in Eastern Europe and who were being systematically starved, humiliated and extinguished.'

This poised, unrancorous recollection, deeply part of his nature and irradiating his mature art, has a tone heard even when the tragedy touches him so intimately. He said in an interview in the *Jewish Chronicle* in 1966:

> 'In 1942 I learnt that my whole family were exterminated in one day. I do not care to talk about it; I hate self-pity. The most tragic things I see as part of being human.'

The transmutation of tragedy into art is his constant preoccupation, whether in his penetrating criticism of fellow-artists or in tracing the springs of his own insights. It is characteristic of this seamless quality in his work that he wrote in the *Jewish Quarterly* in the Spring of 1980:

35

'Auschwitz, more palpably than the *Inferno* or *King Lear*, declared the helplessness of man in the face of evil; the Jewish artist has taken this tragic destiny and fashioned out of it a body of art which stands beside Dante and Shakespeare and makes the like affirmations.'

*

A radiant interlude separated the Glasgow 'Memories' from the significant period among the Welsh miners of Ystradgynlais. Yet the drawings and the handful of paintings produced in the Highlands and the Western Isles remained unseen until they were shown in Cyril Gerber Fine Art in September 1984. He went first to Skye, in the autumn of 1942 and the profoundest impression was made upon him by the brilliance of the light and the play on the Cuillins:

'At first they looked soft, as though sagging, and the edges were not very clear. Then the outline, too, hardened and the whole splendid mass stood there before my eyes against a soft yellow light . . . To such memories one remains indebted for ever.'

Josef has always written vividly, of people in their daily work, of artists and their craft but—when we remember the comparative rarity of landscape in his own work—some of the most striking of his prose is devoted to the variety of landscape in which he has worked. One of the most vivid is his description of the Scottish fishing villages:

'The recurrent images are still with me . . . A group of fishermen in yellow or black oilskins standing on shore, sitting in the boat or moving about their tasks. A dream-like tranquillity. A planet all its own. In the atmosphere of this planet one forgets the distant hustle and one is reminded of more durable rhythms. Each figure self-contained in a grand form. Each group telling the simple tale of human bondage . . . and all this is happening in slightly moist, soft Highland light . . . In time the Scottish fishermen alongside the Welsh miners and continental peasants were, at least to one man, a source of joy.'

Josef Herman, *The Quay, Arisaig*; coll. Eluned Brown

Now, that passage has the complexity of a novelist's art and the ambiguity of fine verse: 'dream-like tranquillity', 'a planet all its own', 'durable rhythms', 'a grand form' and then, in sharp dissonance, 'the simple tale of human bondage.' From these recollections of the Western Isles we understand more clearly the conjunction in his Warsaw memories of the 'living charm, a hypnotic lore' which he tells us he derived from Chagall, and his tragic union with those who died in the ghetto.

This experience in the Highlands is a too-little regarded element in Herman's work. Toil is dominant: the weight of a catch poised at the hip and straining the torso, the labour of quay-side fuelling, the curved drag of ropes and nets—and all captured in light. The chiaroscuro of Warsaw had been exorcised and the depths of the coal-pit had not yet been explored. It was a tranquil interlude.

*

37

Josef Herman, *The Miner*

Before his arrival, in 1944, at the Welsh mining village of
Ystradgynlais, Josef Herman's philosophy of his art had already
begun to mature. Of Permeke and the other Flemish painters he
had met on first leaving Poland, he could now say:

> 'Their pictures carry their iconography to a moral depth and this
> is more than painting for aesthetic ends.'

Life with the miners of South Wales confirmed this moral purpose for Josef Herman, and Dr Jack Lindsay (for some years a near neighbour of the Hermans in the Suffolk countryside) summarises the qualities of the new work that emerged:

'By discovering the miner as a concrete type, Herman had discovered himself as an artist with a deep distinctive view of reality. He was no longer looking back to the past; he had recreated the past in a more comprehensive vision of the present.' [Introduction to the 1975 retrospective exhibition, at Glasgow, Edinburgh and Cardiff]

It is characteristic of Herman that this new maturity is seen in terms of his craft:

'Between 1944 and 1951 my way of drawing was under the shadow of Rembrandt's pictorial ways. From 1951, as I now see it, my drawings became more sculptural, my works more controlled for that sculptural end, the contrasts stronger and the line lost all remnant of 'beauty', a thing I did not regret. Beauty and I were in long-lasting conflict but not until 1951 did I get the better of it.'

He settled rapidly in Ystradgynlais, living at first in the Pen-y-Bont inn and then converting a derelict 'pop factory' to a studio and living space. Very soon the toil of the miner was one with the artist's craft, producing an unique account of an industrial community, all the more valuable today in coal-mining's tragic decline.

These works are no mere exercise in industrial archaeology. In *Related Twilights* Herman quotes with approval Munch's credo for his own paintings and their subjects:

'They must be living people who breathe, feel, suffer and love. I will paint a series of such pictures in which people will have to recognise the holy element and bow their heads before it as though in church.'

Herman gives a more penetrating account of his own ideal when he wrote:

Josef Herman, *The Miner*

'I always desired the timeless moment when life stands still and this endlessness I try to paint.'

This 'arrested eternity' is present in the haggard features and the tragic endurance of old age in the Warsaw drawings; in some of the Highland studies a fisherman's toil is poised, suspended for our contemplation; but it pervades all the South Wales drawings—and it has never left him as he explores the labours of vine-dressers, potato-pickers, the peasants of Mexico or Spain and those framed in the antiquity of Greece and Israel.

Herman's subject is never merely 'toil' and these Ystradgynlais studies have sharp particularity and clear definition; 'Miner' is a toiler of epic dignity, the grime an honourable mask; the working postures are all explored, crouched with a pick at the coal-seam, pushing the underground trucks, squatting at the foot of a wall or relaxed in the leisured parody of the cramped attitudes of coal-cutting. And about them and their families, the landscape, dominated by two eminences, the man-made waste-tip and the God-made Craig-y-Farteg, 'a monument to endurance and silence.'

It was probably rash of me to suggest that landscape featured less prominently than man in Josef Herman's work. The truth is that man and the landscape that frames (even enshrines) him are so fused as to be inseparable. In his essay 'A Welsh Mining Village' (printed in the catalogue of the Welsh Arts Council's exhibition in 1962 and reprinted in *Related Twilights*) Herman searches for the analogues which will focus and define for him the quality of the Welsh miner.

'The miner is the man of Ystradgynlais.

Already in his appearance, although at first sight liken to other workers, the miner is more impressive and singular. Sometimes I thought of old Egyptian carvings walking between sky and earth, or dark rocks fashioned into glorious human shapes, or heavy logs in which a primitive hand had tried to synthesise the pride of human labour and the calm force which promises to guard its dignity.

It would be true to say that the miner is the walking monument of labour.'

41

Yet, behind this perception of the miner's monumentality extends the landscape, eroded, burnt, erupting in waste-tips, bearing in both light and shadow its own peculiar mystery, impregnated by the human struggle of which it is the setting; hence Herman's judgment of his own art:

'Endurance and silence are as frequently in my landscapes as in my figure-paintings. I do not need a war to make me think of heroism. It is our endurance of the everyday.'

If Ystradgynlais is the landscape, the prose in which it is described is painterly:

'Violet roofs at the foot of green hills. Pyramids of black tips surrounded by cloud-like trees the colour of a dark bottle.'

while the single dramatic moment is swiftly captured:

'A woman walking on the bridge at the end of the street, the wind blowing against her: the white shawl rises from her shoulders and spreads like two huge wings.'

and there is the dramatist's ear for the acute turn of speech:

'There you are' said to me a man with a soft voice of secrecy, 'such is life here, mostly grey but there is also a drop of gold in it.'

Though life and work for Herman's eleven years at Ystradgynlais rarely lost his perception that "The pain of living must never be too far from artistic expression", this was always transfigured by the visionary quality, which we see in this passage from *Related Twilights*. It describes the first impact on him of the "images which were crucial to my decision to stay there."

'It was in 1944, either a June or July day . . . I vividly recall the heat of that afternoon and how deeply I was struck by the quiet of the village around me.

There was hardly a soul to be seen. In the distance low hills a

42

copper-coloured sky—how often I later returned to the colour and mood of that sky! Its light reddened the stone walls of the cottages and the outlines of the stark trees. The railings and the cement blocks of the bridge had golden contours.

Under the bridge, out of a cold shadow, trickled a pool of water which got thinner and thinner as it ran on amidst the dry stones and glittering pebbles. Then, unexpectedly, as though from nowhere, a group of miners stepped onto the bridge. For a split second their heads appeared against the full body of the sun, as against a yellow disc—the whole image was not unlike an icon depicting the saints with their haloes. With the light around them, the silhouettes of the miners were almost black. With rapid steps they crossed the bridge and like frightened cats tore themselves away from one another, each going his own way. The magnificance of this scene overwhelmed me . . .

This image of the miners on the bridge against that glowing sky mystified me for years with its mixture of sadness and grandeur and it became the source of my work for years to come.'

*

The issue of the *Radio Times* for Friday, 20 January 1961 records that at seven o'clock on the Welsh Home Service there was to be a discussion, directed by Dyfnallt Morgan, the subject, 'The Springs of Creation' and the participants, Josef Herman, Daniel Jones, Gwyn Jones, Jonah Jones and Moelwyn Merchant. The *Radio Times* further promised answers to the two questions: What are the impulses which prompt certain people to find a creative outlet in some branch or other of the arts? and, Do they stem from emotion or is the process a rational one?—pretty comprehensive, for wide exploration, and I have no doubt that Daniel Jones, then at the height of his music composition and Jonah Jones, still articulately remembering his work at the Eric Gill studio, would have been noble foils to Josef Herman. Unfortunately, I can remember nothing of the discussion! The broadcast's sole significance for me is that it was the occasion of my first meeting with Josef Herman and began the closest possible friendship which has lasted, to my great enrichment, for over a quarter century.

He had now left Ystradgynlais (in 1955), first for London and then later in the year of the broadcast, for Holly Lodge in Little Cornard, Suffolk. Fortunately we were both members of the Welsh Committee of the Arts Council—forerunner of the Welsh Arts Council—and met as often as he felt he could afford the three days from his studio which a meeting in Cardiff cost him. One such meeting took place on 3 May 1963; the topics for consideration could not have been very engrossing, for, as I sat next to Josef, I found him engaged in covering a sheet of our scribbling-paper with a pattern of eight drawings, which included a labourer in a landscape, a mother (even in the two or three square inches, a Mexican or Spanish mother) carrying her child, and two men—I should say from Ystradgynlais, —in animated conversation. I saw his hand poised above the sheet, about to crush it into a ball and interposed my hand: "May I have it?" He replied in a puzzled "Of course" and, framed, it stands before me as I write, probably the most valuable product of that committee in those years!

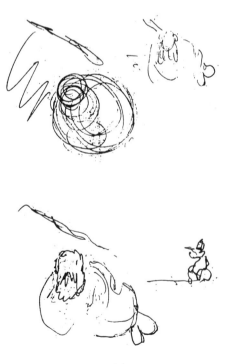

Josef Herman, *Lear Destroyed* (4 drawings); coll. the author

45

In 1963 the world of literature was girding itself for the Shakespeare Quater-centenary the following year. Because I had written *Shakespeare and the Artist* (O.U.P. 1959) Gabriel White of the Arts Council of Great Britain invited me to prepare an exhibition for the A.C.G.B. headquarters to celebrate Shakespeare's four hundredth birthday. Since the argument of my book had been that the world of Shakespeare criticism had been too verbally dominated and that academic criticism could learn a great deal from artists, designers for the stage and book illustrators, I greatly welcomed this opportunity to demonstrate the force of what I had called 'visual criticism', and two further things emerged from conversation with Gabriel White which confirmed my purpose for the exhibition. The first was the assurance that funds would be ample to enable us to gather in London the finest of the Shakespeare visual material; the second inducement from my point of view was the ready agreement to my request that I be allowed to commission an entirely new work to conclude the material of the exhibition. The sole condition was that the Arts Council should approve my choice of artist; I assured Mr White that they would have no difficulty in approving, since I proposed inviting Josef Herman.

Josef had done little or nothing of this kind since his nineteen-forties recollections of Yiddish plays and novelists. Though I knew of his devoted reading in at least four languages, I knew too that he held literature and the visual arts at some distance from each other. He expressed this very vividly in an essay I invited him to write for *Essays and Studies,* (English Association and John Murray, 1977):

> I learnt to read at the age of four . . . since then there has hardly been a day during which I have not read something . . .
>
> Yet, however my mind may have been instructed—I love ideas—my heart remained illiterate and essentially primitive.

Those who know Josef Herman's command of European literature will smile at that word 'illiterate'. He gave the explanation:

> Reading absorbs me completely, my imagination and all; but it does not urge me to work. The urgent flame which makes me

paint must come from life itself. I paint emotions which I do not find in reading. In this too I am a primitive. Painting has come down to us from pre-lingual times. Still today it is akin to dancing or miming, a 'silent language' with its own basic signs.

Though this was written fourteen years after my invitation to him to paint a picture for my exhibition and he had never spoken of the subject with this clarity, I felt that I was on difficult ground. Herman describes our first meeting on the subject:

'What about something from *Lear*?' Merchant asked, hinting, perhaps suggesting, perhaps trying to stimulate my emotions. 'Maybe, yes, this appeals to me . . . something from *Lear*,' I mumbled. The weekend ended and Merchant left.

I had not long to wait before preliminary drawings came my way. It is invaluable to hear in Herman's own words the process by which this came about:

I read and re-read *Lear* about a dozen times. The more I read it the more I was convinced that following the text would lead me nowhere, to an illustration perhaps, but nothing more significant. I put the book aside and began brooding over something more like a synthesis. In this mood I was sitting at a table facing a blank page. Half dreaming I felt my hand making circular movements . . . I soon had the shape of a bundle. A sad, human bundle. Now I got excited, my imagination 'inflamed' in the way Delacroix so thoughtfully described the process. Now I saw clearly everything I had to draw. Eventually the human bundle lay passively midst rocks and stones on bare earth, a heath on which nothing could grow.

These first sketches I now have at my hand as I write and they still seem to grope towards the tragic vision. At length they emerged into the clarity of two or three stark drawings (pp. 44-5).

With this much to go by, I began painting. In the distance, far from the human bundle, on the horizon, I painted the Fool sitting on a low heap of pebbles, playing a flute, totally unconcerned with Lear's fate. The sky, lyrical and soft, an eventide all rose and red, the colour of a peach; like the Fool, nature too was unconcerned with Lear's lot. Lear was intensely alone.

Now, this is strangely ambiguous. It is Josef Herman's practice in painting to lay down a ground which establishes the 'tone of the painting' and then, eschewing the inert media so regularly used today, he paints in a very large number of glazes which allow colours and tones to glow through. In the final painting of 'Lear', Herman had laid down a very hot ground, a glowing earth-base to the whole painting which would burn through the glazes which carried the central image of the king in his desolation. Does it matter which was his intention?—a hostile desert environment, establishing hostility to the tragic king, or a radiant nature, 'unconcerned with Lear's lot.' This ambiguity, the holding of disparate truths, is found in all great art.

Finally, Herman summarises the central quality of the completed painting:

> There exists no such scene in Shakespeare's *King Lear*. But everything in the second act suggests the gradual intensification of Lear's loneliness and grief which culminates in the wretchedness of madness. Except for the moment of dying, human isolation can go no further.

This work, 'Lear Destroyed', has all the gravity, the compassion, the desolate sense of human tragedy and the nobility of its endurance, which we saw throughout the Glasgow and the South Wales studies. Herman's own personal experience of tragedy, setting aside all self-pity and dramatisation, distils into his work a sympathy and an epic grandeur exceedingly rare in contemporary art. It is not uncharacteristic of his intuition concerning the arts that *Lear*, like the miners, gave him a vision of noble endurance, and that in music a constant revelation for him is the austere grandeur of Sibelius's second symphony and the choral entry in Beethoven's 'Ninth', the Ode to Joy. His own art has the same equipoise, of passion with patience, of toil with tranquillity. Few have so nobly rendered the joy and the pain of human endurance.

*

Related Twilights is the record of a life reaching towards maturity; it is also a critical account of Herman's contemporaries in art; above all it frames a series of word-pictures, from Mexico, Spain, France or Israel, in which a candid and apparently wholly unprejudiced eye looks at man in his landscape—or seascape—of toil. When we have learned to live with the Herman of Warsaw, Glasgow and the Welsh mining valleys, we are in part prepared for his search into the heart of alien cultures which miraculously become his own. There is a quality of syncretism in his make-up which reaches out to any peasant labourer anywhere, explores his life and adopts it as part of his own. Hence the unique power of his art, whether in words, line or paint.

In the chapter 'A Mexican Village' he tells the legend of Diego the outcast wanderer. His mystery is prepared for with a bardic skill:

> The mountains divided and a narrow creek between them was visible, opening into a vast plain studded with a variety of wild cactus, all dark and green . . . In no other place have I felt so much a stranger, no other place has ever seemed to me so impenetrable and so mysterious. Now the sun was one circle of fire. A rider was moving in our direction across the plain with the sun behind him . . . In the plain the rider looked small and insignificant but when he came nearer he was majestic . . . He had a calm face, only his eyes spoke. He looked at me and I felt sad. I returned his greeting. He exchanged a few words with Roberts in that strange-sounding patois and went on his way.

The sequel to that opening is just four pages long; it might have been novel-length.

If there is one figure wholly complementary to the miner in Herman's work, it is the vine-dresser. It has haunted me since I saw the sombre dark-hued landscape with the solitary figures bent to the pruning, in the painting in Cardiff's National Museum. It takes its original setting in the chapter called 'La Rochepot', and again the landscape has the definition of a finished painting.

> The whole panorama was coloured in various shades of copper ... The vast fields were the colour of a biscuit, and the symmetrical, long, low rows of twisted bushes were either dark grey, or black as charcoal: no sign of a leaf on any of them.
>
> Behind lay the vague outline of the hills, smooth in texture, their colours ranging from ochre to vermilion. And beyond them rose the hard walls of the mountains, as hard as the figures of the peasants who bent over the vines.

'Figures bent': it is Herman's invariable rendering of toil: bent over the cobbler's last, bent at the coal face, bent at the potato picking, bent at the drawn net, and, in the solitary labour of the vineyard, bent over the branches and the pruning-knife:

> Watching a figure bent over the low vines, noting the rhythm of his hands—one holding shears, the other the twig to be cut— reminds me of some sacred ritual ... Should I succeed in synthesizing its grandeur, I could call it justly 'Pruning the Vine' and be certain that it is a poetic record of all such incidents, that I have captured the universal in the particular.

Israel made on him a special demand, stirring in the blood but with an ironic denial of the expected pattern. The potentially tragic ambiguity is captured in one vivid paragraph:

> To sit on the white stones of the Judean hills, at twilight, when all matter merges in the finest shades with the air, and the late sunlight pours all over the valley, gilding the rocks with the sheen of mirrors, warming the landscape into a glowing red as though seen through a bottle of wine, to sit in this atmosphere and contemplate the antiquity of the land—it is a temptation difficult to resist. For even more than Greece, Italy or Spain, the atmosphere of Israel is heavy with the ever-presence of history. Yet immediately below the eye, and beneath the pearly wall of hills, Israel has the faint buzz and all the appearance of an unfinished factory.

Josef Herman, *Pruning the Vines*

Josef Herman, *Yemenite Girl*

51

But for all the ambiguity and the irony, Herman reaches a humane judgment on the citizens of Israel:

> On the whole life was neither lavish nor rich . . . For the incentive here is neither milk nor honey. It is something more fundamental . . . It springs from the group feeling which reassures the individual that he is not alone on this forsaken earth.

And this was the intuition he had learnt in the ghetto, in Glasgow, in Mallaig or Stornoway and in the broken landscape of the coal-pits. The pattern, whether he writes or paints, is of a piece, heroic in its understanding of man's brevity and toil.

*

In 1968-9 Josef Herman's travels in Mexico, studying its rural art and, more important perhaps, the life of the peasants, had impressed him deeply. In a letter to me from Little Cornard the following year, he places this Mexican experience in relation to his life in South Wales:

> I am still in Mexico! Whatever I paint bears some relation to my experience of this continent. I must have absorbed more than I thought I did. When in Mexico I could hardly make a decent drawing. Painting was out of the question. I was too ill. Then two years later and like a flood it came wildly dashing out of me. Subject after subject. The ways of creation are indeed very obscure. A mystery to me. After Wales it is the second great experience in my professional life. And so I am swaying from miners to Indian peasants, from the rich Welsh twilight to Mexican dawns.

This is a remarkable conjunction 'miners to Indian peasants' —and the relationship between them seen as one of the two 'great experiences of his professional life.' Again the imaginative compassion which gave him the insight to make this relationship is expressed in terms of his craft and its handling of atmospheric

Josef Herman, drawings on Post Cards, sent to the author from Spain.

landscape. But unspoken is the constant social concern, the moral values which gave these toilers their final significance for him.

During the miners' strike of '84-'85 he and I spoke a great deal about the issues involved. He deplored the violence even more than I did; more deeply he grieved at the destruction of the miner's way of life and the communities which enshrined it. But this was—as always for him—expressed mildly, apparently without passion, but it was clear, as he spoke of his memories of hardship, danger, and the deep affections he had known in Ystradgynlais that he was more deeply stirred by this tragic strike than he could well express.

Throughout the 'sixties and 'seventies the related topic that drove him to draw and to paint in urgent protest was that of nuclear disarmament. The ironic distaste with which he repeated the barbaric clichés—'balance of terror', 'limited aggression', 'the nuclear shield' —expressed a little of the emotional energy that marks some of his finest paintings of these later years.

The first concrete knowedge I had of the power of this conviction of his came with a reproduction of his large painting, 'Aldermaston', shown in London and Zurich in 1963. It is a massive work (beyond its canvas size of three feet by four); a vast crowd of marchers curves through the body of the picture and—in affectionate parody of Trades-Union processions,—three large banners dominate the protesters: the first, almost black, with the CND device in white covering its surface; the second in plain red, without any device; and the third, cutting vertically through the horizon, an intense blue with a black cross extending through its whole height. The people and the symbols are left to formulate their own rhetoric and the single-word title sufficiently expresses its purpose.

At Christmas 1982 I received from him the card which he had drawn for the two organisations, Jews Organised for a Nuclear Arms Halt (JONAH) and Artists for Nuclear Disarmament (AND). It is a dove with an olive branch emerging out of a dark chaos, and we are brought up sharply, out of its serenity, when we open the card to read the verse from a Negro folk-song:

> God gave Noah
> The Rainbow Sign:

No more water—
The fire next time!

and, in Josef's Hebrew characters, the recipients of the card are wished 'a year of peace.'

At this present time his studio is dominated by a very large panoramic picture and the many studies of its 'subject matter'. In a letter written in the very early morning of 19 November 1986, he told me:

'At the moment am very involved with the large panel, a sort of symbolic homage to the women of Greenham Common. It is going so well that I am praying—well, a sort of praying—for things to continue this way. This of course, depends very little on me. It is already bright enough to start painting.'

The tenderness of a woman with her child, the bitter contrasts of barbed wire and rich plant-growth, the conflict of symbols, of war and peace, these are again stated in the rich, unrhetorical manner which is the most moving quality of Josef Herman's work. It will always be for him 'bright enough to start painting'.

Joseph Herman. Drawing for the Catalogue of an exhibition "Homage to the Women of Greenham Common", the Angela Flowers Gallery, London, 1989.

The 'forties and 'fifties were lively times in the Church in Wales, with a very vigorous group of young clerics, all friends and of similar age, and determined to establish a thoroughly Welsh and Catholic Anglicanism in a tradition which we knew united us with the rich literary, artistic and liturgical tradition of mediaeval Wales. The *Western Mail* at this time commissioned a series of ten biographies of these young clergymen with portraits by David Bell, then Director of the Glynn Vivian Gallery in Swansea and Art Director of the Welsh Committee of the Arts Council. Nine of these essays were written by me and the tenth (in which I was the subject) by G.O.William, later Archbishop of Wales. All were unsigned. (Most of these young men very soon became Deans and Bishops in the Church in Wales.)

During this time a church youth organisation, 'Cymry'r Groes', was set up and I founded and edited its magazine of the same name. In it I aimed to print the best poetry, art and literary criticism (my colleague Leslie Bethell in University College wrote a regular film review) and indeed any topic from ecology to brass rubbing which had any bearing on the young person's perception of theological relevance was seized upon. Among the early contributors were Norman Nicholson and Anne Ridler and we were fortunate that the church authorities allowed me substantial funds to maintain a quite lavishly illustrated magazine.

Editing *Cymry'r Groes* led directly to one of my closest friendships, John Piper had already become one of our best-known painters, both as a 'war artist' and the considerable commission from the Queen (the present Queen Mother) to record the great variety of Windsor Castle architecture. I had seen reproductions of his early work, including some of the Windsor drawings in the volume devoted to Piper in the Penguin series, 'Modern Painters', and in the introduction read that his wife's maiden name was Myfanwy Evans, and that much of his landscape painting was produced in Wales. This led to my writing to him, enclosing the early copies of the magazine, and asking if he would write me an article. He replied at once (14 January 1946) offering me an illustrated article, 'The Artist and the Church' which, with its plates would occupy eight pages of the magazine. Though at the time deeply involved

David Bell, *Moelwyn Merchant* (pencil), coll. the Author.

with designs and sets for a Britten opera *The Rape of Lucretia*
(produced at Glyndebourne by Eric Crozier) the material arrived
promptly and the article appeared in the July issue that same year.
With very direct simplicity he laid down his principles for 'religious
art':

There is a feeling that art in church must *teach*; but surely if it is good art, it does teach, without laying down laws or doctrines, or telling stories that may be better said in words. If we apply the same rules to art in church as we apply to the more naturally abstract art of music—if we say that it must be good, and must be done to the glory of God, then that is as far as we need go.

There is an admirable summary of Rouault's art (and a reproduction of his 'Crucifixion' lithograph) and the article concludes:

It is indeed a wide and unsafe bridge that has to be crossed before the best artists do their best work for the Church. But there is hope that it might be done. If any churchman of authority knows a good artist who is a sincere Christian—let him give that artist his head!

Very soon I was invited to meet the Pipers before the opening of an exhibition of his at the Leicester Galleries. I waited for them on the doorstep and was introduced to the other visitors to this very private show: Henry Moore, Mr and Mrs Graham Sutherland, William Coldstream and Philip Hendy—I believe there had been that afternoon a meeting of the Tate Gallery trustees; whatever the occasion of their gathering, if a bomb had dropped that evening on that gallery at Leicester Square, a major part of British art would have been wiped out.

Unaccustomed to all this distinction I withdrew into a corner of the main gallery, to hear a quiet voice at my side: "Would you like to come around the show with me? I've not yet seen these pictures" and for half an hour I was treated to a warm-hearted commentary on all the pictures by Henry Moore. His consideration for my diffidence and the generosity of his comments on Piper's work I was to learn were wholly characteristic of him.

That night I slept (the first of many times) on a bed in the studio, beneath two large landscapes in oils and within the warmth of the Tortoise stove. It was very splendid to wake the next morning to the presence of some forty or fifty Piper works and to realise, more strongly than in the show the previous day, the impact of their intense vitality.

Very soon I had an even richer opportunity to understand his profound commitment to English landscape and architecture. Rupert Hart-Davis invited us both to prepare an illustrated edition of Wordsworth's *Guide to the Lakes* and in the autumn of 1950 we set out to explore the whole of the Lake District, making the Salutation Hotel our headquarters. It was an excellent omen that the engravings in the entrance-hall of the hotel were Wilkinson's views of the Lakes which had accompanied the first appearance of the *Guide* in 1810. Wordsworth's essay was an anonymous introduction to *Select Views in Cumberland, Westmoreland, and Lancashire by the Rev. Joseph Wilkinson* . . . and published by Ackermann. It was not until 1820 that it appeared as Wordsworth's work to accompany his volume of verse, *The River Duddon*.

My briefing was formidable. For weeks before our visit I had read large numbers of the eighteenth—and early nineteenth-century *Guides* and had to be prepared to tell John before we started out each day what artists had worked at that lakeside and what literary association it had. We began our quest for 'prospects' on a hill to the south of Windermere. John swiftly sketched the terrain in ink and then drew the shrubs and hedgerows in the foreground. His method intrigued me by its simplicity: the trunks and branches were drawn swiftly and dipping his thumb in a knot-hole in our bench (it has been raining, as it did almost throughout our visit) he pressed it on the still wet indian ink, spreading foliage over the naked branches. I was naively astonished: "That's a remarkable trick!" "Ah, you should see the effects I get with butter!"

Every day I learned techniques in a field quite unknown to me until then: 'stopping-out' with sharpened candle and greasy crayon before washing the paper with diluted ink—at the crags about Wastwater this produced a powerful effect, dramatically enhanced by his use, in the next stage, of collages built up with marbled paper of his own making. Processes familiar enough to artists were to me a kind of magic, splendid mysteries, as I realised with what atmospheric intensity a landscape could be rendered in a very few minutes, capturing a mood with more than photographic fidelity.

We were fortunate after some four days to capture a true Wordsworthian moment. I had pestered John every day since we arrived to find the lakeside where Wordsworth had stolen a skiff

John Piper: Drawings for *Wordsworth's Guide to the Lakes.*
(1) Loughrigg Tarn   (2) Duddon Valley
(3) Styebarrow Crags, Ullswater   (4) Wastwater Screes

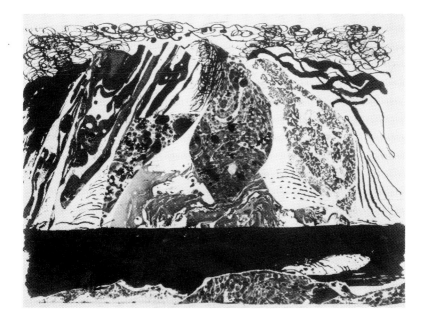

and, on rowing out into the lake, had been menaced by the towering mass of a mountain behind him:

As I rose upon the stroke, my Boat
Went heaving through the water, like a Swan
When from behind the craggy Steep, till then
The bound of the horizon, a huge Cliff,
As if with voluntary power instinct,
Uprear'd its head, I struck, and struck again,
And, growing still in stature, the huge Cliff
Rose up between me and the stars, and still,
With measur'd motion, like a living thing,
Strode after me.
(*The Prelude*, Bk I)

John had been curiously reluctant to make this secular pilgrimage but agreed at last. To our amused astonishment, when we arrived at the shore, *there* was a skiff, in the very spot from which Wordsworth might have taken it. The drawing (omitting the small craft) and the subsequent collage from which the plate was made for printing, had an irony absent from the other drawings; for the reeds which fringed the lake were rendered in staves of music cut from Victorian sentimental songs—this one had the title, 'Oh come where waters shine' —my importunity had been repaid.

The resulting book was handsome in its miniature way.

*

My visits to Fawley Bottom were now more frequent and I began to realise that for all John Piper's power in painting landscape and secular architecture, his insight into ecclesiastical architecture was perhaps profounder. Indeed, in many ways, his designs for stained glass, transmuted by the skills of Patrick Reyntiens into radiant ikons, seem to me to be the summit of his work. I was truly fortunate to have been intimately concerned with four of these works.

During the German bombing of Plymouth the centre of the town had been devastated and St Andrew's Church left a gutted shell.

John Piper was commissioned to fill the windows again with stained glass, the climax of the work to be the 'St Andrew' window. He determined on a double cruciform pattern, a traditional cross imposed on the mullions of the window, with, superimposed upon that, the 'Saltire', the Cross of St Andrew which was formed by the intersection of the 'Ladder' and the 'Reed bearing the Sponge'. This provided a complex, symmetrical pattern of spaces into which the Symbols of the Passion were to be placed. I was fortunate to observe the penultimate stage of the design. A full-scale replica of the window-space had been hung in the studio, showing the mullion verticals and the cruciform patterning. The Passion symbols had been painted on individual sheets and there followed the fascinating process of distributing these units over the surface, with considerations of colour, intensity and weight, balanced against iconographical considerations in juxta-posing these symbols. The result was one of Piper's most satisfying creations.

The second project was less taxing, although theology again fully extended its demand. The commission was for glass to fill the nine lancets of the east window in the chapel of Oundle School. John determined on nine aspects of the Person of Christ and there was much discussion of the groups into which they would fall. It was an additional pleasure for me that these talks introduced me to the priest, Victor Kenna, who had prepared John for confirmation and was a near neighbour of mine in the diocese of Exeter. Since Kenna was one of the leading authorities on ikons and on Cretan seals, it was not surprising that a strong flavour of Byzantium was clear in the final windows. The grouping of the lancets had a most satisfying pattern; the revelation in Christ is explored in three groups of three: The Way, the Truth, the Life; The Vine, Bread, Water; Judge, Teacher, Shepherd.

The third project was not for glass but for a tapestry to hang on the screen behind the high altar of Chichester cathedral. The panelling and canopies of the screen itself seemed to impose a symbolic pattern which could not be ignored: a large central panel, flanked on each side by two narrow panels. I remember my excitement on receiving his letter describing the physical problems this patterning gave him. I cancelled my tutorials for the morning and very clumsily, in an annotated drawing, put my suggestions to

John Piper, *Drawings for the pamphlet on the Oundle Chapel Windows*

John Piper, *Reredos Tapestry for Chichester Cathedral*

him for a lay-out. My drawing indicated a large design in the central panel for the Trinity: a circle, a cross and a wing of fire, the three held together by the intersection of an equilateral triangle. For the four flanking panels I suggested horizontal divisions, with symbols of the four Evangelists above and the four elements below. I confess it was a high moment for me, at my next visit to Fawley, to see my drawing pinned above John's working table and in the event this was the lay-out, especially transfigured by his sense of colour, which went to the weavers to be made into the final tapestry.

This of course meant that in Chichester cathedral, in close proximity to the two carved Saxon panels which were the glory of their period, the worshipper may see three great works of contemporary art, the painting 'Noli me tangere' by Graham Sutherland, a window in stained glass by Rouault and this tapestry by Piper.

I should hazard a guess (I have never asked him) that Piper's most challenging commission was for the windows in the north and south walls of the choir in Eton College Chapel. For Evie Hone's

65

superb east window was already in place and would seem to challenge the presence there of anything but plain glass. I knew also of his great respect for Evie Hone's work, for he had written about it in the *Cymry'r Groes* article and reproduced there her drawing of the Crucifixion from his own collection.

Again the spaces seemed to demand a double balance and symmetry—within the windows themselves and in confrontation across the width of the choir.

Letters shuttled quickly. The first from John on Eton (27 May 1957) was also crowded with other work:

> I'm glad America plans itself well, and hope to see you before you go. We go to France again August 5th, and I hope to have done the Eton designs, and some Coventry as well, before I go. Then Llandaff perhaps in the autumn. So much work in hand!

In fact, exhibitions and designing extended this timetable and on 9 January 1958, he writes:

> The show took every minute till November, and since then everything that waited for the show has had to be done, especially unveiling of Plymouth and selling the Coventry designs to 3 different committees there. This is now done and contract signed. We spent Christmas in N. Wales (top of Traeth Mawr, nr C. Williams-Ellis). I was v. impressed by the incumbent of Portmadoc's Christmas H.C. . . .
>
> There is such a lot of Coventry to do that I ought to get down to it.

On 19 March 1958 Eton surfaced again:

> I have to get down to Eton very soon, in order to get the designs finished (in 1st state) by May. There are several problems to solve: the main one that I can only use one Miracle or Parable in each window, I think, as I don't want to overweight the design by the ideas . . . . Of your suggestions, I can certainly do Water into Wine, & Stilling the Waves, but devils are so difficult and Raising from the dead not much easier. Yet your scheme is

obviously right. What I would welcome would be your four parallel, or antitype, Parables for the Miracles you have suggested . . .

A p.c. would be most useful!

I replied (at greater length than a postcard) on 20 March. I first laid out in parallel the Miracle and Parable relationships John wanted:

Miracle	Parable
Water/Wine	The Sower : Wheat Tares
Stilling the Waters	House on Rock and Sand
Healing the Blind	The Prodigal Son
Raising Lazarus	Dives and Lazarus

I explained the changes I was suggesting and then—

To be more systematic about it: the four windows on north and south would now read eastward, beginning with 'the first miracle that he wrought' and ending with the two resurrection themes . . . There is a proper theological progress from the Miracles of Nature . . . through the Miracle of Healing to the conquest of death . . . the sequence also in Christ's life. Each of these is a contribution, as I said in the earlier note, to the Epiphany theme, 'shewing forth His glory' . . . I should like very much to see the Blakean image in the background to the miracle of healing the blind: 'men as trees walking' . . . very potent, but which I can't remember any artist's having attempted.

John replied to this:

Oddly enough, Men walking as trees was suggested by the Headmaster about 6 months ago, as a good visual symbol—and I forgot about it. It is excellent.

At the end of my letter I had said:

There are many other inter-relations which I find in the two series [I had already written at too great length] but they may be too verbal and conceptual to be useful to you.

67

On 21 March John replied:

> . . . Just what I wanted. I think the shape is now taken of the whole scheme and I shall try to stick to the main outlines as you state them . . .
>
> Come and see some of the sketches soon. And my newly-repaired barn for Coventry, which goes on apace.

I was in Fawley on Friday, 18 April and indeed work was 'going on apace' and splendidly. I was able to see the first full-scale patterns for the Baptistry windows in Coventry cathedral together with his resolution of all the Eton problems. When the windows were in place, it was a final grace that, though his style differed so markedly from that of Evie Hone, the total space at the east end of the chapel had a superb unity. To hear, nearly thirty years later, a string quartet played as a substantial part of the College's early morning worship was to experience the setting for a rare quality of contemplation.

*

John Piper was notably generous in my own academic concerns. I had been researching and writing for some years with a view to publishing a book, *Shakespeare and the Artist*—it was in the event to be Geoffrey Cumberlege's last book published by the Oxford University Press and Vivian Ridler's first as Printer to the University. I had already explored many thousands of drawings, paintings, book-illustrations and theatre-designs and I wished to lock up my argument, that an artist's insights can at least match the verbal expositions of the literary critics. To this end I wished to establish this 'visual criticism' by exploring one of Shakespeare's plays with an artist whose literary interests did not conflict with his art. John Piper had already been involved with Benjamin Britten's operas, with settings for productions at Aldeburgh, Glyndebourne and Covent Garden and when I asked him to join me in this experiment he immediately agreed.

We met for some three hours over a meal in London when, (acting the part of the director of *Measure for Measure*) I told my

John Piper, *The Miraculous Draught of Fishes* (stained glass); Eton College Chapel

artist-designer what my aims would be to render the abstract themes behind the plots: the majesty of justice and the emergence of a beneficent equity out of the potential tragedy of the play. John said he needed a month to explore these ideas and on 10 March 1949 (precisely a month to the day) I received a five-page letter with many drawings, which outlined precisely the concepts he and I had worked over. Justice was there in a central 'throne of state' with a baldachino which could be flown for the dark prison scenes:

> The whole set should be pretty open—even in the Duke's palace—to get a contrast with the prison scenes . . . Then one would get a really enclosed sense in the prison by dark lighting and a *suggestion*, merely, of rich colours . . . Keeping a Gothic feeling throughout might symbolise sufficiently the Duke throne—altar—Throne of God sense?

The next stage was to reproduce these ideas from the painted versions —which were already wholly satisfying—to black and white drawings which would reproduce in line in the book. The Press did the rest and that chapter, thanks to John's insights, is a wholly satisfying summary of the necessary collaboration between word and image—and, by extension, between artist and critic.

*

As I brood over John Piper's amazing output and especially in the context of the Tate Gallery's massive celebration of his eightieth birthday in 1983-4, I am torn between my admiration for his atmospheric landscape art and the profound spiritual insight of his work in stained glass and tapestry—but perhaps that expression of divided admiration is erroneous. It may yet be seen that the delicate evocation of landscape, even his sense of transience and 'decay' is part of the spiritual insight which transfigures his works in Chichester, Coventry, Plymouth, Oundle and the Metropolitan cathedral in Liverpool.

In these last years it has been my good fortune to be invited to write an introduction to the Marlborough Gallery catalogue of recent paintings which showed at the same time as the Tate

70

John Piper, *Stage Setting for 'Measure for Measure'*, for Merchant's *Shakespeare and the Artist*

retrospective, and to the catalogue of his 'religious' works shown in Lichfield Cathedral in the 1984 Festival. I conflate them here as my most adequate expression of the magnitude of his contribution to our art.

*

71

Buildings, like people, have their span of development, their birth, growth and decay; their life-span may be ten times that of a human being but it is a life-span with the same inevitable end. But in their exterior forms, ancient buildings do not always mirror the intensity or the quality of the life within. There are human parallels. Rembrandt's self-portrait in the aggressive equipment of a young warrior has in fact less interior vitality than the last self-portrait, where, out of the hint of seeming senility there gleam eyes of marvellous acuteness. So many of John Piper's buildings show a similar paradox and a parallel acuteness.

For many of the buildings in his paintings and drawings appear to be in the last stages of dissolution, ruins where once there was architectural splendour. 'Fountains Abbey' seems little more than an etched shadow of its former massive structure. Yet Piper's paintings assert a double denial of apparent decrepitude: the buildings have gathered over the centuries an accretion of nature's life, a patina of organic growth, and this patina the painter renders with loving fidelity; and further, they have maintained, perhaps more starkly in their skeletal form, the driving vitality which informed their builders, the spiritual force of early monasticism or the aggressive determination of military fortification. Piper's paintings are the vibrant records for our own day of ideals which were once potent and of which a sensitive artist can still make us aware.

A phrase has long pursued much of John Piper's art—'pleasing decay' was a useful cliche and established a critical toe-hold on some of his work; but if it implies a mannered affection for romantic dissolution, or the superficial twentieth-century equivalent of an eighteenth-century Gothique folly, it is greatly short of the mark.

For 'Romantic', as a critical term, has for Piper very concrete associations, as he declared in his book, *British Romantic Artists*:

Romantic art deals with the particular. The particularity of Bewick about a bird's wing, of Turner about a waterfall or a hill town, or of Rossetti about Elizabeth Siddal, is the result of a vision that can see in those things a significance beyond ordinary significance, something that for a moment seems to contain the

John Piper, *Snowdon Landscapes;* coll. the author

Wood engraving by Reynolds Stone after drawings of Snowdonia by John Piper

whole world, and, when the moment is past, carries over some comment on life or experience besides the comment on appearance.

This is equally true of Piper's art, his 'particularity' in the rendering of building or place. For the 'spirit of place', that complex interaction of nature with the passionate meddling of human occupation, has been dominant in his work. And the paintings are the more intense when the 'human occupation' has been his own and his family's. 'Garn Fawr', his Pembrokeshire home, establishes with precision the spare geometry of that ancient upland place, a settlement centuries-old in the bleak hill country. And behind all this rendering of places and their natural setting has been the persistent curiosity of a mind of historical acuteness and literary exploration.

Churches have, from his earliest days as an artist, exerted a peculiarly powerful influence on him; and rarely indeed have they been merely topographical records; spare and economical, stating no more than they are intended to state, they convey to us the balanced forces of the architecture, the thrust and counter-thrust of arch, column and buttress; we see precisely the physical problem which the architect was to solve—and much more.

For, in humble parish church or the greatest cathedrals we see structure with such precision that we can date it with ease but we see also an interior light which characterises all the finest of Piper's paintings.

This identification by the artist of the special quality of awe we feel within these 'machines for worship', 'where prayer has been valid', can be seen to greatly varying effect. The sombre grandeur of St Mark's in Venice—the majesty of polyphony appears to echo in the massive vaulting and the shadowed spaces hinted in the interior of the drawing, is so very different from the unpretentious domesticity of so many of his English and Welsh parish churches. 'Prayer has been valid' in each setting but our eyes tell us what our ears seem to hear: that Palestrina reverberates through the one interior and the simple pieties of psalm-settings and village choirs still sound within the others.

John Piper, Christmas Card

John Piper, Christmas Card

Central in John Piper's work is the nature of light and its power to transmute the commonplace. Nowhere is this seen more nobly than in his designs for stained glass and his collaboration with Patrick Reyntiens. There are two great categories of glass which he has mastered. In the one, in Coventry and the Metropolitan Cathedral in Liverpool the 'subjects' are abstract, stained light and its spiritual significance; on the other hand, at Eton College, Oundle and Plymouth, iconography and narrative symbolism are dominant. Yet both categories are of course united by one fact, the translucence of glass. In the Coventry baptistry window, blazing light at its centre is the heart of the subject-matter, God's glory framed in the lower, earth-bound panels and the ascent to infinite blue of the upper panels. This simple concentration on the divine radiance is carried a stage further in Liverpool; there the lantern appears to revolve through the colours of the spectrum, with the bursts of clear light coming three times, the radiance of the Trinity.

All this prolific work in every medium of art is one man's repayment of the massive debt which the Church owes to artists and saints of the past. John Piper has established another debt which church and secular authorities must repay in their turn.

*

When I returned to Wales from the University of Exeter, I had further generosity from John, when I set up the Llanddewibrefi Festival. I had determined that the whole festival should be of the highest quality in context and performance; at the same time I wanted participants and audiences to have a more permanent remembrance of the events and we determined on a well-illustrated brochure to be printed by the Gomer Press. John came across from Garn Fawr for a day and produced one of his finest drawings, our

John Piper, Collage for the brochure of Llanddewibrefi Festival

John Piper, *Llanddewibrefi*; coll. the author

church glowing with an interior radiance. For the lithographed
cover which he supervised he produced a collage which very
precisely rendered the mystery of the original drawing.

Kyffin Williams, *Moelwyn Merchant* (oil, detail)

Kyffin Williams is a late representative of that 'other Wales', *y boneddigion*, the landed gentry who preserved the religious and cultural traditions of our country through centuries of change and the inexorable pressure of the powerful English culture, with no more than Offa's Dyke to stem the assault. These gentle folk, with the country clergymen often drawn from their ranks, preserved this literary culture even through the rigours of the eighteenth century, as Eluned Rees's invaluable research into the sponsors of Welsh literature in that age has shown.

Kyffin Williams is very conscious of this stock, as his witty and penetrating biography, *Across the Straits* (1973) illustrates. It also shows the falsity of the division which some Welsh social historians have described between the 'diverse' cultures of *Gwerin* and *Bonedd*. This division has sometimes, in popular mythology, been driven so far as to make anything *gwerinol*, 'of the people, the folk, the peasantry' wholly desirable, and the aristocratic tradition of *y bonedd* wholly alien. Yet Saunders Lewis speaks spontaneously of 'the aristocratic tradition of Wales'; the very metres of our complex poetry, frequently practised today by cultivated members of *y werin*, speak of a civilisation in which church and landed gentlefolk were the patrons of high art.

And so with Kyffin Williams; consciously of *y bonedd*, he is at least as much at home with the farm hand and the quarryman—as his portraits eloquently show—as any of our self-consciously demotic artists.

Kyffin Williams, lino-cut Self-Portrait; coll. the author

Across the Straits opens with a witty deflation of any pretensions which his natural family pride might foster:

> Like every other man in North Wales, I can trace my descent back to Lludd ap Beli Mawr. The English perversely insist on calling him 'Lud'; they invest him with kingship and say he built London around 120 B.C. If I include the female line, I go back on my father's side by way of fifty-nine generations, and on my mother's by sixty-two. This, I believe, makes me her fifty-ninth cousin three times removed.

In less teasing vein he pursues the historically verifiable and we learn that among his ancestors he numbers more than a dozen country parsons, two of whom were Chancellors of Bangor Cathedral and one, the Rev. John Williams, his great-grandfather, was born in 'my parish' of Llanddewibrefi. There was also Morys Kyffin the bard, there were royal chaplains, governors of colonies, army officers and copper magnates. It is all told with ironic pride, the same warmth and compassionate but ruthlessly truthful insight which informs all his portraiture.

The true history begins in 1666, with Wymffre ap William John ap Rhys, a blacksmith of Llansadwrn in Anglesey.

> Wmffre was a lucky man, for outside the smithy on the brow of the hill, where the road starts to wander down to Beaumaris, he found a pot of gold. One day he was having difficulty in shoeing a fresh young horse, so he tethered it to the stump of a dead tree. The horse pulled and lunged until finally the whole stump came out of the ground, and there in the hole Wmffre saw a golden bowl.

Wmffre prospered, bought a rich farm, changed his name to 'Humphrey Williams' and became, at ninety-three the first member of his family to be buried in Llansadwrn churchyard, "though since then we have been laid there in such profusion that but for our bones the east end of the church would probably collapse".

Kyffin Williams, *Welsh Landscape* (oil)

Two of Humphrey's grandchildren became, respectively, chaplain to Princess Augusta of Wales at Windsor, with three Anglesey livings, and the other "cornered the whole of the British copper industry and died an M.P. and a millionaire".

Clearly his great pride is in his great-grandfather, James Williams, a fellow of Jesus College, Oxford, and rector of Llanfairynghornwy, where, with his talented wife Frances, he set up the Anglesey Lifeboat Association, winning the gold medal of the National Institution for a particularly daring rescue.

But all this must be read in these lively pages, an invaluable record of a noble part of our Welsh heritage.

*

Kyffin's exploration of the Welsh countryside, for his drawings or the densely-textured oil-paintings, is confined almost wholly to Anglesey and the masses of Snowdonia—though one of his finest topographical drawings was of Llanddewibrefi and, lithographed,

83

became the cover of the brochure for the second Llanddewibrefi Festival in 1977. His method was to paint background swiftly and equally swiftly to mould contour and mountain texture with thick-laid oils applied rapidly with a palette knife. He has the country-man's innate understanding of weather and the problems the hill-farmer and the upland shepherd contend with. His studies of storm and snow, animals and men held in the power of the wind are vividly evocative of Snowdon at its most menacing. The power of human endurance is vivid in the drawing for the Snowdon National Park poster, the thrusting effort of a farmer in a snow-drift. It gives me a great if ironic pleasure that these subjects are among the sought-after canvasses at the Royal Academy every year. His instinct for bird-flight is equally ready and I have known him identify a bird at a distance where for me it was barely detectable— whether a hovering red kite in the hills above Llanddewi or the clumsier flight of grosser carrion birds above the marshes towards Tregaron.

This wildness can be offset by a tender study of a sleeping sheep-dog or the racing scurry of a knot of wild ponies. And of course there are the Christmas-cards, frequently carrying animal studies from Welsh legend or the *Mabinogion*—I especially treasure 'Pryderi and the Pigs'.

This is the same tender precision, his unsparing but delicate truthfulness as he paints his portraits which are such a valuable record of his contemporaries; and these are not exclusively the notable public figures—though they are rendered powerfully and without flattery. But equally truthful and with humane insight are the portraits which may properly be called *gwerinol*: the painful humility of the half-smile, the quiet waiting in the passivity of *Blind Boy*, painted forty years ago; or the nobility of labour accomplished in the portrait of *Hugh Thomas*, in the collection of University College, Bangor, which takes one back so gratefully to the similar insights of Josef Herman, of *Mike* and the other studies of miners in South Wales, which show the same understanding of 'the dignity of human labour'. Of the portrait of Hugh Thomas, Kyffin writes:

I found him standing with a sickle in his hand, trimming a hedge. His wife had just died and I could see from his eyes how sad he

84

was. He was a typical Celt, tall and spare with a drooping moustache that accented the melancholy of his face.

I painted him in the rickyard of his small farm, while he sat on a stool against the stable door. The sunlight poured over the hills to streak between barn and stable, picking out his neck and cheekbones, the back of his cap and the edge of his big moustache. He didn't question me and showed little interest in what I was doing. When the light failed and I had to stop work, a slow smile was all I got as he wandered away into his fields.

but he is held there on canvas, a portion of Welsh life kept at least as nobly as any of the tragic peasantry that struggle through the poems of R.S. Thomas.

A fragile nobility is seen in another manner in the portrait of Anna. Here the delicate features held in the sculptured frame of dark hair are mobile with the eager questioning eyes and the breathless parting of her lips. It is a living moment captured with all the finality of great portraiture.

Seeing and admiring his work in the past had not prepared me for the experience of having him paint my portrait. We were staying with him at his home in Llanfairpwll, on the western shore of the Menai Straits and with the ever-changing panorama of Snowdonia rising sheer from sea-level. We had had lunch after a quiet morning and he then invited me to his studio where, for a while we explored landscapes in oil and wash and then he sat me before a canvas which seemed to me of daunting size. Tube after tube was squeezed out on to the palette, to be applied with a knife to the canvas in what seemed to me like controlled and measured fury. Never for a moment did that penetration of analytic gaze leave his eyes. It seemed to me that I was perhaps a living object, a structure of masses and planes to be rendered in a paint that was almost three-dimensional, sculptural upon the canvas. This united itself in my mind with the similar experience with Josef Herman: both portraits resulted in a poem, 'No dark glass', in which I had to say;

> Whether I like it or not
> I look into no dark glass
> at no assumed mask;
> I must learn to live with it

5/50

Kyffin Williams, *Gwastadnant* (print); coll. the author

Across the Straits is also the record of Kyffin Williams's struggle to find himself when the onset of epilepsy led to his discharge from the army. "You are abnormal anyway; why not become an artist?" was the verdict of an army medical officer, one of those vastly prophetic judgments that can occasionally spring out of unbelievable stupidity. Kyffin took the advice, went to the Slade School, (where he was the Robert Ross Leaving Scholar) and became Art master at Highgate School where some of his eminent pupils still remember him warmly (I especially cherished my first conversation with Anthony Green, R.A., who, so many years on from Highgate, spoke

86

of Kyffin with grateful affection). A little later he became independent of teaching and gave himself entirely to his passionate devotion to the Welsh landscape, its cottages and stone walls, the granite and slate of its uplands, and the lives of those who tear their living from its soil. This devotion has made his painting a social record of a depth that ensures its enduring as one of the most valuable of painterly documents in our day. With *Across the Straits*, (a book that demands to be read at least once every year) the paintings and drawings, eschewing all the fashionable slickness that mars the work of so many of his contemporaries, look to the heart of a Welsh life which his ancestors cherished and which is rapidly withering into oblivion.

*

Kyffin Williams, *Anglesey Cromlech* (oil); coll. Eluned Brown

Kyffin Williams, *The Countryman* (lino-cut); coll. the author

Kyffin Williams, *Pryderi and the Pigs* (lino-cut); coll. the author

Saunders Lewis, in a brief introduction to a mixed exhibition of Welsh painting wrote:

> The square mile around the ancestral homestead is the secret and the inheritance of the Welsh artist. You'll find it in this collection of pictures. John Elwyn and Kyffin Williams and Will Roberts and many another, they also have their intimate square mile about which they too have family secrets to tell. Welsh names in painting are specially apt for the walls of houses, for intimacy and companionship, like a song overheard.

Very true and though Gwynedd, Kyffin's Gwynedd, is rather more than the 'square mile' about a homestead, he has unstintingly let us into his family secrets and the passion of his inheritance. But the passion has extended far, to another and seemingly alien Welshry.

It was my privilege in 1977, in the Festival at Llanddewibrefi to mount what was, I believe, until then the most comprehensive exhibition of his paintings in Wales. The National Library of Wales made available to me their extensive and unique collection of the Kyffin Williams paintings and drawings of *Y Wladfa*, the Welsh settlement in Patagonia. He had gone there on a Churchill Fellowship and returned with a mighty collection of paintings (and notes for paintings) which record another culture, wholly Welsh in origin and fusing in subtle ways with the native people—and, like its Welsh origins, it too is imperilled by the twentieth century. Here we find settlements, farmsteads, many sturdy Welsh farmers and native peasants, extensive almost desert landscapes and intimate cultivation where men might pursue their inherited crafts. Set those works beside the prolific record of North Wales, its land and its people, and we are left wondering whether our gratitude to Kyffin Williams is the greater for his being one of our most accomplished artists or one of our acutest social historians.

CERI RICHARDS AND GRAHAM SUTHERLAND

Swansea, in the early part of the century: Daniel Jones, composer, Dylan Thomas and Vernon Watkins, poets and Ceri Richards, painter—three of the four major arts brilliantly represented by near-contemporaries in a relatively small Welsh town. And there were inter-relations and overlappings between their arts, with Ceri Richards a substantial focus of the vigorous life. Himself an accomplished pianist and organist, a great deal of his painting and lithography was concerned with music and musicians, while another major aspect of his work related to the poetry of his friend, Dylan Thomas and this was the occasion of my first getting to know Ceri Richards.

There are, of course, very many works in all the major arts whose origin is in another work of art, sometimes in the same medium, more interestingly in a different medium. Musicians borrow themes from other composers and their 'variations', however brilliantly conceived, remain anchored to the original theme; Picasso is indebted to Velasquez for 'Las Meninas' and after some three hundred studies and variants, produces the one definitive work which unites the conceptions of both artists. But this 'act of translation' is most potent when it takes place across the arts, when Benjamin Britten transforms *A Midsummer Night's Dream* into an opera or Ceri Richards takes a poem by Dylan Thomas or a composition by Debussy and translates them into paint or lithograph. It is interesting that so much of this complex activity has taken place when verbal translation, poetry from one language to another, has once more attained the stature of a creative activity in itself. The act of translating from one language to another is in fact a valuable analogy when we are considering the handling of Debussy or Dylan Thomas by Ceri Richards. Those millions of us who have found themselves from infancy to be strictly bilingual, very frequently find themselves also immersed in distinct cultural settings; in my own case my Welsh 'placed' me in a predominantly Latinate, Romance tradition, while my English related me to a largely Nordic and Germanic tradition—with most interesting consequences. Each act of translation, if we are formally engaged on a literary work, is a distinct creative act. The impossibility of literal equivalence is no weakness but a challenge. At the level of

Ceri Richards, "Do not go gentle..." (water-colour); coll. the author

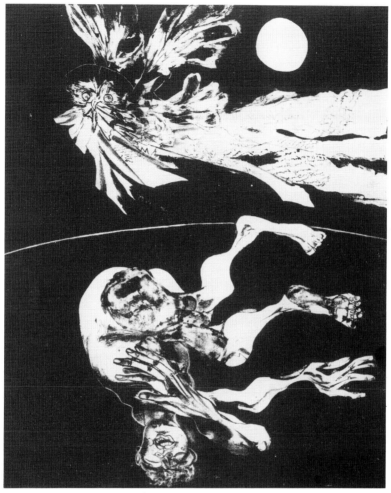

Ceri Richards, "Do not go gentle . . ." (lithograph)

simple conversation there is a subtle shift of tone and reference between the two languages. In more formal terms, in preaching or lecturing, I have found that if I have given the 'same' sermon on a single Sunday, in English and in Welsh, although the structure and 'content' will be the same, both the tone and impact will be quite different. And at the level of poetic translation, after the first struggle to attain approximate identity of 'meaning', the translator is indeed engaged in creating a quite new object. It will have its own integrity and requires no necessary identification with the original work, even though, for many readers, responses will be richer from their understanding of both versions.

This then is the creative point at which relations between the arts are most intense. Here we have to be wary of the word 'illustration'. In nineteenth-century editions of Shakespeare or Dickens, the plates required the words to fulfil the illustration; but to observe the work of Blake as he draws on Dante, the Bible, Shakespeare, is to see creativity which matches the intensity of the 'original'. Blake's 'Pity' and its companion colour-print 'The Triple Hecate' have such complexity, and range so far beyond the single line or phrase in Shakespeare, that they are in every sense complete and independent works of art.

My contact with Ceri Richards over his handling of Dylan Thomas's poem, 'Do not go gentle into that good night' had interesting beginnings. I had been invited to review Professor Edgar Wind's *Pagan Mysteries in the Renaissance* and apart from its brilliance in teasing out the significance of the 'mysteries', I realised that its critical significance was a profound stimulus to my concern for inter-relations in the arts. Our common ground led Professor Wind to invite me to take his place when he failed to undertake a Granada television broadcast in the *Context* series and I broadcast in the Renaissance 'slot' with the title, 'The Nature of Man'.

Meanwhile a conversation with Gerald Barry, fresh from the enormous success of the 1951 Festival and then at Granada T.V., showed very clearly how difficult it was to foster this cross-fertilisation in the arts. When I asked why television paid so little attention to non-dramatic poetry and prose, he spoke the current wisdom on the matter, that television was too essentially visual and that poetry was heard best on radio. I put to him the case for televised work of that kind and, the following year (1963) Granada T.V. invited me to prepare and broadcast ten programmes under the general title 'Word and Image' and they ranged from Chaucer ('Portraits of People') by way of Shakespeare, the Picturesque, Wordsworth, Coleridge, Eliot and William Golding to Ceri Richards's handling of the poetry of Dylan Thomas. Granada—and especially Janet Wadsworth and Pat Owtram who directed the programmes—took the great trouble which made the series an exciting success.

When it came to the programme 'Light and Dark', the exploration of 'Do not go gentle', I was fortunate in being able to buy from Ceri Richards the drawing preliminary to the two large paintings in the Tate Gallery and the Whitworth Art Gallery in Manchester; both in his studio and in subsequent correspondence I was able to learn a great deal of Ceri Richards's reading of the poem as he proceeded through drawings to the large paintings and subsequent lithographs.

The active relationship between the arts had always been a motive-force in Richards's work. An early painting, 'Homage to Beethoven', had anticipated the elaborate series of drawings, paintings, constructions and lithographs based on Debussy's prelude, 'La Cathédrale Engloutie', many of which were shown at the Venice Biennale in 1962. 'Do not go gentle' was perhaps his most powerful treatment of a literary theme.

Thomas's poem is ingeniously articulated, while the form is subjected to extreme emotional pressure. This may be felt in the multiple ambiguities of the opening line. What is the grammatical function of the word 'gentle'? Does it signify 'gently'; or imply 'gentle one' as a synonym for his father to whom the poem is addressed? And the 'good' of 'good night'; is death a 'good night' to be desired, or a 'goodnight', a long farewell, not to be welcomed? Ambiguities are pursued through the poem:

Grave men near *death*

anticipates in its tragic punning the further line '*see* with *blinding* sight'. This comes to its sombre climax in the opening lines of the last stanza:

And you, my father, there on the sad height,
Curse, bless me now, with your fierce tears, I pray

where the father-son relationship echoes the tragic cry of Esau to his father Isaac, when Jacob has cheated him of his birthright:

And when Esau heard the words of his father, he cried with a great and exceeding bitter cry, and said unto his father, 'Bless me, even me also, O my father.' (*Genesis* 27, 34).

Ceri Richards's preliminary study has a ground-work of blue wash, intensified towards the base and half-framed by a bare bough on which an owl perches, holding in its beak a shroud, out of which a dead body tumbles into the void. Visually this seems partly to deny the specific plea in the poem's opening line (which Richards incorporates into the margin of the design) but it answers to the falling, muted tone of Dylan Thomas's own recorded reading of the poem, even in the plea, 'Rage against the dying of the light'.

In October 1962 I wrote to Richards and raised with him the contrast between the resignation, even perhaps the tranquillity of his drawing and the violence of the poem. On 28 October he replied:

> I was asked in 1955 by John Berger to make a drawing for this fine poem. I was profoundly moved by this poem and reflected deeply on it. What is most important, I didn't want to illustrate it superficially by keeping step literally with the obvious meaning of words like *rage, rage* (where I would render this by a fanfare of trumpets blasting away in the face of the Inevitable)—that rendering came into my mind most obviously and directly, but I felt this was superficial.

Richards's instinctive use of the words 'illustrate', 'superficial' and 'rendering' at once imply the distance that he set between the illustrator's craft and the artist's translation of an original work in one medium into the terms of his own art.

Indeed, Daniel Jones, himself a composer and commenting on Richards's Debussy and Beethoven studies, wrote:

> The vocabularies of music and painting overlap with terms like 'tone', 'colour', 'composition', 'structure', 'rhythm', 'bright', 'dark', 'thematic'. These are mere metaphors, rescuing language from failure, but they can lead deceptively from analogy to identification. Ceri Richards was not a man to fall into such a trap. He was too good a musician, too appreciative of poetry, to confuse those arts with his own. He saw in them a parallel equivalence, springing from the same source in nature and only at that profound level finding identity.

96

When Ceri Richards and I were corresponding, he was of course writing to me at seven years' remove from the work itself:

> At this distance in time I cannot reassemble what I felt then—I am attempting to do so—but this poem cannot be seen in retrospect at two different removes and give one the same sort of awareness.

Nevertheless, his attempt, despite this disclaimer, is illuminating:

> My rendering is my personal one and a seriously felt one—and here comes the difficulty—myself as an artist am interpreting this poem in visual terms designed to create a special and equivalent feeling arising from the poem—I wouldn't dream of saying that I was giving exact definition to the inflections and beauty in Dylan Thomas's poem—that is presumptuous, but I parallel the poem and its effect on me by a creation in my own terms of drawing.

There follows in his letter a valuable passage in which he tries both to answer my question about his initial response to Berger's request and to recollect his mature response to the poem:

> I can only recall something of what I remember writing to John Berger about the poem, for he didn't anticipate my interpretation —but by recalling it now it would seem that I am repeating and possibly reinventing a situation of creative response to the poem —which can be a sort of distortion.
>
> I believe I was moved by the poem into feeling a quality of the pathetic and tragic futility of resistance to the natural cycles of life. Dylan mentions the different modes of living and how they affect the last moments of life—I felt I could see the isolated and pathetic passivity of man on the threshold of Eternity—I hope very deeply that I say those last words with deep reverence and seriousness—but I think this (is) what I conveyed in my drawing—the body of man is tossed out of the shroud into the void—his resistance quietened.

97

Richards had perhaps felt that my question concerning passivity and the tone of 'Rage, rage' somehow implied a failure on his part to render the pressure of the poem; in fact his 'reading' (with which I wholly agreed) exactly echoes Dylan Thomas's own interpretation of the falling close. Richards's response to my question is interesting.

> You dont think this ('his resistance quietened' in the previous paragraph) is the equivalent of the lines 'Rage, rage against the dying of the light'—I believe I veered away from the literal force in Rage—and thought of the sensibility, the depth in the words 'Do not go gentle into that good night.'

All these considerations did not exhaust for me the fascination of Richards's response to the poem. The posture of the limp and tumbled body in the drawing (and—though to a lesser extent—in the larger versions in the Tate and Whitworth) inevitably for me recalled the flayed body of St Bartholomew in the Sistine Chapel 'Last Judgment'. I had found Edgar Wind's exploration of 'The Flaying of Marsyas' the most gripping of his analyses in *Pagan Mysteries*. There he shows that the flaying of St Bartholomew at his martyrdom and the flaying of Marsyas by Apollo were both regarded by the neo-platonists of the Florentine Academy, with whom Michelangelo had a profound sympathy, as an expression of the soul's release from the trammels of the body; indeed Michelangelo has totally identified himself with this pagan-christian myth by making the head of the flayed saint a self-portrait of the artist.

I suggested to Ceri Richards that in this—perhaps unconscious—echo of one of the profoundest moments in renaissance iconography he had added a further dimension to Dylan Thomas's poem, to his evocation of that moment when man inevitably goes gentle into that good night. His reply was characteristic:

> You mention a Greek myth, 'the Flaying of Marsyas' and the Michelangelo—I wasn't deliberately aware of either of them, and that you should find that they seem to occur in the overtones of your drawing is quite legitimate—a true work of art is a crucible

98

which can contain the past, present and future, and we see its contents according to our sensibilities.

*

A year or two after my exchange of letters with Ceri Richards, the International Professors of English Conference met at the University of Venice and I was invited to lecture on my favourite topic, 'Visual Criticism'. It was a fascinating environment for a lecture, for I was in a room in the Cà Foscari, at the bend of the Grand Canal which gave the only uninterrupted view down to the Rialto Bridge. The previous day, in the wake of my work on *The Merchant of Venice* for the Penguin edition, I had gone to the Ghetto Nuovo and (imagining a Shylock of historical reality) I traced a possible route from the Ghetto to the Rialto and so to judgment. It was hard to maintain my concentration on my argument and my fellows, when a half-turn of my head gave me one of the loveliest and most evocative sights in Europe, the Grand Canal.

Ceri Richards and Dylan Thomas were admired artists and my argument seemed to be accepted. I therefore felt justified in pursuing the argument in a very different order of experience.

Hymnology and the long tradition of theological wit, culminating in metaphysical poetry in the seventeenth century, have accustomed us to certain conceits which have become almost universal when the image of Christ's Cross is contemplated. The witty contrasts are all subsumed under the central tragic irony: the Death of the Lord of Life. From that *discordia concors* the others all follow: the union of the tree of life in Eden and the tree of death on Golgotha; the Cross as the throne of the King, with the extension of that conceit into the kingly purple robe mantled about Him by the blood of His wounds; the weight of sin's ransom measured out on the balances of the cross-beam—these are some of the images which traverse meditations on the Passion of Christ. Within the English tradition they may be found very early in the *Dream of the Rood*. The power of the tradition is however more clearly seen in widely separated hymns.

In the second half of the sixth century Venantius Fortunatus composed a sequence for the ceremonial reception by S. Radegund of a fragment of the true Cross. Two couplets, in both the Latin and the familiar English version, establish the most powerful of the images:

> Arbor decora et fulgida
> Ornata regis purpura . . .

> Beata cujus brachiis
> Pretium pependit saeculi

> How bright in purple robe it stood,
> The purple of a Saviour's blood . . .

> Upon its arms, like balance true
> It weighed the price for sinners due.

Twelve hundred years later Isaac Watts, in one of our noblest hymns, employs the same incongruities to point the nature of Christ's sacrifice:

> Did e'er such love and sorrow meet,
> Or thorns compose so rich a crown?

> His dying crimson like a robe,
> Spreads o'er his body on the Tree.

Here Watts has added to the imagery of Venantius Fortunatus another commonplace: 'Or *thorns* compose so *rich* a crown.' The irony is both biblical and theological. Thorns were no part of God's original creation but were the first manifestation of the Fall. There could be no greater showing of divine grace at the crucifixion than that this malformed and aggressive intrusion into the natural order should become the symbol of Christ's regality, the Crown of Thorns answering with propriety to the regal purple of streaming blood, which in turn graciously parodied the imperial purple derived from the dye of the *Murex*.

These matters have been the substance of iconography in paintings of the crucifixion and one of these relations has a special

Graham Sutherland, *Thornheads*; coll. the author

interest, the extent to which Graham Sutherland has derived from Grünewald's Colmar altar-piece. One element in Grünewald's study, the crown of thorns, was however developed well beyond its original significance; it had been important but not obtrusive in the Colmar study; Sutherland now explored its formal possibilities very much further. Before undertaking the painting he made numerous drawings of thorn and gorse, their forms becoming ever more anthropomorphic as he developed the series of Thorn Heads (there is at least one drawing, in my own collection, in which two Thorn Heads have begun a macabre conversation), until, with the actual painting of the Crucifixion for the Church of S. Matthew, Northampton, the Crown of Thorns takes on a central symbolism, enhanced by the rectilinear abstraction of the background and the solitariness of the crucified Christ. After the completion of the painting other lithographs and drawings prepared for the next major development in this theme in Sutherland's work, the Crucifixion at the base of the great Coventry tapestry. Here the most fascinating of all the developments from Grünewald has taken place. If we compare the two paintings of this theme by Grünewald, that at Colmar (the Isenheim altarpiece) and at Karlsruhe, we see that the latter has a significant difference: the arms of the cross are bent downwards as if in response to the profound tension of the crucified arms and the pendent body. If the lines of force in the painting be isolated they are seen to establish the form and tension of a cross-bow, of which Christ's body constitutes the bolt. This theme is not alluded to, so far as I am aware, in any other crucifixion, nor does Sutherland take it up in the Northampton study, otherwise so deeply indebted to Grünewald. But in the succeeding years it is all-pervasive, and many of the studies for the Crucifixion within the Coventry tapestry have explicit reference to this motif.

The two painters, Sutherland and Grünewald are as clearly dependent upon a tradition of imagery as the hymn writers who explore the theme more conceptually; Sutherland's work, wholly of his own age in style and temper and in no sense derivative, yet makes penetrating critical comment on the work of the earlier painter to whom he is indebted and in the course of developing his own theme, Sutherland, whether consciously or unconsciously, isolates an aspect of Grünewald's comment on the Crucifixion which might easily in itself escape notice, extending its emotional significance as he simplifies the treatment, until in some of the drawings the whole structure of Christ on the Cross is reduced to the single dynamic function of an arrow placed in a cross-bow.

When, some years later, I came to make a poster-poem of 'Thorn Heads' I was fascinated to find that Graham Sutherland, while wholly realising his debt to Grünewald, was quite unconscious of the cross-bow image which so powerfully united the two artists' work.

3

THE MIDDLE YEARS

Through all the last half-century I have had an especial affection for the parish of Llanhenog in Gwent. A long strip of high ground, about seven miles long and no more than a mile and a half wide, it had superb views in every direction from the height on which the church stood. And there were other good things. The field below the church was known as the Careyder Field, a corruption of the Welsh Cae y Derwen, The Field of the Oak, for there at the bottom of the field was a derelict stump of a tree with one branch bearing leaves, an oak which was recorded—so they said—in the Domesday Book. A mile or so along that road was Glen Usk, the former Mackworth residence, an excellent Regency building which still glows across the valley to the Usk road.

In 1938 I was Lay Reader-in-charge, a rare duty and from my ordination in 1940 I was first Deacon-in-charge and then Priest-in-charge and fortunate throughout that time in my Church Wardens, Major 'Birdie' Partridge and Colonel Dean, who then lived in Glen Usk.

The former had been a Welsh international Rugby player and early in my ministry a history of Welsh rugby appeared in which a party after a French match in Paris found 'Birdie' waltzing around the floor with a statue in his arms. This was too good to miss and after morning service the next Sunday, I began:

"Major Partridge, I was reading this week a book on Welsh rugby and—"

"It's a lie," he said but his eyes glinted.

*

There was always laughter when we met Major and Mrs Partridge (her eyes almost disappeared in merriment even when she simply smiled); but there was a period of harsh potential tragedy. Their son was reported 'Missing, believed killed' in the North African campaign but they came with equal faithfulness and little hint of their suffering, to every Sunday service. Then came word that he was a prisoner-of-war and finally his release. Their joy was the joy of us all.

*

Colonel Dean was High Sheriff immediately after the war and as his chaplain I attended 'crime' at the Assizes. I was at that time very young and the last case before lunch on the last day of 'crime' clearly perturbed the judge on my behalf. It was a peculiarly difficult rape charge and when we went to his robing-room, he turned to me: "This is a liberal education for you, chaplain." I felt my professional standing impugned and said, "Priests are liable to hear of life's seamy side." "We can take it, then?" "Oh yes, we can take it." Colonel Dean had suggested that it would be courteous to stay on for the first civil cases until tea-time and as ill-luck would have it, the first case was a rather grim divorce suit. The next dialogue was dramatic:
Counsel: "And what then did he say to you?"
Wife: "What, Sir? The *very* words!"
Judge: (looking happily down at me) "Yes, of course; we can take it!"

*

There were pleasant domestic moments back in the parish. One Sunday morning I was to baptise a baby from a household where I thought—correctly—that an older child was also unbaptised. At the font, Moira, the older child, was an embarrassing commentator and finished the baptism of her younger sister by abortive press-ups on the back of the font. When therefore I reached for her, she thought retribution had come and began a loud crying which was sustained through the time when, I'm afraid, I rather violently made her a Christian.

There was a sequel. I hadn't to go to the University on Fridays and spent the morning teaching in the tiny Church school, staffed solely by Mrs Daniels and her daughter. I was disturbed every Friday to

104

find that at my first appearing, Moira would disappear around a corner and when I asked her older sister why this happened, she confessed: "Moira can be naughty and if she's specially naughty, we say to her, 'If you're not a good girl, Mr Merchant will baptise you again'" and in all the years since then I've not been satisfied at the sacramental theology hidden in that threat.

The happiest and most lasting memory also concerned the school. Sir H.M. was chairman of managers, though then over eighty years old. After a very early divorce he had married one of the parishioners and they then lived on the north border of Gwent. After one meeting I asked him why he didn't sometimes make his communion at my altar. "Oh, my dear boy, I'm divorced and excommunicate." This seemed to me tragic after some half-century and he agreed that I should speak to the Bishop.

Now, Bishop Monahan, whom I greatly liked and admired, had two topics that dominated his sermons and a good deal of his conversation, the Doctrine of the Trinity and Canon Law, with its impact on belief and behaviour. I never actually heard him say, "Canon Law says this about the Trinity" but I felt it was not impossible.

I had arranged with the bishop that Sir H. should see him in the morning before our next managers' meeting and I waited near the church, in some concern for his arrival. He came striding up the road with the most contented of smiles. He put his arm round my shoulders and said:

"Oh my boy, this is the happiest day of my life and we shall be with you next Sunday." But then his face clouded as he asked:

"But tell me, my boy, who *is* Canon Law?"

*

Though the church was a hard three-mile walk from our home in Caerleon, the family was very involved in the services. One Sunday morning, as I was in the pulpit about to begin my sermon, Christina, aged about three and speaking no English, showed every sign of giving me a bad time in my preaching; I felt I needed a promise:

"Christina, wyt ti am fod yn ferch dda?"

"Na!"

"Christina, wyt ti am fod yn dda—neu fe fydd Momma am fynd â thi allan. Wyt ti am fod yn ferch dda?"

"Na!"

The English reader no more needs a translation than my intensely amused monoglot English congregation who knew that defiance was in the air and my wife took her out of church, crying wildly.

I lost the next round also when I got home. 'Tina was sullen and I asked her (in Welsh) hoping for repentance:

"Who was talking too much in church this morning?" The words were only half out of my mouth when I realised my error and the reply came firmly: "Daddy!"

*

Holidays were not easy to purchase in the days after the war, when a young family, Christina and Paul, had to be brought up on a relatively small salary. One summer a solution was suggested by the Vicar of Capel Curig, in the heart of Snowdonia: that we should exchange our home in Caerleon for his vicarage in the north. This had several attractions for me; it was a small parish in terms of numbers, services were in English and Welsh in the little church, the parish was bounded on all sides by mountains, and the vicarage was large enough to take my parents and ourselves. We did a deal with them: alternate days throughout the month, of child minding, leaving them fifteen days to explore by 'bus the coastal towns of Conwy, Llandudno, Rhyl and the mountain towns of Beddgelert and Betws-y-coed and further afield if they wished, while on the other fifteen days, Lynne and I were free to attempt the 'fourteen three-thousands'.

For we had been reading *I Bought a Mountain*, in which, in addition to a fascinating account of his farm (which was in 'my parish') the author describes his training for and conquest *in one day* of the fourteen peaks above three thousand feet in the Snowdon range. If he could do it in one day, could not we perhaps in fifteen?

We explored the ground with maps, binoculars and conversation with farmers in my congregation—who thought it pretty peculiar that a quite decent-looking parson should so wish uselessly to expend his energy. To seek out straying sheep? yes; but for fun?

But there they were, a confrontation for us like Everest ('because it's there'). Along the road Tryfan, the shapely, so attractive contours, and across the Bangor road from Tryfan, Carnedd Dafydd, Carnedd Llywelyn and Pen Llithrig y Wrach, which looked a comfortable scramble; and then the two Glyders ('large' and 'small', though 'small' was also over three thousand feet). These two climbs, Glyder Fawr and Glyder Fach were to give us the finest panoramic views and one day of low-lying mist, a staggering view of a rolling white sea with most of the three-thousand peaks rising like islands about us.

The first climb was Tryfan, so near the Vicarage as we began the lower slopes. Some of the way was quite tricky scrambling for beginners but we managed the peak: one, and thirteen to go.

Snowdon itself counted as two, for there were two ascents: the climb from Pen-y-Gwryd, the mountaineers inn, the initial letters of which gave its name to the Pyg-track and Yr Wyddfa itself, the central peak of Snowdon, approached cravenly, if you wished, by mountain railway. We started from the main road at Pen-y-Gwryd, and went along the lower, easy stretches of the Pyg-track. As we approached the steep scramble to Crib Goch we saw a rather professional-looking party in full climbing gear coming obliquely to meet our path. The leader came towards us.

"Where are you taking the young lady?" He was looking curiously at our rubber-shod light shoes. "Up Crib Goch and on to Yr Wyddfa" I replied, a little tentatively. "Well, follow us. These lads are on the final test as Sea Scouts and I'm afraid we have no ropes to spare you."

Ropes! This was a new aspect of the 'fourteen three-thousands' I had scarcely anticipated but one couldn't lose face at this stage. We followed steadily, making quite good time in their wake, watching their direction and holds and of course we were not wasting time roping up! We got on to the ridge. To my view it looked sharp as a knife with a drop on one side to a lake and on the other a land-slide of scree—and it seemed to stretch ahead for miles. Here I learned my most humiliating lesson: Lynne had a splendid head for heights and I had none. She walked securely along the 'knife-edge'; I cravenly went down a yard, using the top of the ridge as a hand-rail. The views were sublime—the true eighteenth-century sublime—

and I can appreciate them now in comfortable memory. But then I had no taste for aesthetics and when we came to the Pinnacles, which had somehow to be negotiated before we began the next task of Yr Wyddfa, I sat in the scree and said—I believe actually aloud—"I can't go on; I can't go back; and I don't care."

The Sea-Scout leader came back towards us and courteously assumed I was resting. "There's just a little jump across that fissure and you're really on your way." 'That fissure', which was just about five feet across, seemed to me to open into an abyss miles deep. Lynne jumped gracefully over it, while the Sea-Scout straddled the other side and gave me a hand. I thought now it was time for sandwiches, to allow the real climbing party to get away; and Yr Wyddfa, the final summit of Snowdon lay solidly and comfortingly before us. We thanked the leader warmly and, on the whole, he seemed not displeased with our progress, even mine.

That evening, in the quiet of the Vicarage, we read the climbing guides for Snowdonia and I sweated again as I read that Smythe regarded the ascent from the Pyg-track to be excellent training for the ascent of Everest. He was of course speaking of winter conditions, with snow and ice along the ridge—but why split hairs?

Towards the end of the month we had done twelve of the fourteen climbs and had only Carnedd Llywelyn and Pen Llithrig-y-Wrach to complete. We began on the latter and had reached half-way when we realised that our sandwiches had been left on a boulder, where we had rested after the first stretch. We had one orange for the day's climb and we decided on the peel for the upward climb and the flesh for lunch on the summit. We got back to the Vicarage hungry but fitter than on any previous day.

Sadly Snowdonia then did its worst. Mist, rain and high winds blotted out our last days and Carnedd Llywelyn remained unconquered. As I have subsequently driven Telford's road to Anglesey, I look at the peak with some regret.

*

"Do you like living in London?"

"Oh, we don't live in London—no-one does. We all live in villages and ours is called Sadler's Wells."

It was a quite unexpected revelation from the art critic, Eric

Newton, when we stayed with him and his wife, Stella Mary, in Cumberland Gardens. As a provincial, I had always envied Londoners their access to art, music and the theatre and the Newtons' loyalty, not to London, 'The Great Wen', but to its many 'villages' was a new and somehow comforting thought.

It was always a delight to talk about art with Eric, his insights into contemporary art, his intuitive acceptance of the genuinely new and rejection of the pretentious or bogus, gave me delight whenever I shared talk with him, and the pleasure was renewed each week as I read his all too brief essays in the *Sunday Times* and amply confirmed by his lectures as Slade Professor at Oxford. I wonder how many now remember the opening lecture when he projected several slides showing successively a few square inches of canvas and invited us to identify the artist from the brushwork?

Stella's expertise converged upon his. Her central discipline is the history of costume and jewelry and she has done some of her most notable work in the attribution of obscure paintings, whether in the reserve collection of the National Gallery or in collections in Europe and America. I remember one judgment very well, which she related when she returned from one such consultant visit: "No, it cannot be as early as they claim. You see that pendent jewel? It's the Order of the Golden Fleece and that Order had not been created at the date they assign for that picture."

So it was that Eric's most substantial book, a study of Tintoretto, has an appendix by Stella on Mannerist costume and she ruefully told me of the devastation they caused on a tour of U.S. galleries, as they deprived them of confident attributions to Tintoretto: "We must have cost them thousands in lost attributions—but after all it was they who invited us to make the judgments!"

Stella and I met frequently at the Summer Schools of the Religious Drama Society (now called Radius) and it was at one of these that we first attempted our 'double act'. Stella's knowledge of costume and her sense of colour, texture and scale led to some notable designs in the theatre (her set for *Coriolanus* in 1946 at the Old Vic is reproduced in *Shakespeare and the Artist*). I asked her if we couldn't play the public game of her designing a Shakespeare play to my demands on her in my role as 'director/critic'. She was very ready.

Our first essay (at, I believe, an R.D.S. Summer School) was *Antony and Cleopatra*. I spoke about the play for about a quarter of an hour and, without any interval and with only a couple of blackboards and coloured chalks, Stella produced a stage set and costumes for the main characters, which vividly met my reading of the play. At the time I was still teaching in University College, Cardiff and we had a particularly good evening in the department, 'putting on' *Hamlet*.

We had already worked together on my pageant-play, *The Two Swords*, for the Diocese of Monmouth during the 1951 Festival of Britain, for the production of which we were fortunate to have Clarice O'Shea. She was already a talented member of the B.B.C. Wales Drama Company and sustained the extensive circuit of Monmouth Churches with fortitude. Stella's costumes, whether in the open-air performances or in churches and St Woolos Cathedral, had a vividness which turned the performances into true pageantry. As I write, a week before Christmas, I have before me her witty drawing of the Nativity—her Christmas card. Mother and Child are stage-centre before a plain back-drop, while the *dramatis personae* peer, questioning the marvel, around the concealing 'flats', while an angel shares the curiosity of the animals, straining over the top of the back-cloth. It is an insight that the makers of the York, Coventry or Chester Cycles would have recognised and perhaps—in an unguarded moment—have envied.

4

TEACHING—HOME AND ABROAD

The decision to apply for the Chair of English in the University of Exeter was difficult. I was very happy in Cardiff, my roots were in Wales and I was beginning to enjoy some of the results of the long, eleven-year haul over *Shakespeare and the Artist* and had just been appointed to the first Readership established by the University of Wales. It would, also if successful, involve leaving behind as young members of the Department in Cardiff the three most brilliant students I have taught anywhere: Lynne Brown, Terry Hawkes and Gwyn Ingli James. They were making Cardiff a lively department and I hated the prospect of leaving it all.

The question of my children was more ambiguous. Christina was about to read French at Cardiff and declared that the best way of going to a university that was not 'home' was to send your parents elsewhere. She redeemed this opinion by coming after her initial degree to the Department of French in Exeter, and took her Ph.D. two years later with a dissertation on *Delacroix as Creative Critic*, a sophisticated parody of *Shakespeare and the Artist*; she remained on as a tutor in the Department of French and had the good sense to marry a fellow-tutor, David Shaw.

Paul was in a trickier situation. He had left the choir at the Royal Chapel in Windsor for Sherborne School and, though taking Russian on his own account and learning Modern Greek from the house cook, he was manifestly on the way to a career in Classics. This seemed later to be confirmed by his reading the Classical Tripos at Cambridge and going on for a year to the University of Athens, a happy period interrupted by the regime of 'the Colonels'. Poetry was now becoming dominant (he had won the Chancellor's Prize for Poetry in his final year) and after a period at the University of Tennessee, he returned to teach English at the University of Warwick.

But this was somewhere in the future. I was appointed to the Chair at Exeter and, hearing that it was in many ways an unhappy department, asked the Vice-Chancellor for an interview before accepting. I was not in a position to 'impose terms' but I did have his assurance that steps would be taken to enlarge the department and that the first opportunity would be taken to promote John Speirs, Harold Mason and Patrick Crutwell to Senior Lectureships, promotion scandalously overdue. Both promises were fulfilled.

The move was made and we were fortunate in finding a handsome Regency house not far from the Cathedral, and in a sufficiently dilapidated condition to meet our purse. Work began on house and department. The first tasks on the house were conducted by a stream of workmen for three months; the first on the department was to get equitable grants for our library and adequate staffing—endeavours not appreciated by the other larger departments who had gained from the quiescence of English.

There were happy moments. It was clearly puzzling that the professor of English should have come from Wales and be also an Anglican parson. A young reporter was sent to the university by the local paper and his only question was this: "Isn't it strange that the Professor of English here should be a Welsh-speaking Welshman?" "Hilarious," I replied "but then this university does things like that. Do you know that the Professor of German is an English-speaking Englishman?" A very puzzled reporter left my room and I don't think Professor Garland bore me any ill-will.

It was perhaps fortunate for me—but I think, on the whole, not fortunate for the British universities in general—that the Robbins Report commended rapid expansion. Since I was now fortunate also in the appointment of our intelligently sympathetic Vice-Chancellor, Sir David Llewellyn (who became head of the British Council later) expansion of my department became possible and I was able to put other projects in hand. It had always been my dream that a Department of English should be a centre of creativity within a university, that drama, fine art and music could be related to our central critical and historical concerns in English Literature.

Roderick Ross, the Secretary of the University, and I, succeeded in obtaining the interest of a wealthy businessman in building for us at the heart of the university estate a full-scale theatre. Lord Holford our architect was very interested in the project and I spent a happy six months preparing a scheme for his realisation which would enable us to have a stage flexible enough to produce any mode of play, Greek drama, Elizabethan plays in their early setting, proscenium-arch framing, a modern open stage and 'theatre in the round', together with a sunk orchestra pit for chamber opera, and cinema projection. We succeeded beyond all expectation.

Meanwhile I had set up a drama sub-department with a lively young actor-producer John Rudlin, to begin work on a combined-honours degree in a course which could draw on the resources of the theatre. As a final coup I succeeded, on a visit to Stratford on Avon in persuading Tony Church to take two years leave from the Royal Shakespeare Company to become the first director of our Northcote Theatre. Grace was added to this theatre when Dame Barbara Hepworth gave us a large bronze sculpture to be placed in a niche in the theatre foyer.

Years of fine productions followed and when Tony Church was succeeded by Jane Howell, with her Brechtian interests and skills, a style had been established which gave the theatre prestige beyond the West Country.

The next step for me was to persuade our department of Music to join us in an Honours degree and to negotiate with the Exeter College of Art a much trickier collaboration. This was to devise a joint-honours course which would involve half the English Honours and half the Diploma in Art and Design (the Dip.A.D.). That Clifford Fishwick was the Principal of the College of Art ensured both intelligent understanding and the cutting of red tape. Roughly the scheme was this: the Art side would involve a choice by the undergraduate at the end of the first term, between painting and sculpture, while all of them took graphics and printing. All undergraduates on the English side took a course on Shakespeare and three periods in literary history, while all students in this degree presented a collection of poems, short stories or plays of their own, set up and printed by them and illustrated in line or lithograph. In all this I had the happiest cooperation from all members of my own department and from three in particular from the College of Art, Eric Cleave in charge of printing, Arthur Goodwin who tutored the painting course and Michael Snow the sculpture. It was a remarkably successful degree and since we wished to supervise their work closely, we allowed only from five to eight students to enter each year. Since we had about a hundred applicants for every place, we had an excellent choice.

The department was now working admirably and I was able to expand work in two other directions. First, on the recommendation of Cleanth Brooks whom I knew at Yale and now, to our great pleasure, Cultural Attaché at the U.S. Embassy in London, I was able to invite Michael Weaver to lead our new venture in American and Commonwealth Literature. After Cambridge Mike had gone on a junior fellowship to Yale and had so impressed them that on their recommendation, Exeter appointed him 'unseen', confirming the appointment readily the following year. He was an excellent critic—his *William Carlos Williams* already published,—and something of an authority thus early on the history of photography and the cinema. I nearly lost him to Eastman—Kodak as we were at the height of our experiment but he stayed, to shape a team with Mike Gidley and our own graduate Peter Quartermain in a pioneering course of study.

Soon after, we appointed Michael Swanton from Manchester to head our Mediaeval Studies (he now holds the personal chair) and once more we had expertise with boundless enthusiasm. For him, Old English poetry *was* poetry and not a treasurehouse of grammatical peculiarities and his vitality soon informed the whole sub-department.

There came a final resonance. Ted Hughes had come to live in North Tawton at no great distance from Exeter and we began arrangements to set up the Rougemont Press, with my son Paul and with Eric Cleave as our printer. Our first publication was an anticipation of *Crow*, with a selection of Ted's poems and we went on to publish Sylvia Plath's *Fiesta Melons*, the first volume of hers which was illustrated with her own drawings. These two books were in immediate demand and were followed by 'manuscript poems' by Jon Stallworthy, Sylvia Plath and Norman MacCaig and a very handsome pamphlet of poems, *Sundials* by Ian Hamilton Finlay. Two further substantial volumes gave me a lot of personal pleasure: Paul's first collection of poems, *Stones* which had two specially drawn lithographs by Barbara Hepworth and an introduction by Ted Hughes; and finally Dorothy Pound's first book, her journal kept when she first met Ezra Pound and again there were plates, lithographed from her drawings and watercolours.

Ted Hughes was now closely involved with my department and began to conduct poetry seminars during a lunch-hour each week, with from twelve to twenty of our undergraduates. These sessions began by my leaving on the table of my room a number of cans of beer and enough pies to sustain them, and Ted listened to their poems and read them his own in progress. He told me of his surprise at the quality of their verse and also suggesting very quietly that perhaps Queen's Building and the atmosphere of formal teaching was inhibiting and asking if I minded that they spend the lunch-hour in an Exeter pub. I thought it an excellent idea and the whole course was so successful that we published a substantial series of 'Exeter Books', sometimes in anthologies of undergraduate work and sometimes devoting a volume to a single student or to our lecturers in the department who were writing excellently.

When Ted Hughes had done this for as long as he felt able, we had Charles Causley leave his Launceston school to become poetry fellow, teaching for a year in American and Commonwealth studies and again involving himself with student verse.

The whole of this activity, formal and informal, produced a tight-knit and exciting department and I was fortunate not only in having a scholarly and loyal group of colleagues but we were also able to attract some of the best undergraduates from a wide variety of schools.

*

As we were well launched on our work in the University, 1964, the Shakespeare Quatercentenary was looming up. On the strength of *Shakespeare and the Artist* I was asked by the Arts Council to mount the 'Shakespeare in Art' exhibition in London and Professor Alistair Smart invited me to arrange a similar exhibition in the Department of Fine Art in Nottingham University. There were two lecture visits to the United States, a visit to Paris under Unesco auspices and a tea-party for Shakespearians in Buckingham Palace.

But in all this activity two events took precedence, a five-week visit to India and a lecture-tour in German Universities.

*

The main activity on the India tour was a series of lectures in universities at Madras, Delhi, Jadavpur and Calcutta. Seminars with Indian academics were exceedingly stimulating and at the same time there was ample leisure to explore the architecture, especially of south India and get some feel of the art which was an almost new experience for me.

Madras gave me one of the richest experiences of the tour. At a British Council reception I had met musicians who invited me to their home and to listen to their rehearsal for a recital that week. They were three brothers and two friends who constituted the group, regarded as the finest in southern India. After the meal I went with them to the austerely furnished rehearsal room, and they showed me the instruments and explained some of the basic musical principles of Indian *ragas*. The room was the perfect acoustic setting for their rehearsal and as the music gathered momentum and force, I was not so much listening to as invaded and permeated by the music. I walked back to my hotel across Madras in a private reverberant world.

The recital in a theatre the following evening was very different. Much of the sound was now dispersed in the large auditorium but substituting for the physical involvement of the rehearsal was the murmurous nodding of the knowledgeable old men with whom I sat and the smiling encouragement of the sister of three of the players, a classical dancer, who turned to me in delight when a passage in the music demanded exceptional skill. They were very pleased when one of the *ragas* was played especially for me, a high compliment in this remarkable setting. I was to experience a similar expertise in Calcutta some weeks later when I was led through the intricacies of classical Indian drama by the whispered commentary of Professor Lal of Calcutta university.

We spent Christmas in the country south of Madras. On the way we broke our journey at Mahabalipuram with its huge frieze of life-size figures, animal and human, 'The Penance of Ajuna' cut in low relief in the living rock. This was overwhelming in its sheer scale:

> But the valley is more moving.
> Here, within sound of the breakers,
> The five temple-chariots in stone,

The Rathas with their guardians:
    Elephant, Lion, Bull,
    A goddess in each niche,
    Wait for the feast.

The enterprise, to fill a whole valley
With sculpture, ceased abruptly,
Twelve centuries ago.
The catastrophe was sudden—
    One sees the very moment
    When the tools slipped from their fingers—
And the design, the act of creation,
Stands open to our eyes.

The granite is fine grained,
The great raw pieces
Poised for the chisel.
Some are blocked out in geometric masses
The interior stresses of the animal form;
Others etched in fine ridges along the contours,
Lines of stone to be struck away;
Finally the form revealed, the creature couchant,
The granite textured to its final shape.

One process remains, the work of the years,
The dark patina of caressing hands
The mute understanding of muscle and stone.

Christmas day was rather trying for me; I was too unwell to eat almost anything; I hadn't been too pleased with our opening 'entertainment' in the early morning when a snake charmer played a pipe to some listless cobras and then placed a boa-constrictor around my neck.

But the Eucharist in the local church—(the rite of the Church of South India) had all the peace one had hoped for and I was now looking forward to Delhi.

We were happily entertained by the British Council at Delhi but the politeness of the situation was disturbed by the entrance of one of my Ph.D. students from Cardiff days, Professor Mohan Lal Chejara, who had been like a member of our family and was now overcome by the meeting after so many years. It was six years since he had left us after completing a most satisfactory dissertation on Wordsworth. He had come to see us at our home in Caerleon before flying back to India the following day. He had been like an older brother to Christina and Paul and they were now dismayed to find Mohan so upset. It came out that he had heard that morning that his father had arranged a marriage for him in a week's time to a young woman he had never before seen. We spoke to him as comfortingly as we could but he went away to a long silence, with no communication for nearly six months. Then came as remarkable a letter as I have ever received; from its first sentence: 'I have fallen in love with my wife' it was full of happiness.

Now, in Delhi, we arranged to meet, after I had lectured in Aligarh, at his first university at Agra. I had been a little fearful of seeing the Taj Mahal, assuming that it would not have the beauty that photography claimed for it. In fact, from the first sight of the building in the distance its radiance was magnificent.

As he left me at Agra, Mohan told me that he was bringing his wife and two children to see me at Calcutta. There I chose to sleep and take my meals not in the hotel but in one of the small cabins in the quiet garden. There, on the afternoon we had arranged, I looked out of my window at a remarkable and moving sight—Mohan walked gravely alone, dressed completely in white, Kamal in a gold *sari* (her marriage dress, she told me later) walked behind him and then, keeping the same distance, the children, as grave as their parents. Mohan stood aside and Kamal bowed very low, murmuring "Mohan's *guru*!" The next moment the beautiful woman was laughing and chatting like one of the children. We spent a happy afternoon, spanning the time since Cardiff, and then two full days, exploring Calutta together.

There were shadows. The poverty was appalling and on my early morning walks before the heat of the day it was an affront each dawn to see the carts which travelled the streets to pick up the bodies of those who had not survived the night at their sole home, the pavement. I went with Kamal and Mohan across the long Hooghly bridge and was astounded at the hundreds who lived their whole lives on the sidewalks of this bridge. I had never thought to have leprous hands raised to beg for my alms and I knew the pained disgust which forced from Mohan the whispered, "India has become a dung-heap!"

But there was the Cathedral and the gentle and learned South Indian Archbishop De Mel. His hospitality was warm and I was severely tested by his invitation to me to spend a year with him on his staff; had Exeter not been at such a critical point in the development of the degress with Drama, Fine Art and Music, I should almost certainly have accepted.

I was at his home one afternoon when news came by telegraph that T.S. Eliot had died. A memorial service was arranged for the following Sunday, at which I preached.

*

As I read over this brief account of my time in India it seems to me that I have scarcely given the impression that the British Council sent me, with Miriam Allott and the Oxford historian, Dr John Roberts (Warden of Merton College) on a tour which was to make contact by lectures and seminar discussions with Indian academics. This of course took place; I lectured on Shakespeare and the three writers, Kipling, E.M. Forster and T.S. Eliot who had made such an impression on the Indian literary scene. The British Council had done work of incalculable benefit to their universities and the parties at their centres where we met the English and Sanskrit scholars were among the happiest features of the tour.

And yet it was India itself that held us, lovely, squalid, learned and devout, heir of a cultured tradition more ancient than ours, yet suffering the birth-pangs of an incomprehensible new age. And because of our common concern in what the Welsh call *Y Pethau*, 'The Things', the things that matter, we were admitted, if we cared to enter, into their joyful and tentative explorations. These matters between us set our academic concerns in their correct perspective.

*

We returned to England in January 1964 and I had to get ready for the various Shakespeare celebrations, and of course the film,

The Bible was in its critical last months of production. The celebrations I most looked forward to were at Bochum with the Deutsche Shakespeare—Gesellschaft and at some other universities.

Post-war Germany had fascinated me in its resurrection out of devastation. Two sights are still indelible. Hamburg in the months after the war: from one of the few church towers that survived the bombing I looked out over the acres of destruction, waves of rubble that spread to the horizon, with the waters of the Alster a ribbon in the wasted fields. It was as if Paul Nash's picture of an immense field of shattered planes, his *Totes Meer*, had been realised before me. Yet a few years later, on the bank of the Alster, a splendid church drew me to a Mass in which the altar was suffused with the sunrise-colour of the finest abstract stained glass I had hitherto seen.

The second memory is of a visit to the university of Freiburg-im-Breisgau. I had taken the opportunity on my journey from Munich to Freiburg to explore the churches of the Barock-Paradies, of the Black Forest. I still had the complex majesty of Steinhausen in my mind, when I came to the university and in an afternoon after my lecture, sat sombrely with the professor of English on a hillside overlooking the town. Though it had been of no military significance whatever, in the last weeks of the war it had been devastated right to the west door of the cathedral, reminding me of the even greater crime of Dresden's martyrdom. I asked my friend, "Doesn't this make you feel bitter?" "No," he said, "I always remember Coventry." The tragic waste of it all.

One of my earliest German visits had been to the Free University in Berlin, founded when a large number of professors and students marched in protest at the political humiliation of the Humboldt University. The atmosphere was lively but not as lively as the visit I made with our Cultural Attaché to the Berliner Ensemble in the Russian sector of Berlin. Brecht's *Lukullus* was not to be missed and in those early days there was no 'Berlin Wall'. Because my passport photograph showed me in clerical dress, I wore a 'dogcollar' for this trip and in the interval of the performance I was the centre of half-amused interest and forced to give a 'press conference'. "What did I think of the Berliner Ensemble—of Brecht—of Helena Weigel

—of *Lukullus*—of Berlin?" It was testing time and I believe we parted as friends. In a strange way their eager questions, the demand for friendly assurance, reminded me of the smiling but questioning faces of Martin Luther King's congregation in Atlanta, Georgia. There were tragic resemblances.

*

It was difficult to envisage the whole task before me when I started work on *Shakespeare and the Artist*. Superficially it appeared to be a simple if arduous history of Shakespeare illustration, but this was not my intention; I set out to analyse all the artists' efforts to illustrate, to interpret, to 'translate' and set for the theatre all Shakespeare's works. To do this and cover the period from his own day to ours took me eleven years and in that time, my research cards told me, I had examined ten thousand works, from the great illustrated Shakespeares of the eighteenth century, through artists of stature as diverse as Hogarth, Blake and Eric Gill—and these had had to be pursued through the museums, art galleries and private collections in this country, Europe and the United States.

The ultimate intention was to establish what I called the method of 'visual criticism', the two-way traffic between diverse works of art, the light which one artist throws on the work of another. It was exciting to see a painting of Coriolanus by Poussin pursue Shakespeare's play through books and theatre productions throughout the eighteenth century from Rowe's edition in 1709 to Kemble's production in 1811; or, even more vividly, to see the flood of illumination a painting by young John Runciman in 1769 gave to the dereliction of Lear on the heath.

There were many personal pleasures to compensate for the seemingly endless drudgery: the apparently unbounded patience of John Gielgud and Paul Scofield as I questioned them about their reactions to the sets designed for some of their major productions. One such interview, with Michael Redgrave, led to near-catastrophe in a performance. It was my custom in those days to use a Penguin edition of a play to make notes on a major production I wished to record, and I had devised a set of signs to 'choreograph' all moves and to define stress and movement in the speaking of the lines. The play in question was Redgrave's remarkable *Hamlet* at Stratford and I planned to see it three times in the week. On the morning after the first performance, I had a long talk with him about his interpretation and, knowing that with meticulous scholarship he explored the notes in the major scholarly editions, I questioned him about his pronunciation, 'tropically' in Hamlet's exchange with King Claudius in Act II, 2:

King: What do you call the play?

Hamlet: 'The Mouse-trap.' Marry, how?
        Tropically. This play is the image
        of a murder . . .

I asked him what his pronunciation 'tropically' implied. He looked surprisingly nonplussed, for it was rare for him not to know every footnote on a crucial word. I told him that I disliked the implication in 'tropically' and preferred the hint of a pun in the suggested '*trap*ically' but an even greater preference was for '*trope*-ically'—in the manner of a 'trope' or small play. He was delighted with the little quirk and that evening in the theatre I waited with interest for the line. It came:
    "Marry, how? Trop . . . trap . . . trope . . . tropically."
It was the first (and only) time I have ever been the occasion for a break in a Shakespeare production and I believe that if Michael Redgrave had not been a most generous man, there could have been another murder on his mind that evening.

*

It was good fortune for me that for just £6 in addition to my Rockefeller Fellowship I was able to travel first class on the Cunard liner *Carinthia* for my first visit to America. I had unfortunately not been able to take up my full year on my Folger Library Fellowship, but it was good to have the three and a half months from the beginning of September. In that time I hoped to supplement work published in *Shakespeare and the Artist* and to gather material for a study of Elizabethan law and the work of Edward Coke in particular.

The journey across the Atlantic was eventful and not the least like the leisurely cruise of my imagining. Off the south Irish coast we encountered a gale-force storm and I could feel no fear, simply awe as, behind the plate-glass observation point, we saw the ship plough almost nonchalantly through the heart of waves which seemed to tower a hundred feet above us. When we had passed through the storm, nature gave us pleasure at the other end of the scale. A small song-bird, unable to make further progress on its migration, landed on our upper deck for a free passage and became our watchful care for the next two or three days.

The food throughout the voyage was embarrassing and every dinner-time I played the game of choosing my five courses from food I had never eaten before—nor have been able to afford since. And of course there were the friendships in the leisurely time, with the Washington attorney, Robert Ashe whose advice was so valuable in my relations over Ezra Pound's case in the next months and the Americanist Marcus Cunliffe with whom conversation was a vivid foretaste of the flavour of U.S. intellectual life.

Since I arrived in Washington on the eve of Labour Day, James MacManaway and his wife insisted on my staying with them over the holiday before settling into my apartment off Constitution Avenue. Though himself a Southern Baptist, Mac took me to Washington Cathedral for my first Sunday service in the U.S. As I walked down through the congregation, I was aware of a tone in the pre-service whispering that was teasing but unidentifiable. The explanation came at the announcement of the first hymn: this was the annual service of the whole Welsh community of the U.S. east coast. The sermon was especially fascinating, a fluent exposition with the strangest New York accent overlaying the native north Welsh! Time in America could scarcely have begun more propitiously, as Mac well knew.

Arrangements for readers at the Folger Library were so lavish that I estimated at the end of my relatively short visit that I had completed as much work as I could have managed in some two years in Great Britain, even with the resources of the British Museum. 'My librarian', the lively and intelligent Elaine Fowler, by-passed for me all the time-wasting chores which made research at British libraries so irritating. One morning we arrived at the same time at the Folger. "What's the assignment for today?" "I saw a reference yesterday to the use of the word 'saint' applied to King David in the *Book of Homilies*. It would be interesting to trace its use through the sixteenth-century editions of the *Homilies*." By the time I had sat at my table and got my notes, filing cards and pen all ready, the first six editions of the *Book of Homilies* were at my elbow, with the call-slips all made out and needing only my signature and by lunchtime I had not only traced my Welsh-sounding King of Israel through all the volumes but also written my brief article for *Notes and Queries*.

Two other stimulating finds punctuated my more long-term studies in Elizabethan law. In the intervals of digesting Coke's *Institutes*, I was refreshing myself with brief searches for Shakespeare illustrations that I may have missed in England and Germany. My first discovery was a bundle of note-books in which George Romney had made extensive studies of the plays. It was his habit to seize upon one dramatic scene and make as many as six to ten drawings of successive moments in the scene, giving the effect of a succession of cinema stills. Two groups were especially striking, the first a sequence depicting the storm which opens *The Tempest* and the second, the appearance of Banquo's ghost at the banquet. In the latter group the menace of the ghost's confrontation of Macbeth and Macbeth's increasing horror has the intensity of a stage presentation.

A little later, a chance remark by MacManaway revealed that the library possessed the original drawings for the exceptionally beautiful Hanmer edition of Shakespeare of 1744. So important were these drawings that I prepared an article with a selection from them which Mac published in *The Shakespeare Quarterly*.

Meanwhile, my meetings with Ezra Pound at St Elizabeth's Hospital had given a new and more personal urgency to my work on Edward Coke. It had hitherto had a solely sixteenth-and seventeenth-century interest, in clarifying for me Shakespeare's pre-occupation with legal and constitutional matters in his plays and especially his concern for legitimate royal authority. Now, as Pound worked on his 'Coke' cantos, my own academic concerns took on a greater personal significance.

*

Louis Wright, the Director of the Folger Library was very happy that Fellows should make contact with other academic institutions in the United States. The first of my weekend excursions from Washington was to affect very happily the next twenty years and beyond. At the suggestion of Father Martin Jarrett-Kerr, C.R., my friend at the Community of the Resurrection, Mirfield, Father Richard Young, chaplain to undergraduates in the University of Chicago, invited me across for a visit. In that brief time I began my long friendship with Professor Nathan Scott and his wife Charlotte and Dick Young introduced me to the Chicago Medical Centre, with its five teaching hospitals and numerous institutes and clinics. This led, the following year to my return for a fortnight to Chicago to stay with Dick Young in the chaplaincy within the Medical Centre. During the next twenty-one years I failed only once to return either to the Medical Centre or the English and Divinity Departments in the University of Chicago.

These later visits, if my host was Dick Young at the Centre, had a stern routine. After the Eucharist in the Chapel, I was available over breakfast to receive telephone invitations to lunch-time or evening lectures at one of the medical institutes. The first of these talks was to the Haematological Institute whose director was anxious to show me their new electron microscope of phenomenal power and versatility; I think they were happy with my talk on *Macbeth*, which was billed '*Blood will have blood*' and I was rewarded with a Dictionary of American Slang which greatly broadened my horizons. My second visit was to the Psychiatric Clinic where naturally my topic was *Madness in King Lear*, on which they had very interesting theories.

After breakfast we did a ward-round, either at Presbyterian St Luke's or Cook County Hospital, or observed an operation—far more lavishly manned than in British hospitals. Back to the centre for meals and discussions and to bed after a normal fourteen or fifteen-hour day.

The Medical Centre authorities were very concerned at their high suicide and divorce rate; they were what they called 'a unitary society' of some twenty-three thousand people, from probationer nurses to senior consultants. Chaplains and sporadic visitors like myself were welcomed but they felt the need for a more permanent non-medical presence and they invited me to be a Professor of Literature and Fine Art, It was a flattering and attractive offer; I had never, in any British university met this great concentration of expertise and dedication to one discipline, and friendship with Dick Young and increasing contacts with the University of Chicago through Nathan Scott made the proposition almost irresistible. But Christina and Paul were at critical stages in their education and it seemed wanton to disturb them. With great regret, I promised simply to return whenever I could.

*

Meanwhile, my research period in Washington work was going on steadily, with my 'home' weekends dedicated to visits to St Elizabeth's and a long time spent almost every Sunday in the National Gallery. These visits included lunch, tea and dinner in the cafeteria, spacing out an exploration of two of the galleries in the afternoon and evening (Picasso and Braque were 'compulsory' each Sunday) and a recital of music in the early evening which supple-mented the recitals every Friday evening at the Library of Congress. There, the Hungarian Quartet's performance of all the string quartets of Beethoven first led me to wonder whether it was worth spending one's listening energies on anything but string quartets—it is a question that still lingers.

Sunday mornings were usually spent in the parish church of Alexandria, Virginia, a street-car ride across the Potomac river. The church had a remarkable history. In 1765 twelve vestrymen were enrolled to consider building a church. Two years later the architect James Wren began work and by 1773 it was completed. Perhaps this efficiency was not unconnected to the presence of George Washington as one of the vestrymen.

On 17 July 1853 Robert E Lee was baptised in the church and worshipped in Christchurch both as a child and later when he came to live in Arlington. It was a reverberant tradition and I was glad to be immersed in its life. The rector of the parish had been ill for some time and the young curate was hard pressed with pastoral work. In the two services on the Sunday mornings therefore, I alternated with him as celebrant or preacher. On my first Sunday

I found myself addressing a large congregation who had been profoundly shaken by the disturbances at Little Rock, Arkansas— for Alexandria was very conscious of its 'southern' identity. In as seemly a way as I could, I told them of our British concern for their 'black problem' and, at the coffee break between the two services, I was approached by a woman of manifestly keen intelligence who said, without any aggression: "I want you to know that I treat my servants as though they were white." I felt impelled to reply, I hope with a courtesy she understood, "I'm glad, but I think they would prefer it if you treated them as though they were black." Our talk went on for the rest of the break between the services and I believe we were friends.

Another of my friends in Alexandria was 'Frances Bonamy', author of the classical 'whodunit' *The King is Dead on Queen Street*, a very gracious hostess and southern lady. Finally, when I left Washington I was given a cross made from the wood from one of the avenue of walnut trees planted when Christchurch was first built and now growing beyond their maturity.

*

From my first visit to Chicago, Nathan Scott and I became close friends. There were many reasons for our friendship apart from a mutual liking. Nathan was formally a member of both the English and the Theology faculties in the University of Chicago (as he is now in the University of Virginia) and in a wide-ranging list of books he has explored with a scholarship that embraces the major European literatures, the complexities of contemporary theological and philosophical debate. I have just finished reading his latest book, his finest, and in *The Poetry of Belief* he has given his clearest statement of the common disciplines which span literary criticism and theology. My visits to Swift Hall each year were therefore both pleasant and creative. My own views, dating back to those fire-watching days with Leslie Bethell, now matured alongside my convictions concerning the inter-relations of art and literary criticism.

It seemed to me, after I had become more and more at home in Chicago that it was due to Nathan Scott that I was offered the

127

Willett Chair in his university. This was a characteristic American professorship, a means of inviting someone the university wanted in residence for anything up to a year, in any discipline they wished to foster. The holder of the Willett Chair was invited to complete his own title and mine was to be Willett Professor of Literature and Theology and involved me formally in giving some lectures in the term which was all I could undertake in view of my Exeter commitments. These lectures explored, with particular reference to Shakespeare, the principles of theological criticism and their relevance to the substance of literature, especially in the Renaissance. When later I was asked to give the Prideaux Lectures in Exeter, I extended the argument by a closer scrutiny of twentieth-century authors, with Eliot, Pound and James Joyce at the centre of the discussion; and when a year or two after this, I gave the Lyttelton Lectures at Eton College, the argument went further to examine the relevance of the more abstract art of music in a consideration of the highly conceptual matters we were arguing in Chicago. Two incidents in the course of my Willett lectures gave me especial pleasure. I was approached gravely by three men who announced that they represented twelve Jesuits who were doing advanced studies in the University and were attending my talks—and they were very troubled! "What heresies have I committed?" "Oh, none; that's the trouble; you're so appallingly orthodox." It was my first glimpse of the wide spectrum of beliefs which could be embraced even by the most vigorous of the Church's priesthood. When later they invited me to a meal, there was some hilarity at the end of our discussion when they accused me of being more Thomist than they could altogether countenance!

Of even greater charm was the smiling greeting of a pretty young woman in a short, flowered frock, who wished to question some points I was making. I asked what she was reading and was taken aback by her reply: "I'm reading for a Ph.D.—and by the way, I'm a Poor Clare!" Jesuits and Franciscans—my world was being assaulted!

Even more important for me than giving the lectures and the associated seminars were the quiet meals with Nathan, Charlotte and their friends. I knew the poetry and the criticism of Elder Olson before I came to Chicago but his hospitality, his passion for music and fine art made our meetings an even greater pleasure. And there was one evening where the Scotts brought the distinguished Mircea Eliade to dinner and the other two guests were his assistant Charles Long and his wife. We were then three whites and four blacks and some of the talk turned on the tragedy of black adolescents in Chicago at that time. Mrs Long declared with angry tears that had her young son been white he would never have been picked up by the police, as he had, with no more suspicious circumstance than that he was black—because a bicycle was missing in their street. But with Mircea Eliade present the talk soon moved to the philosophy of 'primitive' religions. This was a new and rich world for me and when I learned that my first, rather informal teaching hour immediately followed Chuck Long's main lecture hour, I went along with him at the earlier hour. To hear him talk of an Australian aborigine's concentration on the magic of a 'churinga stone' held in his palm, or a West African's conviction that the sky, the heavens were infinitely above one's head—at least a hundred yards above— was for me to enter unknown modes of being described by a man who knew them in his blood.

*

Chicago is a city of very great beauty, coming, for me, close behind Cambridge, Edinburgh, Venice and Vancouver as cities to capture the heart. But Chicago has the great liability, that you freeze nearly to death for five months of the year and grill nearly to death in another five. I have walked at the lake-side near the university campus between walls of ice some thirty feet high built entirely from waves frozen by winds direct from the northern tundra and for weeks in down-town Chicago, working at the Newberry Library, have walked dizzily in temperatures of 100° and over.

There were however 'times off' of great refreshment. Kitty Picken, one of my undergraduate students, had her home on the campus and her parents were generous not only in their enter-tainment but in ministering to my wish to pursue a project at every visit, outside my university concerns. One year it was to study the architecture of Frank Lloyd Wright. Our apartment was in a post-graduate building next to Wright's Robie House, his striking experiment in the prairie style. But the Pickens extended this experience well outside the confines of Cook County: after the houses, including Lloyd Wright's house with his studio in the suburbs, we went out to the spectacular Taliesin East and the oddly beautiful building of the Johnson's Wax company. Nothing, even in the other architecture of the Lakeside Drive, compared in imaginative impact with these buildings, except perhaps the Pan-Am Building in Kennedy Airport.

*

One year I missed the University of Chicago for a summer course further up Lake Michigan at Lake Forest. Though my assignment was again Shakespeare, it was good on this occasion to meet academics from Union Theological Seminary in New York. Their lively, often provocative examination of religious drama was stimulating and talk among the senior members of the course was liable to go on too long.

One day I decided to travel down to Chicago to have lunch with Nathan Scott and had left the 'phone number of the hotel where we met with the Lake Forest people. I was nonetheless surprised when a call came for me—would I please come into his studio to be interviewed by Studs Terkel. "Studs Terkel!" said Nathan—"the most important radio interviewer in America!" What on earth had I done to earn this distinction? It seemed that someone at Lake Forest had commended me to him, without telling me about it, so that I went to the studio in complete ignorance both of him and the topics he wished to discuss.

There was no problem. In his very small studio, almost completely covered with awards and decorations he had received, Studs Terkel was the completely accomplished interviewer. He had 'done his homework' and seemed mainly interested in the fact that I was Welsh. His interviewing manner was the finest I have ever heard—he spoke very little but placed the provocative question at precisely the point when our talk needed a thrust forward. I found myself talking about Wales, its language and religion; about music

130

and the theatre; about my undergraduates and my hopes for their creative lives. It was wholly enjoyable and we reluctantly parted, old friends of an hour's standing.

*

New Haven and especially the home of Tinkum and Cleanth Brooks was my frequent 'staging post' as I left on my way to Kennedy airport and home. The occasion on my first visit to Yale was a lecture on 'Visual Criticism' and it was not until we were driving out into the country to his home that Cleanth told me the dismaying number of professors of English who had listened with such patient courtesy, and that three of them, Robert Penn Warren, Louis Martz and Norman Pearson were to be his guests at dinner that evening. As we drove into the grounds of his house—a skilfully converted seventeenth-century farm-house—we were halted by a small figure in shirt and riding-breeches with an axe over the shoulder. When Cleanth had introduced us, Tinkum turned briskly to the house, throwing over her shoulder, "Killed three copperheads this morning." Her recent death takes away one of my most endearing friends.

The evening meal was prepared in the garden, Cleanth preparing with scholarly expertise the largest steak I had ever seen, just one steak for the nine of us and grilled over wood-chippings and charcoal to an unbelievable perfection. Talk was unaffected and moved wittily from topic to topic; my ambiguous status, as Robert Penn Warren's wife thought it, poised between university and church, drew from her the deliberately provocative question: "What sort of a priest are you, anyway?" Tinkum and Cleanth, both good Episcopalians were not displeased with my rather tentative answer, "Not a very holy one, I'm afraid, just like most." It wasn't anything more than a semi-colon in the conversation, but it sufficed.

On Sunday morning I was taken to the little Episcopalian church and Cleanth stopped me at the door. "I want you to meet our churchwarden, Leslie Hotson." Somehow it seemed to me that *The First Night of Twelfth Night* took on a fresh life—such a lively and unpompous book.

131

And it was at that visit that Norman Pearson opened for me the possibility that I might make my own small contribution to the release of Ezra Pound.

*

Wichita, Kansas, the centre-point of the United States, was the venue in 1961 for a liturgical congress which brought together some of the finest liturgists in America. As we expected, it was dominated by the genial scholar, Professor Massey Shepherd of the Divinity School of the Pacific. There was adequate leisure between the working sessions and I had a great deal of talk with Massey Shepherd at the point in our English liturgical argument when the new services were being considered. At the end of the Congress he asked me to join him in the University of the South, Sewanee, Tennessee in 1963 at their most interesting summer session which enabled American clergymen to take M.A. and Ph.D. degrees by attending the required number of summer courses. (My lectures were on religious drama and were published in 1965 as *Creed and Drama*). There was a splendid 'family' atmosphere, for many of the clergymen, from both New England and the Deep South had brought their wives and children and just down the road at Chattanooga there was a music school which my daughter Christina attended as often as she could find transport. This produced a tragically embarrassing incident: we had become very friendly with a young black curate and at breakfast one morning Christina asked him if he would drive her down to the music session. He agreed but I thought with a little reluctance. In a few minutes he sought me out and asked me to explain to Christina that he would not dare to drive her on that open road in the current temper of the South, for they were liable in a country village to get shot at, on the assumption that he was abducting a white girl. Christina was passionately angry, for the young man was so manifestly a dedicated clergyman, and of what significance was his colour?

This was the prelude to an invitation to me to take a weekend in Atlanta, Georgia with the vicar of a city church, Frank Ross of All Saints. He told me that if I preached economically in the morning

132

service he would probably be able to drive me across the city to the church of one of his closest friends, Martin Luther King. I was duly economical and we drove rapidly across to Ebenezer Baptist Church just as their service began. They were singing the first hymn and a dozen smiling blacks (we were the only whites present) thrust open hymn books into our hands.

I knew of Martin Luther King's reputation as a preacher, a fiery eloquence informing the careful scholarly structure of his sermons. We were to be surprised. His address lasted perhaps three minutes, was very quiet and deeply moving. It declared simply that the following morning, he and the *white* mayor of Atlanta (he stressed the colour) were to go to the White House to plead with the President the case for black civil rights. "Pray for us, as white and black together, we make our plea." Here, in the gentlest possible tones of that wonderful voice, was the source and indeed the substance of the oratory which flowered in his most powerful speech, 'I have a dream'.

We spent much of the lunch-hour talking with him, his wife Coretta and the children; through all the quiet domestic conversation there glowed the fervour of a man whose vision—and martyrdom—was to transform the social structure of the United States. As we left he gave me an inscribed copy of his volume of sermons, *Strength to Love*. This was for me a meeting as full of power as that so different meeting with Karl Barth, twenty five years earlier.

When I returned to my rooms in Sewanee I knew, as I read his opening sermon, 'A tough mind and a tender heart' that I had met on that Sunday morning one of the greatest prophets of our century. The sermon ended:

> When days grow dark and nights grow dreary, we can be thankful that our God combines in his nature a creative synthesis of love and justice which will lead us through life's dark valleys and into sunlit pathways of hope and fulfilment.

*

The Chicago Symphony Orchestra was celebrating the retirement of Pierre Monteux, probably the most aged conductor then still active, and Nathan Scott had secured tickets for himself and me. It was an attractive programme but we were all waiting for the second half which was to consist simply of Stravinsky's 'Rite of Spring', which Monteux had conducted at its first performance in Paris, two generations before.

The smiles of the standing orchestra as he came on for the performance were a sufficient indication of the players' affection but they also needed to feel a substantial trust. For this was not the version of the 'Rite' with which we and they were familiar but the original version which Monteux had received from Stravinsky for that performance which left Paris in an uproar.

The conductor was the only member of the orchestra without a score and the performance was electric. We had participated in an event which spanned the creative experience of our century as it bestrode two world wars and three generations of music-making.

*

Father Dick Young invited me one Saturday in Chicago to come the following morning to Eucharist at a black church of which he had charge—and would I like to be the celebrant? He picked me up early and we drove out of the university campus to a large house in a black area. Two large rooms on the ground floor had been made into the chapel of their community centre; it was neatly furnished and the altar was made ready. I vested fully, the chasuble a plain and beautiful vestment. Dick was to be deacon and gospeller and I was attended by two little boys, the shining blackness of their faces enhanced by the white of their surplices.

The singing was no surprise—I expected the rich and fervent sound and had already heard it, first when Paul Robeson gave a recital in Cardiff in my first year at University and then in Atlanta, Georgia, in Martin Luther King's church. But I had not expected the simple and devout precision of their ceremonial, their economical and reverent movement about the altar, with no ungainly curves, no hesitation or unsought pauses; it was liturgical ceremony which drew no attention to itself, an unobtrusive frame for the words and music.

So we proceded to the Epistle and I was taken by my two acolytes to my President's seat, eastward of the altar. Then the unexpected

134

happened, to the great pleasure of the congregation. Having carefully arranged my chasuble over my knees, one of the acolytes, with a broad smile—excusing himself or just simple delight?— jumped on to my knee and snuggled into my vestments. I think the congregation heard little of the Epistle but perhaps they reached a fuller grace in seeing this spontaneous gesture of affection.

After the closing hymn we went to the dining room where the communal meal was ready. On the way from the chapel the complement to the previous incident almost caused catastrophe. The little acolyte, having unvested in a room upstairs, was now coming down for the meal but saw me as I came out of the chapel and from about the sixth step of the stairs, launched himself into my arms. I fortunately saw him coming and made a clean catch.

*

The phrase 'Rites of Passage' can have strange overtones. Of the transition from one way of life to another it has serious things to say and it is as well to be conscious of the rites and to perform them. Passage from one country to another by way of the scrutiny of Customs Officers is another matter; the phrase has now to be modified to 'Rights of Passage', though ritual is still its undertone. I am sensitive on this subject, for the customs counter has had several embarrassing moments, with strong comic elements. Two of them may be worth relating.

The Lutheran College at Hamburg had invited a number of Anglican theologians in their several disciplines to discuss doctrine with their Lutheran counterparts. They said, however, that they were weak in 'the Theology of Society' and 'of the Arts' and invited two of us, Dr Langmead-Casserly and me, to represent these areas, without Lutheran counterparts.

Casserly invited me to join him in the drive across the Low Countries and North Germany and to meet him on the quay at Dover. I was disconcerted, on arrival at the meeting-point, to see five tyres strapped to the roof of his car and a covert inspection showed that they, like the four on the wheels, had little or no tread. I mentioned this tentatively and Casserly replied, "There's no canvas showing anywhere", which was apparently his standard.

135

The drive to and from Hamburg saw the tyres reduced to the four wheels and since Casserly had no German, I had to negotiate the wheel-changes with the garage-hands. 'Kaput' became a key word in our converse and I learnt that Goethe and Heine were inadequate verbal currency on an Autobahn.

Meanwhile the conference had gone extremely well and the Lutherans told us on the penultimate day that it was their custom to give gifts to their guests but they didn't know our tastes; would we please go into Hamburg and buy ourselves a gift and here was money to pay.

During the previous years I had bought a case of virginals and an almost complete consort of recorders: a sopranino by Dolmetsch, and a descant, treble and bass by Schott. A tenor recorder would complete the consort and the Lutheran gift should enable me to purchase it. I was right, and a tenor of beautiful tone was bought and was packed, in its three sections, in its canvas and leather case.

Casserly and I parted company before the Channel crossing and I was not to see him again until he became a professor at North-Western University and invited me across from Chicago to lecture in his department; his scholarship and natural verve were as exciting as his driving.

There were not many passengers on the crossing from the Hook, for it was late autumn, and I thought my laudable habit of writing out a complete list of all purchases, with prices in both foreign and British currency, would ensure my quick passage through. The officer scrutinised the list and then froze like a pointer. "Recorder?" he said, "a tape recorder at *that* price?" "No", I replied; "a recorder is a musical instrument." "Yes", he said, "I *know* what a tape-recorder is." I tried to explain what it was, while he told me that I owed vast duties. At last, "Open it up", he said.

When I opened the case and he saw the expanding bell-shape of the third section—"This isn't musical; it's a sub-machine-gun," he said but I saw a slight smile. "Very well; put it together and demonstrate that it's for your use. It will save you £25 if you can."

By this time all the passengers were through customs and were gathered behind me, while all the customs officers were grinning spectators on the other side of the counter. I assembled the recorder and played them the first verse of 'God save the Queen' to the most flattering applause. At £25 for one verse of the English National Anthem, I reckoned that I was probably the highest paid wind-player in Britain that day.

*

It was unusual for me to arrive at O'Hare Airport from Montreal —in fact I can't remember another occasion than this—but there I was, taking my suitcase towards the customs counter, from where I could see, outside the barrier, Father Dick Young, my host, waving in welcome.

It seemed to me that the customs officer eyed me rather searchingly as I approached and he kept glancing across at me as he dealt with the young woman just ahead of me. I understood from her answers to him that she was seeing into Chicago the dancing shoes of a ballet company and since, I understood, the 'points' of these shoes were sometimes used to smuggle drugs, her consignment was very thoroughly searched. Then it was my turn and I felt that by this time his scrutiny was positively hostile. I was told to open all baggage and—this had never happened to me before—he leaned over and patted my pockets—'frisked me' is, I believe, the Chicago term. I looked across in some bewilderment at Dick Young to find him laughing quite helplessly, which increased my irritation. It was clear from the officer's look that he was comtemplating an invitation to me to be body-searched but after another long scrutiny, he ungraciously waved me away. I walked across to the barrier and Dick Young.

"What was all that about and why was it so funny?"

"The morning paper warned O'Hare that a leading drug-handler was leaving Montreal for Chicago today, carrying a large consignment and *dressed as a clergyman!*"

Sub-machine-guns at Harwich, drugs at Chicago: it was clear that my experience was broadening perceptibly.

*

The Shakespeare Conference in Vancouver in 1972 had to work very hard to compete with the beauty of the city, the bay and the background of the Rockies. The 'papers' were, I suppose as good as they always were on these occasions; I can remember none of them but I do remember the almost daily visit to the park where I saw—with ample time to absorb both their craft and their significance—the comprehensive collection of totem poles and other Indian crafts and domestic work. It was an entry into a world I have never since wished to leave and when Eskimo art was added to these, the North American continent took on a wholly new aspect.

More domestically, a dinner at nightfall on the boat-restaurant in the harbour showed a sight as we looked south which was both breath-taking and unreal; breath-taking because in the sunset light the cone of Mount Stanley hovered above a cloud-base as if suspended in air; unreal, because it looked not like nature but like a fragment of Japanese art. It was all the prints of Fujiyama brought before our eyes.

Then there was the drive into the heart of the Rockies; the fact that we were in a vehicle on a well-made road, implied a taming, a 'civilising' of the wild but the scale, the peaks, the extent of the tree-line, snow above the black-green of pines, all these were the Rockies of our imagining.

Yet the week was dominated by an experience which put all academic considerations into their proper dimensions. The heart of the week was the first showing of Grigori Kozintsev's *King Lear*. In those years he was the leading classical film-maker in the Soviet Union and we had already seen *Hamlet*, still for me the only rival of Michael Redgrave's performance in Stratford. I had also read *Shakespeare : Time and Conscience* (E.T. 1966), with its acute study of *King Lear* and *Hamlet*. Kozintsev's courage, both artistic and political, was shown by his use of Boris Pasternak's translation of *Hamlet* as the basis of his film-script, and his employing the Yiddish actor Mickhoels as his Hamlet. Two brief entries from his diary during the shooting of the film reveal his temper and attitudes:

The boiling cauldron of history: wars, rebellions, the changes of power, and the flight of hopes; the iron of violence, . . . will all this be in the film?

There have been hundreds, if not thousands, of interpretations of *Hamlet*—stage and literary—and today every one of them . . .

evokes the impression of insufficiency: Shakespeare's hero is deeper, spiritually richer, has other qualities. What is the secret of the inexhaustibility of this figure?

... Shakespeare wrote life, which contained an infinite swarm of germs for ever-new ideas.

I carried to the film theatre that afternoon the memory of one moment in *Hamlet*: the shot of Hamlet's speaking of the kingdom's corruption and, as he spoke, leaning spread against a wall of rock which was fractured by a fault, nature's response to the flawed common weal.

Canadian Broadcasting had asked me to review the film of *Lear* immediately after the showing and I was to be interviewed by Phyllis Webb, one of the most original and brilliant of the new school of Canadian poets. I saw the film through, and the stunned silence at the end was eloquent of its impact on an audience of scholars rarely subjected to such intensity. I then waited outside for Phyllis Webb. There was no sign of her and since the C.B.C. studio was waiting for us, I went back to search the auditorium. I found her at last, huddled in her seat and mastering a storm of tears at the impact of the film. I persuaded her to come to the car and as we reached the broadcasting studio, she was once more the completely accomplished professional—and in place of the scheduled half-hour, we gave the broadcasters an uninterrupted hour of tape. Rarely indeed have I seen an interpretation in visual terms which penetrated so delicately to the heart of the play as this film did.

That evening I dined with Kozintsev and in the remaining days of the conference we spent a lot of time together and before we left had decided to collaborate on a book on Shakespeare in Film, which we hoped to begin the following spring. When I returned to Exeter I found the British Council again generous to me and it was arranged that I go to Moscow to make final arrangements for the kind of collaboration we envisaged, and in the interim Kozintsev sent me a large collection of stills from *Hamlet* and *Lear*.

Difficulties over visas reduced my time in Moscow to five days and I found when I arrived that Kozintsev was gravely ill—he died just a few weeks later. Even the cathedral *ikonostasis* and the Rublev ikons in the Tretchiakov museum did little to fill the gap of his absence, and the grief and fears of his artist friends in Moscow emphasised the loss which the world of art was soon to sustain.

*

When I was in the Kremlin, walking among the splendid ikons in the churches and cathedrals sited within that remarkable nucleus of Moscow, to see their ikons, set singly on the walls or on the massive *ikonostasis* before the sanctuary, was a wonderful experience—except for one thing: they had become dead, museum objects. As I moved through the lifeless churches I watched the faces about me and felt sure that I was one of the very few who acknowledged the original function of the ikons as objects of veneration. A few hours later I was in the Tretchiakov Museum, a very important centre, in that all the works in it have been painted or carved by Russian artists, a microcosm of Russian art. Three places in that museum between them constitute a parable. First, the floor below ground where there is a unique collection of Rublev ikons. In a very real sense I was happier than I had been in the Kremlin, for these ikons were freed from their liturgical significance, removed from the reminders of a dead church. Rid of the necessity of any spiritual gesture—a homage I would gladly have paid them within the glory of Eastern Orthodox worship—I was able to look at this master of ikon art coolly and objectively, with critical detachment. But I was virtually alone in this gallery.

I went upstairs, reaching the eighteenth and nineteenth centuries and here we had a hive of artistic activity: shrill-voiced and earnest teachers standing before appalling historical paintings with groups of bemused schoolchildren being permanently corrupted by these lessons on 'historical realism', I managed to find a third room, quite small and to one side, where some Russian painters of the first years of this century had been looking closely at Impressionist painting; this room was full of light and liveliness and artists had painted because they wanted to paint. I said to my interpreter—a young woman of about 25—"Now this is painting, the first real painting I have seen since those Rublev ikons in the basement." She looked at them in blank incomprehension and brought out the tired old cliché we have all heard: "But they do not look like anything!"

Indeed it is possible, in Russia or the West, so to indoctrinate a whole generation, without any political overtones being particularly obtrusive, as to make it quite certain that they will never again look at a painting with an innocent, unclouded eye.

Now it is as well to be unambiguous about all this. I am as unlikely as anyone to be completely at home in the Russian revolution! But I would say that I can forgive that revolution a great number of its honestly-held opinions before I can forgive the corruption of the sensibility of a whole generation. I believe they can survive the attempted destruction of their theology and liturgy better than the killing of their artistic sensibility. This may well be because religion is tougher, more durable than sensibility; all the more reason then for guarding the latter.

*

I have often been subjected to that cool, searching, analytical look by which a portrait sculptor or painter determines the planes of one's skull, the texture of person revealed in the living expression. This is the same analytic look I find in the eyes of an artist or an appraisal of a poet as he reads the poems of a fellow-craftsman. And it comes from a realisation of process, of the slow gestation of a work of art. This has become to me the most absorbing of questions: what happens in the progress of the creative act? Jon Stallworthy has a fascinating study—he is himself a fine poet—of the developing power of the successive manuscripts of W.B. Yeats's poems; there is an equal absorption in watching the early stages of a painting or sculpture, in assessing that moment when the work seems to take on a profound independent life of its own, and then the final excitement of the craftsman's resumed power as he shapes the final form—in word, paint or stone—that he had originally conceived. The composer Alun Hoddinott tells me that a symphony or concerto may begin for him in a bird-call in the dawn chorus, or the dissonant relations of two foghorns on the French coast; they take their complex shape with many other buried fragments and ideas; but the shaping, the final formal creation is that of the skilled craftsman.

These intellectual explorations are the common ground of the artist and critic; the artist has always explored the nature and

141

conditions of his craft and the critic—so often faced only with the completed work in its impregnable integrity—can benefit from a knowledge of the process by which that final form has been reached.

*

I have come full circle, from my unhappiness at the denial, within the glories of the Kremlin, of some of the cultural roots of that great people. It would be false pride which asserted that our concerns with the arts are a final antidote, a panacea which solves our ills— both politicians and the Church may also take a necessary hand in the process. But artists have their profound part. In the terms which I have used, Picasso's Guernica is a work of powerful intellectual organisation, a work in which our minds can recognise the cool, analytic look of the artist which has the violence of a blow. For most of us anger is hot, impulsive, and that kind of anger can be dangerously ineffective. But Picasso's anger was disciplined and coolly effective within its painterly control. In the French exile of this passionate Spaniard there was the tragic power which we recognise in the angry geometry of 'Guernica', the painting which first revealed to my generation the brutality of man's warfare, his ultimate inhumanity.

It is instructive for us to turn to Shakespeare's *Lear*, the summit of man's art hitherto. Superficially this tragedy might well say, 'Isn't life awful?' but in fact it says something profounder: 'Isn't life awe-ful?' It might speak of the terrible in man's life, in fact it speaks to our knowledge that out of terror comes awe and out of awe a profound compassion. For Lear knows on the heath a sympathy for 'poor naked wretches' and when he meets Cordelia again with his renewed sanity, to her plea for a blessing he responds, "I'll kneel and ask of thee forgiveness." I have seen great performances of this play by Michael Redgrave accompanied by the music of John Gardner and the visual terrors of Leslie Hurry, by Gielgud and by Scofield, and in the overwhelming film by Kozintsev. But whatever the performance, we know that in the presence of that play our human relationships, our loves, our public and private sympathies, can never again be quite the same. As with

142

Keats we 'burn through' that tragedy, art has taken us into a dimension where triviality is appallingly irrelevant and life so much more tensely significant. Shakespeare, like Picasso, has revealed some of the central concerns with which we in our humbler ways are busy, as we sharpen the critical and creative abilities of our pupils and ourselves. I should like to think that at the end of a teaching lifetime, devoted mainly to the critical analysis of words at their most powerful, I might, like my pupils, shape a poem or a piece of stone to a valid pattern. This creative power is the true end of our critical disciplines, and the key to our common responsibilities.

Sheri Martinelli, *Ezra Pound at St Elizabeth's*; coll. the author

5

WRITERS

EZRA POUND

To read English in a university in the early years of the 'thirties was a curiously ambiguous experience. On the one hand there were the accepted curricula in every School of English, with little variation: Old English, Middle English, the 'backbone texts' of Chaucer, Shakespeare, Milton, Wordsworth and Browning, with forays into Elizabethan drama, the eighteenth-and nineteenth-century novel and—by the early 'forties—a tough reading of the Metaphysical poets. On the other hand there were the looming figures of our contemporaries—Hardy, Lawrence, Eliot, Yeats and Pound, those writers whose vitality and 'contemporaneity' was ours, and it was bewildering that they were for us 'extra-curricular' (MacDiarmid and Bunting were never mentioned).

Thomas Hardy had died when I was in the sixth form and I had gone at once to the Carnegie Library and borrowed and read in chronological order all the novels. It seemed to me that you didn't pick at your food, you crammed your mouth with it and got the full flavour. (On the same principle, a year later when I heard as an undergraduate that I was to read *Hamlet* and *The Duchess of Malfi*, I read every Elizabethan and Jacobean revenge play I could find—in three weeks. This made me unwell.)

Poetry was the most testing experience for those of us who found, in our early reading, the Edwardians to be our contemporaries. Now there were new and strange experiences, 'smells of steaks in passage-ways', obscure visits to Byzantium, the curious acquaintance of Hugh Selwyn Mauberley (the *Cantos* were not yet in our hands to confound us still further); Yeats gave us the occasional echo of an earlier lyricism and T.S. Eliot provided us with clues in *The Sacred Wood*—and, gratefully, we were soon to meet the American 'New Criticism' and especially the civilised voices of Cleanth Brooks and Robert Penn Warren—but Pound, what were we to make of him?

An early grasp of his powerful seriousness came at the heart of *Hugh Selwyn Mauberley*. There I read the quatrain:

> Faun's flesh is not to us,
> Nor the saint's vision
> We have the press for wafer;
> Franchise for circumcision.

Here was a glimpse of dereliction—grievous for me at the age of seventeen —and at the same time a transparent diction that revealed a new range in contemporary poetry. There was irony, a sophisticated pursing of the lips, in the first poems I had read by T.S. Eliot; but here, in four lines by Ezra Pound there seemed to be passed a final judgment on the vacuity of our age as we slid towards the tragedy of war. We were alienated from the natural order, the faun's domain; we could not bear the intensity of the mystic vision; for eucharistic partaking we had the dubious press and for initiation we took part with the even more dubious politicians. (The conjunction 'press for wafer' prepared us for greater particularity in Canto XLV:

> with usura, sin against nature,
> is thy bread ever more of stale rags
> is thy bread dry as paper,
> with no mountain wheat, no strong flour)

This comprehensive rejection of our popular *mores* raised massive expectations. There came the first *Cantos*, the war, the broadcasts in Italy, the infamous incarceration in the American Army Disciplinary cages in Pisa and the equally infamous thirteen-year incarceration in St Elizabeth's Hospital in Washington D.C. As we read the *Pisan Cantos, Section Rock-Drill* and *The Women of Trachis*, written in these conditions we wondered at the quality of human endurance. This overthrew our customary view of 'a poet'. This man suffered and was prophetic.

*

It was not possible, even for his most intimate friends, to have an uncomplicated relationship with Ezra Pound. There were the passionate intellectual convictions, economic, political and legal, and above all the critical intelligence and the creative pressure which produced the voluminous literary essays and the *Cantos*. Indeed, passionate conviction was the overwhelming impression which every meeting with him conveyed, a passion of such intensity that it was difficult for an ordinary human being to breathe in it, to maintain poise.

And yet there were confounding opposites: the gentle courtesy and the sweetness of the smile with which every friend was greeted; and the apparently invulnerable calm which allowed him, in the thirteen years' confinement in the St Elizabeth's mental hospital in Washington, to push on almost to the conclusion of his massive work. Whether in controversy or creation, Ezra Pound moved with the power which Wyndham Lewis described—in a phrase which gave its title to one volume of the *Cantos*—"His rock-drill action is impressive: he blasts away tirelessly."

Despite his tragic circumstances, the omens were good for my visits to him in Washington, for T.S. Eliot had briefed me carefully on the personal issues and the pattern of friendships which surrounded Pound in face of official animosity. I was myself going to Washington on a Folger Fellowship to complete work left over from my *Shakespeare and the Artist* and to begin work on Elizabethan and Jacobean law at the Folger Shakespeare Library. Since this meant a detailed concentration on Edward Coke at precisely the time that Ezra Pound was exploring work for his *Coke Cantos* (107-109), this led to the most powerful link in our conversations and letters.

It was also fortunate for me, in view of later happenings in my four months in Washington, that I travelled to America on the Cunard liner, *Carinthia*, with members of the American Bar Association, one of whom became a good friend in Washington.

I arrived in the last week in August, 1957 and carried with me, from Dr Overholser, Director of St Elizabeth's Hospital, permission to visit Pound; this I did on the first Sunday afternoon in September. It was hot and brilliantly sunny and Pound, very lightly dressed, hurried across the lawn to greet me. His first words

147

startled me: "How's Possum?" and for the first few minutes, Eliot dominated our conversation. During the rest of the afternoon there was much coming and going of visitors but two people remained throughout, still and almost wholly silent, Dorothy Pound who was with him throughout all the visiting hours for the thirteen years and the vivid young Marcella Spann, who was helping E.P. with the anthology, *Confucius to Cummings* (the 'Spannthology' of his subsequent correspondence). Conversation quickly turned to my projected work at the Folger Library and the happy coincidence of work on Coke's *Institutes*. Though I was not at that first meeting aware of the central importance that Coke was to have in the closing *Cantos*, it was obvious that I could help a good deal with references and photostats.

My visit the following week was on a less sunny afternoon and he took me to his little room in Chestnut Ward, where he was somewhat protected from the interference of other inmates by a partition which seems now in retrospect to have consisted almost entirely of books. There, at his cluttered table, we read the *Cantos* which he 'annotated' as we went along. It was fortunate for the peace of our talking together that he was no longer in the terrible conditions of Howard Hall, 'the hell-hole' of his early years at St Elizabeth's.

These first conversations and the notes I received from him at the Folger, clarified for me both my own researches and the significance of Edward Coke in the structure of the *Cantos*. My own explorations centred on the legal elements in Shakespeare's work, as they reflected the turbulence in the judicial thinking of his day which saw some of the profoundest changes (and the bitterest conflicts) in our whole legal history. Academic and practising lawyers were aware of the interrelations and potential conflicts between Common and Statute Law, Civil Law in the Roman tradition, and the corpus of Canon Law, but with the accession of James in 1603 the situation changed dramatically. With a sound knowledge of Scots Law, which was based on Roman Civil Law, James wished to introduce its operation into English legal practice; and in this he was backed by academic lawyers, like Dr Cowell, Regius Professor at Cambridge. The conflict was now fairly engaged, with powerful adversaries: Francis Bacon, Lord

Ellesmere, the university Professors of Law, the King himself and—most powerful of them all—Edward Coke, determined to maintain the primacy of English Common Law and the authority of the statutes. The King had been flattered by Cowell's definition of the royal prerogative, "that absolute height of power that the Civilians call majestatem, subject only to God". To this assertion Coke rejoined in his personal attack on "Dr Cow-heel", that "the King has no prerogative but that which the law of the land allows him."

This concern for Coke must be set in a wider context. Now that we have all the *Cantos*, even to the *Drafts and Fragments*, it should be possible to match the final, massive achievement against the often-quoted projected summary: "to write an epic which begins 'In the Dark Forest', crosses the Purgatory of human error, and ends in the light" and to set this in turn against his description to his father, in a letter of 11 April 1927, of his plan for the close of the work: "The 'magic moment' or moment of metamorphosis, bust thru from quotidien into 'Divine or permanent world', Gods, etc.". Critics have in fact been reluctant to cope with the dilemma that the *Cantos* were consistently conceived by Pound as a unified whole but that to the very end of the work the 'quotidien' overlays the paradisal vision of 'the divine or permanent world'. In particular, the fact that the brooding presence of Sir Edward Coke, felt over some decades of creativity, should now emerge to dominate in full focus three of the final *Cantos* (107-109) has seemed so confounding that critics have seemed tacitly to ignore his presence. This is the more remarkable after the publication of the essay by David Gordon in *Paideuma* (Vol 4, Nos 2 and 3, 1975, pp. 223-299) in which the relation of Edward Coke to Confucian thought in Pound's work is magisterially explored. The continuity of Coke's presence, the congruity of his thought with other personae who dominate the *Cantos* is there wholly demonstrated. And yet Sir Edward Coke has seemed to fail to capture the critical imagination to the same degree as Adams or Jefferson, Malatesta or Confucius.

An obvious practical reason for this avoidance of a major issue is the difficulty of assuming Coke's assured significance in legal history. The last decade of Elizabeth's reign and the first two decades of the Stuarts' were seminal for the subsequent history of law and society in England; they were also turbulent and confused to a degree that is confounding to the legal historian. It is not the least of Pound's merits as an historian that both in the middle *Cantos* and in the closing sections of the work, he penetrates beyond the detail to the essential principles which underlay Coke's work. Nonetheless the story, as we shall see, is not clear and defies the neat categories which scholarship craves and which the earlier personae of the *Cantos* in large measure allowed.

But there is a problem beyond that of academic difficulty. Both latent and expressed, the parallels with the *Divine Comedy* have manifestly shaped much of the argument over the structure of the *Cantos*. Michael Alexander has succinctly expressed the analogy— and by implication the expectations it arouses:

> The Cantos are also arranged with some deference and reference to Dante's *Divine Comedy*—the gradual ascent to knowledge and illumination via Hell, Purgatory and Paradise. Again, the model is intermittently invoked; this is a humanist *Commedia*. (*The Poetic Achievement of Ezra Pound*, Faber, 1979, p. 124).

True; and we should therefore expect illumination to lead to a transcending of the mundane; yet the 'quotidien' persistently intrudes; the harsh and all too mundane concerns of Coke in his confrontation with James echo the immediate concerns of Pound with the day-to-day. Is this an irreconcilable dilemma? Is the preconceived pattern, with its expectation of some kind of 'beatific vision' impossible in the very fabric of a humanist Commedia? and does the consciousness of this dilemma define something of the tragic mystery of the last fragment but one?

> That I lost my center
> fighting the world.
> The dreams clash
> and are shattered—
> And that I tried to make a paradiso terrestre.

The last words of *Drafts and Fragments* assert the long-sought truth: 'To be men not destroyers', but over the closing years of creation

150

there broods a darker matter, most movingly expressed in the fragment of CXX published in the latest New Directions edition of the *Cantos*:

> I have tried to write Paradise . . .
> Let the Gods forgive what I
>   have made
> Let those I love try to forgive
>   what I have made.

Where in this final stage of the *Cantos* does Coke find his just place? Does his work in any way bridge the gap between aim and achievement? Have the *Institutes*, the massive commentary, 'Coke on Littleton', any key to this sense of final, if partial failure? Is a 'humanist Commedia' a 'paradiso terrestre' a self-defeating vision? or do the final *Cantos* and *Fragments* rather contain within their very fragmentariness a reconciliation, a conclusion which unites the visionary and the 'quotidien'?

The work on Coke was to throw for me abundant light on legal issues in Shakespeare, but for Ezra Pound it was the pivot on which the argument of the *Cantos* turned, and the intellectual excitement of these weeks was intense. His concern for the integrity of constitutional rights had shown itself in earlier *Cantos* in the figures of Jefferson and Adams. The 'Usura' *Cantos* had explored his preoccupation with the integrity of money and the state's involvement in economic principles; but here was an issue dramatised in figures at the highest levels of statesmanship and law. For this was drama which stretched from the struggle between King James, Edward Coke, the Courts and Parliament through to the execution of King Charles. Pound was happy to relate this long-drawn epic to my own concern for its impact on Shakespeare. In a letter to me (17 September, just a fortnight after our first conversations) he wrote:

> Shx/against Unlimited (Sovereignty)
> 33 years from S(hakespeare)s death to
> decapitation of Charlie

and this appeared, with interesting expansion in Canto 107:

> OBIT in Stratford 1616, Jaques Pere obit,
> in 33 years Noll cut down Charlie
> OBIT Coke 1634 & in '49
> Noll cut down Charlie

Until this time, most of his Coke references were at second-hand but the letter of 17 September ends with a suggestion for my own explorations:

> What about Coke as per enc/IF you
> are reading thru him.

The enclosure was a sheet of jottings, dated '15 Sept' and begins:

> COKE on PRINCIPLES
> Jury trial/from Athens, by majority
> Division of Powers/Anselm vs. Wm. Rufus . . .

but a more important extension of the principles of jury trial follows:

> Nature of jury, Peers, i.e. capable of understanding the issues
> Vicinage, capable of understanding the circumstances?

and these two concepts of jury service, of trial by a man's peers and that they should be from among his neighbours ('Vicinage') were central in Coke's writings and in Pound's concerns.

November was a critical month in Pound's exploration of Coke. On 1 November, when he had read extracts from the *Institutes*, he wrote to me: "Coke's mind marvellous for lucidity." But on 7 November he expresses irritation at the difficulty of meeting Coke's work in academic legal circles. I had asked him on the previous visit what one could do to secure his release from St Elizabeth's; his reply was characteristically oblique and impersonal:

> Dear M/what to do? (Tuesday) Get the "intelligentzia", i.e. 3 or
> 4 of 'em to FACE the issues, the reality the problems of the

ang/sax heritage. ignorance of Coke on MY part/known only in
J. Adams reference until 30 October 1957 . . . I think my ten
Adams Cantos were printed in U.S. in '39, a few bits in earlier
Cantos/Jeffersonian until I found Adams/Plea for Blackstone by
Cairns, must have been Mich. Law Rev about 15 years ago/long
silence . . . Next job is to get Coke back into circulation/among
other items and that can hardly bring the FBI down on any
innocent enquirer . . .

It was clear that Coke had become a symbol for the constitutional
and economic struggle which Ezra Pound felt was still continuing
three centuries after 'the decapitation of Charlie'. Indeed the
letter goes on in a more personal tone: we need—

A census of men capable of grasping a legal PRINCIPLE in midst
of pragmatic morass . . .
horrible lack of intercommunication between clercs NOT
engaged in la traison . . .
benedictions, glad to have seen you/cant get 40 years history in
one hurried hour.

This tone was maintained in a letter of 10 November: "that I got to
Coke via the Sacred Edict, a measure of decay in brit/yank/
education." But two days later there was a jubilant note for me at
the Folger Library:

Set of 4 vols of Coke, sighted in London/also that C/on Littleton
fills the first.

This meant that in a short while he was to have the two central
works which were to be the backbone of the *Coke Cantos*; from this
point onwards, Ezra Pound's references to this period in English
political and legal history had a more pointed precision than those
of the earlier Jefferson and Adams *Cantos*.

In purely formal terms Pound's *Cantos* come to no neat
conclusion, no full close. It is true also that the last completely-
wrought *Cantos* bristle with detail and that out of the broken terrain
granitic passages obtrude:

153

> Nor can the king create a new custom
> in the fine print (*Canto* 107).

But the *Drafts and Fragments* with which the whole work ends have a different kind of conclusion, a new emotional and visionary pressure, a gathering of themes which defy formal coherence. The previous three *Cantos*, 107-109 (the '*Coke Cantos*') constitute one entire statement of argument which crowns the intellectual structure of the *Cantos* as a whole: that law is over-riding; that particular laws are manifestations of the universal rule of law, through which alone justice, order, the decencies of daily living can be achieved. A richer and more tranquil mind than Coke's and contemporary with him, expressed this insight in its fulness; Richard Hooker's *Ecclesiastical Polity* comes to its most lyrical conclusion in a vision of the universality of law:

> Now if nature should intermit her course, and leave altogether, though it were but for awhile, the observation of her own laws . . . what would become of man himself, whom these things do now all serve? See we not plainly, that obedience of creatures unto the law of nature is the stay of the whole world?

To this Pound would have assented, indeed did assent in *Canto* 107, with Confucian reference and English particularity:

> That is our PIVOT
> Statute de Merton.

To all the insights set out in the *Coke Cantos* the *Fragments* are a lyrical coda, in which there is also found a place for passages of tragic backward-looking. There is no Paradiso here, nor even a Paradise Regained but an entirely new vision which is both terrestrial and celestial, the city achieved and realised: 'a city remaineth', 'a Body politique'. It is perhaps not too much to say that Magna Carta is the final concrete embodiment of the whole structure of natural law which the *Cantos*, in their long exploration, were seeking, a structure by which the city is walled, itself a metaphor of the cosmic order. The fragments that remain, gathered in the profound silences of Pound's last years, point the joy by means of the tragic undertones, the regrets, the omissions, the mistaken by-ways. Had the *Cantos* been theologically motivated, had the main trend of Pound's long search been that of Dante, the closing beatific vision could have excluded in ecstasy the memory of error and failure. The Cantos could come to no such comforting end; this 'humanist Commedia' had to take into its fabric, to our enrichment, the tragic tone of recollection, a tone which enhances the moments of lyrical vision. Mary de Rachewiltz writes of the presence of her father: "He brought with him a dimension of—no, not stillness, but magnitude, momentum." Nowhere is this magnitude more amply shown than in the transition from the gritty understanding of Edward Coke to the resolution of the *Drafts and Fragments*:

> seeing the just and the unjust,
> tasting the sweet and the sorry.

*

These fragments that remain to us counterpoint the joy and the sorrow and Pound chooses not to forget the errors, the mistaken by-ways. In his tragic last letter to me, out of the long silence held, he reminds me, "You gave me your priest's blessing" and goes on to speak of the entry of evil into life. It is true for him that 'A city remaineth' but its secure peace has been hard-won. William Cookson speaks of these last years: '*Drafts and Fragments* a poetry on the brink of silence. It is deep with a clear depth that is the opposite of obscurity.'

*

There had been two short breaks from my work at the Folger, lecturing briefly at Chicago and Yale. At the latter visit I was the guest of Cleanth Brooks and a dinner party at his home in the country included Robert Penn Warren and Norman Holmes Pearson, who was compiling a checklist of Pound's writings and was an intimate friend of the poet. There was a great deal of talk about E.P.'s confinement at St Elizabeth's and after my return to Washington. Pearson wrote to ask me whether I would join in the pressure on the administration to release Pound. The previous years had seen cumulative pressure from US scholars and writers but he felt it might be valuable that the US Attorney General (William P. Rogers) should hear from someone from Great Britain who was an academic and a priest and with US standing as a Rockefeller Fellow, working at the Folger. I wrote to the Attorney General asking for an interview, first checking my position with Robert Ashe, the attorney with whom I had travelled to America on Carinthia. He greatly approved but warned me that I was unlikely in the future to get an entry visa! (This happily proved to be untrue).

In my letter I briefly and, I hope, simply, repeated the arguments that the Attorney General would have heard many times over the years: that Pound was a distinguished and influential poet, in Europe as much as in the US: that it harmed America's reputation for justice and tolerance that he should simply be locked away without trial.

It was, not surprisingly, an uncomfortable walk to the Attorney General's office and it was with a sense of high drama that I was abruptly faced with a wider issue of domestic politics—the racial troubles at Little Rock, Arkansas, which were over the next decade to change the social fabric of America. The Attorney General was waiting for me and with great charm excused himself from meeting me more formally; President Eisenhower had sent for him urgently to the White House, since affairs at Little Rock had reached a critical stage. His assistant was, however, briefed and waiting to meet me.

The next half hour was deeply uncomfortable. The young man (I forget his name) was clearly affronted that a mere clerical academic (and from Great Britain!) should question the judicial integrity of the US. The long and acrimonious exchange (I have often wondered whether it was taped) may be summarised in two fragments:

"How dare you question our treatment of Pound?" "How dare I not, when I feel sure we share a common sense of justice?"

Our voices were not exactly modulated and I left the Attorney General's office through a kind of guard of perturbed officials who hovered in the corridor. I reported the interview to Robert Ashe, to Norman Pearson at Yale and most urgently that evening to Dorothy Pound. The next three or four days were occupied in packing and travelling to New York to board *Carinthia* again, for my return to Great Britain.

Two letters before I left gave me enormous pleasure. The first was written on 12 December:

> Slow post to giv uy time to arrive IF uy git aboard a boat in NY. (There followed a number of requests for my work when I returned and a note of a gift of books he was sending me) . . . and will be sent to you after Xmas rush, during which D.P. wants to avoid the concentration of animal life at the p.o. and benedictions for yr/noble efforts. EP

Dorothy had added a written postscript, which, I confess gave me equal pleasure:

> . . . Your visits have been such a comfort to us: "Somebody who knows something about some things" to quote E . . . Saluti cordiale.
> Dorothy Pound.

This was followed up on 14 December with a covering letter to drafts of *Cantos* 99, 107 and 109—work on Coke was beginning to bear fruit. Even in a 'good-bye' letter which begins:

> 14 Dec/Dear Moelwyn
> Gtly relieved @ sight of Cunard stationary/which, I take it indicates you were actually on boat and not in Co. offices . . .

He goes on with an elaboration of the related themes which concerned us:

> Shx/ and Coke/law/sense of wrong in unlimited monarchy/ french revolution Voltaire etc. had NOT the Mag. Charta to

157

stand on, and J. Adams say they wd/flop. in short the serious element in Shx.

Meanwhile things ground on in the political sphere and on 16 March, 1958, and the following Sunday, 23 March, articles appeared in the *Washington Sunday Star* and the *Washington Post* which clearly indicated that official opinion was softening. The *Washington Post* article included the sentence:

If the psychiatrists so conclude, we can see no reason why he should not be released under conditions that would assure him proper care and supervision.

and on 1 April the Attorney General indicated publicly that the Justice Department would probably drop the charges against him.

On 7 May he was released from hospital and on 30 June he, Dorothy and Marcella Spann sailed for Italy.

*

There had been other preoccupations during my Sunday or Tuesday visits to St Elizabeth's. The 'Spannthology' (*Confucius to Cummings*) was in swift progress and I ventured to suggest to him that he should include some poems by Dafydd ap Gwilym (which in a rash phrase, I described as 'Welsh gems'). He at once demanded translations from me but these were held up by other work and on 3 May, 1958, he sent me an air-letter:

Dear M/gawbreSSZ and purrzurv uy, But alzo gordaaamit/where are those poems by Herb/ of Cherbury and/or the welsch jems, that are now past date line for the Spannthology? . . .
      benedictions
             EP

The 'Welsh gems' were not in fact to appear until they were printed as 'Dafydd lies in Ystradfflur' in *Planet 23* (1974); on 25 June he wrote: "Spannthology finished and sent to N. Directions."

*

No-one could be left unmoved, unchanged by contact over the years with Ezra Pound. His was a route into poetry and its human—even its political and economic—significance, which a friend could follow or be confounded by it. Few could agree with all his arguments and theories; none, no honest reader, could refuse him the admiration due to a magisterial creative intelligence. Donald Davie, whose *Ezra Pound : Poet as Sculptor* (1946) is still one of the most satisfying studies of his work, makes as his final estimate of his stature: "Dryden and Keats and, yes, Shakespeare are the appropriate fellows for this poet of our time who magnanimously lent his energies to the language that we all share, rather than bending that language to his own egotistical purposes."

*

There must be a postscript to this narrative. I was fortunate that brief studies I wrote in the years after my return from Washington were scrutinised by Pound's daughter, Princess Mary de Rachewiltz and translated by her for publication in Italy.

Back in Exeter I kept in the closest contact with Dorothy Pound and her son Omar and there were golden days in Exeter and on Dartmoor. Out of these visits came two publications. We had set up in my department a series of booklets (The Exeter Books) and the ninth of these was an anthology of translations by Omar Pound: *Poems from the Persian and Arabic, 500-1400 AD* (Edition of 300, 1967). Omar has a delicate wit and a secure grounding in Islamic studies. I especially enjoyed the sly epigram of a poem:

> *In the Heart of the Desert*
> A foolish man rides here
> With my saddle
> And on my camel.
> (al-Tirammah, c. 660)

Soon after this, in 1969, Ted Hughes, Eric Cleave, my son Paul and I founded the Rougemont Press which in the next few years published the first volume of poetry by Sylvia Plath which were illustrated by her own drawings, the first publication of *Crow* by Ted

Dorothy Pound, *La Madonna della grazia* (water-colour); coll. the author

Hughes and volumes and 'manuscript poems' by Norman MacCaig, Jon Stallworthy, Ian Hamilton Finlay and others. On one of her visits to Cambridge (Omar's home) Dorothy told me of a notebook which she had kept in 1909-11 when she first met Ezra Pound in London. At that time also she knew Wyndham Lewis and was soon to meet Gaudier-Brzeska, who both greatly influenced her own drawings and paintings. She allowed me to select long passages from the journal and over twenty of her drawings and paintings (with one little sketch by E.P. of four basking cats); these were published under the title, *Etruscan Gate*, in an edition of three hundred in January 1971. It was a pity that Pound never saw his wife's first book; he would have enjoyed it.

It was as unpromising—indeed embarrassing—a commission as I could imagine: to vet a play by Christopher Fry for its theological orthodoxy!

This extraordinary request came from the Religious Drama Society with whom I had done some work at their summer schools. They had wanted to commission a play by 'a serious dramatist' which could be suitable for playing in a variety of churches by a small professional company. Christopher Fry was invited and wrote for them *A Sleep of Prisoners*. He agreed also, with his usual grace, that the clerical academic of whom he had never heard, should scrutinise the text, testing for heresy. I had explained to the R.D.S. (who after all numbered E. Martin Browne among their leading members) that the 'orthodoxy' of an artist was not the same thing as that of a bishop, that exploration at the fringes of customary belief was the artist's duty and privilege. They agreed, but still—would I, please?

The text came and I read it with fascination. It solved, with the ingenuity of a professional man of the theatre, so many of the traps laid by 'religious drama' and especially by plays intended for church performance. What could be more disarming than Fry's solution? —to lock captive soldiers in a church and have them work through, between waking and sleeping, the tragic dilemmas of Adam, Cain, Abraham, David, all those 'figures of wisdom back in the old sorrows', from Creation, the Three Children in the fiery furnace, to the crucifixion of Christ—an exploration of 'what makes for life and what makes for death'.

The speeches were lively (I especially liked one soldier's complaint that the church uncomfortably suffered from "the smell of cooped-up angels") and I was hard pressed to fulfil my task of detecting heresy. After careful searching I found this statement of man's spiritual destiny:

'The enterprise is exploration into God.'

In itself this was impeccable but could it perhaps be deemed partial, even inadequate? Ought it perhaps to have a further line?:

'And God's exploration into man.'

Feeling rather like a judge who deliberately, in a dubious case, introduces a legal impropriety into his summing-up for the jury, in order to have the verdict overthrown on appeal, I put my question to Fry. With a great courtesy he accepted my theological criticism but said that the introduction of such a line (he refrained from saying "such a flat-footed line") would impair the rhythmical run of the speech. I was delighted to agree with him.

We met and liked each other and some months later I drove with him to Winchester to see a fine performance at St. Cross. The leisurely drive to and from Winchester (he then lived at Trebinsiwn in Breconshire and I in Caerleon, Monmouthshire) enabled us to have a great deal of talk and apart from the sheer fun of his 'verbal games to be played on a car journey', I learned a great deal about his ideas and aspirations in the theatre. One thing surprised me: though accustomed to the stage both as professional actor and director, he feared to lecture before any kind of audience. It was therefore a triumph for me when I induced him to talk to our literary society in University College, Cardiff and he has had no relapse since that evening.

*

Enough has been written, by theatre and academic critics to establish Christopher Fry's place in the body of contemporary drama. Critical caprice made it difficult in the early years to define his true bent. Among those 'professionally' engaged in producing religious drama (and perhaps most notably E. Martin Browne who produced all of T.S. Eliot's plays for the theatre) Fry was consistently esteemed and performed. *The Boy with a Cart, The Firstborn, Thor with Angels* and *A Sleep of Prisoners* established his secure reputation. Then *A Phoenix too Frequent* and *The Lady's not for Burning* were assumed to have established the new Fry manner and tone, with, as one critic absurdly put it, "an Elizabethan splendour of phrase"; from this point onwards he was deemed to be the master of pyrotechnic wit and he should write no plays in any other manner. The drabness of the war years made this verbal scintillation the more welcome but there followed a sense of surprise and even frustration at the wholly different tone and quality of *The Dark is Light Enough* and *Curtmantle*—in my judgment by far his greatest plays and sufficient in themselves to establish his position as one of the finest dramatists of our generation.

The assumption that *The Lady's not for Burning* was the Christopher Fry play par excellence had two unfortunate consequences: with the advent of Osborne's *Look Back in Anger* and the 'kitchen-sink drama' that followed it, verse—and especially this effervescent verse of *The Lady*—was considered outmoded and improper in the theatre; the second and perhaps graver consequence was the ignoring of the serious, even tragic quality of *The Lady*. If critics and theatre directors had looked a little more closely, they would have realised that Fry's dominant mode in his plays was tragedy, that comedy and tragedy were interwoven in a relationship which enhanced each mode.

The thinking behind this essential unity of tragedy and comedy is more clearly seen in a comment he wrote on Teilhard de Chardin's phrase, "an organic crisis in moral evolution." Fry writes:

> We know that the way we mature is through a series of crises, of one sort or another. We reach an obstacle and learn to overcome it; our thoughts or emotions become knotted, and we increase ourselves in order to unknot them; a state of being becomes intolerable, and, drawing upon a hidden reserve of spirit, we transform it. That covers as it were, a tension of imprisonment before the vigour which sets us free; a sensation of death, before the rebirth.

The Dark is Light Enough has a sufficiency of wit in its working out but this exploration of the Hungarian revolution of 1848-9 has as its latent theme Fry's detestation of violence and especially the aggression of war. The plot has all the bitter irony of human relationships across racial frontiers when conflict divides the nations. The country-house of the Countess Rosmarin is near the Hungarian border; Richard Gettner is married to her daughter and is a fugitive from the Hungarian army. To the officer who seeks Gettner the Countess declares the core of her faith:

163

I shall never make
Myself, or my friends, my way of life
Or private contentment, or any
Preference of my nature, an obstacle
To the needs of a more true and living world
Than so far I have understood.

In this 'true and living world' there is one sure law:

One man over another has no kingdom.

The gravity of her profession of faith is tested at the moment when Gettner, surrounded by his former friends, seems at the point of capture:

Gettner
Have a respect for my life.
For the sake of your sleep to come, don't betray me.
Go to your imaginations, gentlemen:
Think of death by shooting.

Belmann
I should more likely weep for stags or partridges.

Countess
Do, then. Weep for what you can.

Fry no longer argues either the intent or the nature of human relationships—it suffices that compassion seize any occasion for the practice of its grace—if for stags or partridges, then much more for Gettner.

I had many reasons for finding *Curtmantle* an even greater dramatic experience. I had spent a great deal of time with Christopher Fry, at his home and mine, discussing this complex tragedy of Henry the Second and Becket, the tension between the two forces of Church and State. I was already immersed in my own researches into Elizabethan law and the similar conflict between Edward Coke and James the First which later was to occupy so much of my conversations with Ezra Pound.

164

The search for law is timeless but if we compare Fry's handling of the theme with either Eliot's or Anouilh's, we find the greater security in Fry's sense of historical fact. For Eliot was essentially concerned with the timeless nature of martyrdom, while the more superficial play by Anouilh ignored the tensions of law for those of a relationship which could be set in any age.

Curtmantle is a weighty, brooding tragedy—the summit of Fry's achievement in the theatre. Behind the temporal struggle of King and Archbishop lies a deeper conflict:

> It's the nature of man that argues;
> The deep roots of disputation
> Which dug in the dust, and formed Adam's body.

We must sympathise with Henry's determination to bring secure and universal law to his realm; the clarity of his mind assumes that the device of uniting archbishop and chancellor in one man resolves the dispute between divine and secular law. Becket more fully realizes the essential instrumentality of man's will, as, in its noblest form, wholly submissive to the ways of providence:

> You're dividing us, and, what is more, forcing
> Yourself and me, indeed the whole kingdom,
> Into a kind of intrusion on the human mystery,
> Where we may not know what it is we're doing,
> What powers we are serving, or what is being made of us,
> Or even understand the conclusion when it comes.

When I asked him to comment on his treatment of history (for *Essays and Studies*, 1977), Fry wrote:

> In the theatre history means people rather than events ...
> When writing about Henry II and Becket, it was not Becket's
> sainthood born of Church-and-State politics that deeply
> concerned me, nor the evaluation of Henry's Customs of the
> Kingdom; it was the degree of self-deception in Becket's thrust,
> and the whole anguish of Henry's parry; so that I was driven to
> ask myself whether, by his dedicated suffering for an ideal (his

165

Passion, in a religious sense), Henry was not the more saintly of the two . . . How much historical fact can be distorted for the sake of theatrical effectiveness is a matter of the playwright's conscience. I believe that keeping faith with the past is more important than the dividends to be got from unjustified flashes of 'good theatre.' They are small change compared with the realities of the human drama *sub specie aeternitatis.*

Before the first performance of *Curtmantle* at the Aldwych Theatre in 1962 by the Royal Shakespeare Company, there was a notable happening in my department in the University of Exeter. Christopher had come to lecture for us and, to illustrate his lecture, he invited me to read Becket to his Henry in a selection from the third act—the climax of their great debate. It was an unforgettable first performance!

What was in fact the 'world premiere' of the play was the production in Holland in a translation by Dolf Vesspoer and directed by Karl Guttmann, founder of the Chamber Theatre at Tel Aviv. It was to celebrate the opening of the new Civic Theatre in Tilburg on 1 March 1961. Christopher invited me to go with him to the opening and the most moving performance was set for me in my first experience of Holland and especially of Amsterdam. The one small blot on the visit was my almost being thrown out of the Rijksmuseum for venturing too near Rembrandt's 'Night Watch'.

*

After his success in writing the scripts for the two films, *Ben Hur* (directed by William Wyler) and *Barabbas* (directed by Richard Fleischer) it was not surprising that Dino de Laurentiis should have invited him to write the script for his projected film, *The Bible*. Fry accepted the invitation but to my astonishment asked that I should be his assistant, helping with the appropriate research and collaborating with Jonathan Griffin and John Whiting in writing the first drafts of the script. Tragically, John Whiting died quite early in our work on the text but Jonathan Griffin and I worked very happily together under Christopher's direction, through all the stormy passages of the film's production.

166

Our first meeting in Dino de Laurentiis's hotel suite in London was a strange experience. A general discussion took place of the films (seven in number?) to cover the whole Bible, and I had my first and very happy impression of Luigi Luraschi, Dino's assistant, quiet and ironically smiling in the background. Seven! Some years later, as the first (and only) film came to its conclusion, Christopher and I reckoned that we should get to the end of the New Testament by about the year 2020, when I would be one hundred and seven years old and he a little older! Into the middle of the discussion, with a dramatic slamming of doors, burst Tony Quinn and after our brief introductions he waved a finger at me: "Write me a big part, a wicked one!" and went out again equally tempestuously.

We were rather dismayed that Dino envisaged a first film ('In the Beginning') to be broken into such sequences as to be directed successively by Bresson, Orson Welles, Visconti and Fellini, designed throughout by Mario Chiari, with music by either Stravinsky or Benjamin Britten. In the event the admirable Chiari was the only one of these to survive these first talks, John Huston eventually directing the whole film and the Japanese composer Toshiro Mayusami composing the music.

But much was to happen before then.

In March 1963 in Rome, it was already becoming obvious that Bresson, having written his own script at Kit's request was determined not to collaborate with any other script-writer. His recent great and well-merited success with his film *Joan of Arc* had established his wide reputation and we were all inclined at first to be muted. There were innumerable sessions, some with just Christopher, Bresson and Dino, others involving us all.

Meanwhile I had met and become very friendly with the Papal representative on the team, Monsignor Salvatore Garofalo, a professor at the Urban University for the Propagation of the Faith and a member of the Holy Office. He had been secretary to Pope John and was as unlikely an Inquisitor as one could meet. We came to an immediate accord and at the first general session with Bresson, after I had spoken of our disquiet at the unscriptural script, Monsignor Garofalo made a brilliant summary of the theological objections and then astounded De Laurentiis and Luigi Luraschi by turning to me and saying, "I hope you agree with me."

167

Luigi confessed to me afterwards that they had anticipated friction between Monsignor Garofalo and me but none with the directors. It was wholly otherwise. Garofalo and I had many meals together and he had arranged a private audience for me with Pope John. It was unhappy irony that in a week or two later the Pope died and Cardinal Montini was elected as Pope Paul VI on the day I was to have been received by Pope John.

Meanwhile the wrangle with Bresson went on, Christopher mercifully maintaining his assured calm. At the last session in which I was involved Dino again asked me to summarise our objections. I felt impelled to say that, apart from credal matters, I was also concerned at his perfunctory attitude to any script. Ironically he said, "Then perhaps you had better write one!" I replied, "We already have." Bresson was enraged and pointing dramatically at me, shouted, "I will no longer work with that man!" to which astonishingly, Dino de Laurentiis replied, "I'm afraid, Robert, you will have to learn to." Bresson very soon withdrew from the production and we were left to regret the circumstances which had deprived us of a fine, if wilful artist and a very great maker of films.

Over the next year it became obvious that the elusive Orson Welles, Fellini and Visconti were not going to fit in with the De Laurentiis vision of the film and, to everyone's relief, John Huston undertook the total direction, bringing unity through his immense and always understated authority.

*

These visits to Rome were not all film business. I stayed, if there was room, in Christopher's flat in the Torre del Grillo, with Trajan's column rising, it seemed, just outside my window. In the flat above lived Patrick Cross and his wife Jenny, both of the Rome office of Reuter's. At my first invitation there to dinner, Iris Tree was also one of the guests, wearing delightfully on her corn-coloured hair her 'Uncle Max's boater'. She was full of stories about Max Beerbohm and his circle and joined Kit and me in our new game of inventing church dedications. I had some success with the Church of San Formaggio in Bocca, which she capped with one dedicated jointly to St Damon and St Runyon. It was a happy evening.

*

Christopher and I liked to have at least one meal each day, lunch or preferably dinner, at our 'local', Angelino's Ai Fori. Dinner usually began at about eight, in the cool of the evening and meandered quietly through until about half past eleven, when Angelino and his wife joined us for a parting drink. These were the quiet hours when the film was usually set aside and Kit spoke of his next play (it became *A Yard of Sun*, his Summer Comedy, set in Siena, on the eve of the Palio in 1946—it was produced in 1970). These were splendid hours of talk in which I learned more about the playwright's craft and the work of the theatre than years of academic criticism had given me.

But it was a lunch-hour at Angelino's which was happily invaded by Jenny Cross. We had been talking once more about *A Yard of Sun* and were rather taken aback by the request that we should help them that afternoon, just before six, in covering for Reuter's the election of the Pope to succeed Pope John. Rome was alive with rumours of the way the Cardinals were moving in their voting intentions and it was expected that six o'clock would signal the election's success. Our orders from the Crosses were that I should stand in one corner of St Peter's Square with an excellent view, diagonally opposite the chimney which would signal the result, black smoke for failure to elect, white smoke for success, and that I was to signal 'white smoke' with a wave and the ancient Roman gesture of 'thumbs up', with 'thumbs down' for failure. Kit was to watch for my signal and run with the news around the corner to Bridget Boland, who had an open telephone in a cafe, to send the news to the Crosses at Reuter's. Jenny warned me that the first puff of smoke was always white (water-vapour, I suppose) and that I was to wait for the second before signalling; at the same time I was to be swiftly alert "because somewhere in the world a newspaper goes to bed every few seconds and we must get ahead of our rivals." I waited anxiously as six tolled but, alas, the second puff was black and my raised arm signalled a negative.

169

That evening we had another meal with Patrick and Jenny and we were told—Kit and I—that we had not done too badly, placing Reuter's just behind the Press Association, so that only one (or perhaps two) papers had been lost to them. The rest of the evening was delightfully filled with Jenny's talk of her father, Robert Graves.

The following morning we were hard at work in the De Laurentiis studios when Luigi Luraschi's secretary ran down the corridor, shouting "White smoke!" It was twelve noon when we gathered before Dino de Laurentiis's television screen, and there, sure enough, was the chimney-pipe puffing out white smoke. After a long wait the Papal Secretary came to the balcony to announce "great joy"—"Habemus Papam." A little English secretary at my side muttered to me in bewilderment: "Habemus, Habemus? I've never heard of Cardinal Habemus!" It was, as we learned—and as rumour had prophesied—Cardinal Montini who had been elected as Pope Paul VI.

*

Three other friends were a constant relief from work and argument over *The Bible*. Dick Fleischer was working on a film at Cinecittá and entertained us regally at the restaurant of the Villa Borghese; dining in the gardens, we had the most spectacular view over Rome, while technical talk and film gossip extended the meal to its customary Roman length. I was delighted that Dick's son, Mark Fleischer, wished to come to my department at Exeter to read English before completing his training as a musician. He was an excellent student and we had also a succession of recitals from him, introducing us to the byways of the classical guitar repertoire.

It happened also very fortunately that during Mark's time at Exeter his father directed the film *Doctor Doolittle* at Castle Combe, and my son Paul, a good cross-country runner, became 'Director's runner', summoning players to their open air shots.

The other two friends were Lorri and Bertie Whiting, Australians quite settled in Rome. Lorri's cooking rivalled that of any Italian chef and most vividly on the palate is the savour of slices cut through a roast kid, stuffed with a lamb, stuffed with a chicken, stuffed with a pigeon—I believe I have the truly imperial succession of the contents, but even more important was my introduction to Lorri's 'abstract' studies, commenting on Shakespeare's *Lear* and two plays by Christopher Fry. I was able to arrange an exhibition of these works in Exeter later that year.

Bertie and Lorri seemed always at hand, at the airport, at the Torre or the Hotel Forum, whenever a little help or comfort was needed.

*

Christopher and Luigi Luraschi were determined that in the limited time I had at each visit to Rome from the department at Exeter, I should get to know as much of central Italy as possible. There were therefore Saturday afternoon and Sunday visits to Ostia, where Kit demonstrated the amazing acoustics of the classical theatre there. We went to Etruria, where, on an afternoon's wandering among the antiquities of Cerveteri, I had my second experience of Etruscan art, the first having been the miniatures in iron by Picasso, cast under the influence of Etruscan bronzes. The spell of Etruria, the mystery of its language and the sources of its art have remained with me ever since.

Equally moving were the experiences of a weekend, crossing the spine of Italy, first to the beauty of Perugia and then on to the Franciscan shrines at Assisi, the atmosphere of the sainthood of Francis remaining amazingly unsullied by the impact of the tourism of our day.

One of these expeditions, perhaps the humblest, was in many ways the most memorable. I was returning home on a Tuesday afternoon from a day at the university, to find my wife anxiously on the top step at the door—"Dino! on the phone from Rome." Could I come the following morning for a conference! No, I was sorry, I couldn't—teaching held me until Friday, when I could travel to London, staying with Kit and Phyl Fry at Little Venice and flying out with Christopher on the Saturday morning. It was agreed.

The first Alitalia flight from Heathrow got us to the De Laurentiis studios by mid-morning and we were all assembled: Dino, John Huston, Luigi Luraschi, Monsignor Garofalo and ourselves, a little stunned, from London.

At first there was an impish exchange between John Huston and Monsignor Garofalo: "That was a tough declaration on birth control last week by your brother Heenan of Westminster, wasn't it?" Monsignor Garofalo was not a bit put out: "Well, yes, perhaps—but he's Irish, you know (this with the briefest smile at Huston, who is of course Irish) and at the Curia we always know Ireland to be the mother-in-law of the Church."

Dino called us to order and nodded briefly to John Huston. "Ah, professor, I need some help in an early moment in the script: 'The Spirit of God *moved* on the face of the waters' or '*brooded* over the face of the waters.' Which is the better version?" I explained briefly that in fact we had little choice, whatever the niceties of verbal interpretation; for at my first visit to the Jewish Rabbinate in New York, to discuss our script, their sole objection of substance had been to our use of the word 'brooded'—it left open the possibility of the heresy that creation in some sort emerged from a 'cosmic egg'. "Ah, that's fine. Thank you so much." He nodded, with a smile, to Dino, who indicated that the 'conference' was over. Two flights, two days, two words—which could have been settled on the telephone on Tuesday.

But the sequel was splendid. Luigi Luraschi had a car in which he proposed the three of us should drive to some part of the countryside I had not seen. I asked if we might go south of Rome into the Campagna, and we could look out for a place for lunch.

We came to a small, rather poverty-stricken village but on the square was a small inn and I suggested lunching there. Luigi was horrified and it was certainly not the Villa Borghese. "Very well," he said, "You fix it up!" I went down to the inn and found the husband and wife at a scrubbed white-wood table, with some of the flat, greyish bread of the countryside and a flask of wine. "May we have lunch here?" They looked amazed and said that they never served food. "But you will be having your meal—may we join you?" They agreed but with extreme embarrassment. We sat, all five, about the table: bread, a scrape of butter and the rough wine. But soon the talk was animated: the life of the village, the affairs of Rome, the film, the Pope. In my recollection it is one of the most memorable meals I have ever had, the bread and the wine shared in a secular sacrament of friendship.

I think it was at that meal that I realised the strong hold Italy had on me—by my standards the last civilised country in Europe, and my definition of 'civilised'—a country in which one can be poor with dignity.

Twenty years later, when I came to write *Jeshua*, one of the few 'invented incidents' in the novel welled up from that hour in an Italian village, when, in the countryside north of Jerusalem, Jeshua and Matthew took such a meal with an inn-keeper and his wife.

*

A moving but tragic journey out from Rome was to Ninfa, the country estate of Prince Caetani. Christopher Fry had spoken to me about his friend, the Princess Marguerite Caetani, American-born and a cousin of T.S. Eliot. Her editing of *Botteghe Oscure* had enabled many young writers in Europe and America to make their first appearance in print and her encouragement had made a significant difference to the young Dylan Thomas.

Christopher wished to see the Caetanis and asked me if I should like to come out into the country to meet them. Lunch was arranged at Ninfa and we were first taken around the gardens by Marguerite Caetani, especially savouring the profusion of roses growing over the ruins of the old village which bordered the estate.

Prince Caetani—Liszt was his godfather—had the quiet dignity of the last of the Caetani family that extended back beyond the days of imperial Rome. The meal was tranquil but overshadowed by a uniform gravity that was rare in the company of Italians. Its source was tragically obvious. Their only son had been killed in the war and a line traversing two millenia of Italian history was broken.

*

Under John Huston's direction and with the additional personal involvement of his playing Noah, the film was now moving well. I was more and more engaged in writing extended briefing notes for Lutherans in Germany and the Jewish authorities in New York, for it was important that these two religious bodies should be wholly satisfied with the seriousness and integrity of our work and I was glad to undertake a visit to Hamburg and two to New York to this end. Dino and Luigi also asked me if I would make a solo visit to

Jerusalem to interest Professor Yadin in the enterprise but this could not be arranged, first because our free dates did not coincide and also because Egypt now became the site for shooting the Tower of Babel sequence.

Two visits to filming locations were interesting but confounding. The first was to the Garden of Eden, a very elaborate re-planting of the dilapidated garden of a mediaeval castle at the sea below Bracciano. An artificial stream traversed the grounds, with artificial weeds and islands, with trees sprayed to give a golden haze overall. John Huston's camera-man assured me that with the appropriate lighting, lenses and filters, paradise would look paradisal. I was more lifted in heart by Luigi Luraschi's remark—"Just think what God could have done if He'd had money!"

There was of course a great number of animals, including a lion "who adores television" and a king-cobra to seduce Eve. On its first acclimatisation visit to the Garden, placed in the tree, it suddenly felt the sun and its own strength and bit the keeper in the arm. This disquieted Eve.

Our talk on the journey back to Rome was subdued; could this setting possibly become pre-lapsarian Paradise? Amazingly it did.

I suppose that my best contribution to the film at this stage was to outline a sequence for the creation of Adam. It was my conviction that a major part of the work had to be done by a sculptor. Working in earth, it should be possible for a large number of shots to follow his work after he had withdrawn from the figure, gradually taking human shape and covered with dust before each 'take'. Then when the inert figure was as near human as could be achieved, the actor would take its place, again obscured by dust. The dust was to be gradually blown away until Adam was revealed, a living body and moving into his world. This delicate sequence was entrusted to the Italian sculptor, Manzu and was, to my prejudiced mind, a complete success.

Our next visit to a filming location was to the trial set for the Tower of Babel. It was designed by Mario Chiari as a dizzying ziggurat, echoing the classical paintings of the overweening structure and especially the painting by Breughel. Chiari, an experienced artist in film and theatre, began with his clearly stated assumption that "no-one engaged in the film nor any member of the potential audience has an innocent eye." We are all influenced by memories of mosaics, stained glass, paintings and mezzo-tint illustrations of the Bible. The enterprise, visually, was to accept this accumulated vision, while at the same time hinting at the primitive, mythical vision before history.

We had made especial efforts to be present at the shooting of the Ark sequences. I knew from Christopher that two large structures had been made, one designed to be shot from middle-distance, with the animals entering the Ark along a special trackway where they could be safely steered, and the other a full-scale interior for the greater part of the shooting.

On successive days I saw the long line in silhouette of the creatures entering the Ark and then the admirable shot of John Huston at the entrance, anxiously watching the threatening sky, as the last creatures made their way in, a slow tortoise lovingly assisted by Noah/John Huston. I was standing just out of shot, near the point marked on the gangway where Noah's hand should rest. One of the stage-hands at the top of the set dropped water from, I believe, a fountain-pen filler on to the back of his hand—the first drop of the deluge to come—whereupon he rushed in and with a last anxious look around, commanded all to be made fast.

The following day Christopher and I had lunch in the Ark with Noah's family. John Huston has a remarkable relationship with animals, wild or tame, and it was both comic and moving, as he passed down the centre of the Ark through the pens, to see the affectionate hug he got from an elephant, her trunk wrapped about his body, and the gaping demand of the hippopotamus for its customary bucket of milk poured directly down its throat.

The sensitive professionalism of Huston and Fry, their mutual care for the sharing of their insights assured the De Laurentiis team of a successful project. Despite the constant use of the term 'biblical epic' in preliminary forecasts of the film—each of the two words used in a pejorative sense—viewers eventually saw it with a surprised respect. For me it was a period of disciplined learning in terms of script-writing and a growing respect for the craftsmanship of the film technicians. Above all, it intensified my regard for Christopher Fry and his capacity for patient creativity.

*

'The Creation of Adam' in the De Laurentiio/Huston film *The Bible*

176

Sculptor: Giacomo Manzu

177

During the last year of the filming one of my duties was to produce briefings for the press and for academic institutions, Christian and Jewish, in the United States. Paragraphs from the last of these, I believe, express our combined intentions in the film.

> Ultimately this is the central problem, to produce public images in the very context where private imagination is most active and at the same time most governed by two thousand years of painting and sculpture. No visual tradition could be more complex. Constantly threatened by iconoclasm, the spiritual fear of any 'graven image' to express the divine, it has grown under the strong necessity to find objective symbols which will focus the great abstractions, of Creation, Sin and Atonement, and also give living form to those beings, human and more than human, who embodied man's spiritual aspirations: Abel and Noah in reverent obedience, Adam and Abraham in worship and sacrifice . . .

The film as a visual medium finds these images, of artists in the past, wholly inescapable, and its sophisticated maturity had to be shown by the freedom with which it moved into this visual tradition, assimilating it, stimulated but not overborne by it. Two statements by Chagall seem to me to summarise all endeavours of this kind. In his autobiography, published in 1931, he spoke of the intense awareness in his childhood worship: "The ikons came to life." Some years later he describes the motive-power of his own art:

> Man seeks something new; he must perpetually rediscover the originality of his own language—a language like that of the primitives, of men who have opened their mouths for the first time to speak their one single truth.

Our collective endeavour in the film was to try to preserve this integrity within the tradition, an endeavour vividly seen in the early sequence when the Italian sculptor, Manzu, though never in shot himself, shaped Adam "out of the dust of the earth."

It was a mundane reason for meeting genius. The preparations for the Granada T.V. series 'Word and Image' were going well, Chaucer, Milton and Shakespeare established; but the tenth programme to be called 'Isolated Man' was to deal largely with *The Ancient Mariner*, with a final reference to *Lord of the Flies*. There was one outstanding set of images for Coleridge's poem, David Jones's etchings for an edition of the work. They so greatly enhanced the significance of the dereliction that I determined to try to meet the artist whose work I had so long admired.

I had first met his work as a painter and engraver before I knew his poetry. The National Museum of Wales had one or two water-colours when I first went to the university and their union of power with delicacy, the sure security of the visionary, prepared me for my first reading, some years later of *In Parenthesis* (which appeared four years after my graduation) and the still more complex work *The Anathemata*. I wrote to him (15 September 1962) and received an immediate and cordial invitation to visit him at Harrow with the most detailed directions to find his house, Northwich Lodge, and with the most engaging apology in advance for the 'untidiness' I should encounter and the hint that "My best time of day for seeing chaps is round about 3 p.m. onwards." The 'untidiness' was simply the homely disorder of a scholar-poet and we were immediately 'at home', talking of friends we had in common, Aneirin Talfan Davies and W.F. Jackson Knight ('Roman Vergil'), our Reader in Classics at Exeter.

He was stimulating on the topic of *The Ancient Mariner* and lent me copies of the etchings to be used in my programme. This enabled me to point a particular insight in David Jones's reading of Coleridge. A previous artist, David Scott, in an edition of Coleridge in 1837 had produced a series of etchings of great power in their realism and one of them, the hanging of the dead albatross about the mariner's neck, gave a dramatic account of his dereliction. David Jones's etching gave a quite different reading. His mariner is young, a more vulnerable bearded figure; the albatross is hung about his neck, pierced by the arrow and with wings half outstretched like a fallen angel. The mariner himself has his arms fully extended as though crucified on the balks of the ship. It was a union of imagery from two ages with which the poetry had now made me familiar. The castaway, derelict man, in a waste land or on a waste sea, in *The Seafarer* in Old English, in Byron's *Cain*, in Coleridge's *Mariner* or in Eliot's *Waste Land*, would in David Jones's vision inevitably be equated with Golgotha.

So it is with his 'Matter of Britain'. Arthur is at the centre of the mythology and myth is translated to revelation when he relates the collection of mediaeval Welsh prose, the *Mabinogion* with the Gospels and in a startling phrase speaks of 'Pedair Cainc y Mabinogi *sanctaidd*' 'the Four Branches of the *Holy* Mabinogion'. It is of course an advantage to be able to read the Welsh words of his work without recourse to the poet's notes and to meet them in such complex relations: the singing tones of the natural features, 'afon', 'moelion', 'nentydd' and the like; the words of the lord's court and its ceremonial, and, linking it all, the language of the Liturgy in Welsh, Latin and the occasional Greek. All the ceremonies are related, in one extended myth, which is the whole of David Jones's prose and verse, and illuminated both by the lettering and the paintings which span all the themes. And in all this body of work I have to say that a 'fragment' 'The Sleeping Lord' from the volume of that name, is the work to which I turn for the essence of this remarkable poet, more even than to *The Anathemata* or *In Parenthesis*. For in that fragment, in which he looks to past and future through the dark shadows of the present, the massive ambiguities that are the springs of his poetry are finally, if questioningly stated:

> Does the land wait the sleeping lord
> > or is the wasted land
> that very lord who sleeps?

*

It is disconcerting when the learned poet takes us into his confidence, invites us to share his journey: *The Waste Land, The Cantos, Briggflats, On a Raised Beach*. It is still more disconcerting when that poet is inviting us to a *requiem*, when looking back he cries *Ubi sunt? Ou sont les neiges?* or when he echoes (as we find in

The Sleeping Lord) the lament of a princess of Powys at the death of Cynddylan, her brother:

> "Stafell Cynddylan ys tywyll heno,
> Heb dan, heb wely."

> Cynddylan's hall is dark tonight,
> without fire, without bed.

Llywarch Hen (6th century).

Finally disconcerting is our realisation that David Jones, as he searches and probes for the sacred truths in 'the Matter of Britain', clothing in pride the legends whose roots are deep, beyond our consciousness, is at the same time intoning *requiem*, singing the dirge of that dying pride. In every Celtic, every Gaelic, every Welsh realisation of lost tradition there is anger above regret, a frustrated kicking against the goad of history.

It is important to hear the tone in which David Jones speaks of this loss. In *The Sleeping Lord*, in a brief verse paragraph, he recounts tensely the 'power-struggle for the fair lands of Britain' and the tidal ebb and flow of 'the warbands' in the long contest for the 'provinces of the West', and the account closes tragically:

> nor is the end yet
> for that tide rises higher
> nor can it now be stayed.

Those three lines are for me both the key to a strand of mourning in David Jones's vision of the sacred Celtic inheritance and a way into the poetry of R.S. Thomas. Through the concerns for art and the grasping of Godhead, through the passionate attempt to reach to the inarticulate countryman, there is a stifled anger in Thomas— sometimes indeed not stifled. "Wantoners" he cries to his dumbly staring congregation; "with oafs and yokels" he sees his country-parson buried, and for 'Protestantism' as he meets it in the raw uplands of Wales, he has the judgment: "the adroit castrator of art." It is difficult to separate these harshnesses from the seemingly less personal anger as he contemplates the drowning of dwellings in the reservoirs of Mid-Wales or the detritus that is the tide-wake

181

of alien tourists. These are no trivial outbursts. The anger is the anger of frustration and is close in its perception though so very distant in tone from that brooding judgment on the tide of invasion, as David Jones realises the inevitable:

nor can it now be stayed.

That is precisely what R.S. Thomas cannot admit. For him the days of Glyndwr, the conflicts of Llywelyn are contemporary conflicts and they need not end in defeat. The resignation of 'ys tywyll heno', or Villon's lament that beauty, valour, nobility, disappear like 'the snows of yester-year', is not for him and this provides the historical tension, the shifting stresses in his poetry as it grows through the years.

In 1972 R.S. Thomas broadcast in Welsh an account of his early days. The opening paragraph was this (as I translate it):

The time: near the end of the first World War, and the place: the Wirral Peninsula, Cheshire. A liitle boy is playing on the beach. Across the sea, to the southwest, high, grey-blue hills can be seen. His father points to them. 'That's Wales', he says. The boy lifts his head for a moment and gazes at them, then turns to his playing in the sand. I am that boy, on holiday from Liverpool with my parents.

'That's Wales', and seen from a distance, with objectivity that characterises much of the image of our country that R.S. Thomas has maintained through all his poetry; a tense objectivity involving also its converse emotion, a passionate involvement.

Some years ago, I aroused fury in parts of my audience, as I spoke to a conference of Arts Associations in Swansea. In the course of my talk I spoke of the three poetic landmarks in the history of literature in Wales: Dafydd ap Gwilym, Henry Vaughan and R.S. Thomas. Now, I was far from devaluing Dylan Thomas or his lively successors in both English and Welsh—poetry in Wales during the last two generations has been in exceedingly good shape and there have been volumes of outstanding quality. But my 'landmarks' still stand. Let me explain.

Dafydd ap Gwilym was a poet of European stature, near contemporary of Chaucer, a borrower of inspiration from Vergil and from Chrétien and kin to those whose language was the gracious wealth of Provence. His Welsh, no more difficult for a Welshman of today than Chaucer is for the English, had the rich allusiveness of one who moved with ease in the natural world and the sacraments of the church. I am more than weary with those writers on Welsh literature who speak of Dafydd as "bardd serch a natur", "the poet of love and nature" —how could a Welsh troubadour be other? But the tense ambiguity that fulfils Dafydd's greatness is the union of that commonplace currency with a passionate religious devotion.

When I went to live in Llanddewibrefi, the ruins of Ystrad Fflur, Strata Florida, were within very easy reach and at my first visit I was struck by the fact that 'Dafydd ap Gwilym lies buried *somewhere* within the walls.' 'Somewhere'—it seemed to me that this was a staggering mislaying of dust and I began the search for the truths of Dafydd. The 'love and nature' were abundantly there, with the passionate pursuit of Morfudd, even as he knelt at his Eucharist:

> Passion of the Mass, the flesh raised up,
> a wanton look at the Host,
> with blind adoration of the lady.

And there were more single-minded devotions: a macaronic version of the *Anima Christi* with each line of the Latin glossed in Welsh:

> *Anima Christi, santifica me*
> O holy, compassionate Trinity,
> single glory of prophecy,
> fair soul of the slain Christ
> cleanse me within like sweet linen.

There were still more intense passages:

> Blood from the pure, pierced side,
> on Christ's tranquil Cross;

183

> Divine breast, hold me,
> sure spring of life, wash me!

These extensive meditations have been so much ignored that the heart of his greatest poem, *The Mass of the Birds,* has been neglected. The 'ritual' takes place in a 'hazel sanctuary' and it is sung, 'this aubade of the dappled thrush' as a

> Matins in the bright glade,
> lyric gospel of love's messenger.

For 'my golden girl' had sent this celebrant and Dafydd's description of the liturgy has all the witty dartings of thought and image of one to whom the ceremonial was a common possession:

> Wordy as licensed preacher
> he flew to the arched hollow,
> his wings draped with a chasuble
> of flowers from the branches of Spring,
> his cassock a wind-blown cloak
> of plaited withies; and—I swear by God—
> no baldachino here but heaven's vault.

There are other ministrants, the nightingale who 'chimed in her throat the sanctus-bell', and the poem ends with a splendid union of Dafydd's complex credo:

> the sacrifice was raised
> above the green glade,
> worship in passion's chalice,
> that pure song
> in its birch sanctuary.

The temper of Welsh poetry at its brilliant height could scarcely be better fulfilled than in that single line:

> Worship in passion's chalice.

184

I have lingered for some time at this first landmark because it may be an unfamiliar place and those who knew Chaucer's London or the lyrics of Provence will have only sparing clues to the grandeur of Dafydd ap Gwilym.

So to my second landmark. Henry Vaughan of Llansantffraed maintained his devotions at the heart of the Brecon countryside, though altars were desolate and Puritan bigotry deprived parishes of their priests. The sacraments of place and season were a commonplace to Vaughan as he remained within his small orbit and it could sometimes extend itself to the point of effrontery:

> I saw Eternity the other night.

But I wish to look at just one poem briefly, that most majestic poem 'The Dawning'. In it he meditates on the time of Christ's second coming to judge mankind: will it be at dawn or dusk or at midnight? The speculation is halted and aspiration is focussed:

> O at what time so ever thou
> (Unknown to us) the heavens wilt bow,
> And, with thy Angels in the *Van*,
> Descend to judge poor careless man,
> Grant, I may not like puddle lie . . .

We know from other poems that Vaughan regularly 'spent his hour' of meditation, not in his study but in the open air, and it is clear that at 'The Dawning' he was gazing across the valley to the highest point of the Beacons, Pen-y-Fan. We cannot make too much of the italics for *Van* (but they do attract out attention) and it seems clear that the dawning of that great day would, for Vaughan, be appropriately localised:

> When thou wilt bow the heavens and with
> the vanguard angels, descend to Pen-y-Fan,
> to judge poor careless man, grant that I . . .

I do truly apologise for the limping, pedantic prose but 'Ban', 'Y Fan', 'the mountain' is a common feature and on the seventeenth-

185

century map of Breconshire, our 'Pen-y-Fan' is 'Pen-y-Vann'. Nor is this by any means the sole place in which the visions, the epiphanies happen within his gentle environs, still relatively unspoilt to this day.

It may now not be so unclear why R.S. Thomas is for me 'the third landmark'. In 1968, in the Poetry Book Society's Christmas Bulletin; he wrote diffidently, "I play on a small pipe, a little aside from the main road." We read that deprecating statement with some irony, for he had already written of Spain and its landscape, of painters in the Louvre and in their Italian home, of philosophers and scientific exploration: and while most of his poems fall humbly within the confines of a single page, the canvas appears vast.

Of the development of his verse (and his growth in stature) I was given modest opportunity to write, in the small book in the Writers of Wales series in 1979. Now, I wish only to pursue those aspects of his work that I feel place him in the lineage of Dafydd and Vaughan. The first of these may be seen most clearly in the Welsh prose work, *Abercuawg*—and I should perhaps say here that without the rare works in prose, in Welsh and English, much of R.S. Thomas escapes evaluation; without *The Mountains*, the introduction to his *Penguin Book of Religious Verse* and to the Faber *Choice of George Herbert's Verse*, the fundamental 'argument' of his work is incomplete.

Abercuawg was a lecture at the Cardigan National Eisteddfod in 1976. It is a delicate, complex work, Thomas's imaginative reconstruction of the poet, Llywarch Hen's Abercuawg, 'that place where the cuckoos sing'. This visionary world is defined in his poem of the same title in the volume *Frequencies*:

> I am a seeker
> in time for that which is
> beyond time, that is everywhere
> and no where; no more before
> than after, yet always
> about to be.

For R.S. Thomas this is no 'mere vision' no quest in dream alone. It is a concrete desire for a Wales that is the fulfilment of vision, where the land has that fecundity that he expressed in his first published volume of verse:

> Notice his poise, from such conscious grace
> Earth breeds and beckons to the stubborn plough.

And when his impatience with his people is at its harshest, the natural order asserts its dominion over them and over his judgment of them:

> And why should you come like sparrows for prayer-crumbs
> Whose hands can dabble in the world's blood?

This, then, is Abercuawg: the vision to which every aspiration must tend, the vision that must order and moderate every political aim and action. This is the conclusion of the lecture in my translation:

> This is man's condition. He is always about to comprehend God: but in as much as he is a creature and finite, he will never succeed. Nor will he ever see Abercuawg. But by trying to see it, by longing for it, by refusing to accept that it belongs to the past and has gone to oblivion; by refusing to accept something second-hand in its place, he will succeed in maintaining its eternal possibility.

I like to think that the birds of Abercuawg could have sung in Dafydd ap Gwilym's hazel sanctuary, that Henry Vaughan could have 'spent his hour' there. And the passion for Welsh identity is found in Thomas's work not only in the rhetoric of the visionary land but in the harsh mountain landscape of Snowdonia. In the essay published by the Chilmark Press in New York in 1968, to accompany wood-engravings by Reynolds Stone after drawings by John Piper, R.S. Thomas defines with great precision the mystery of *The Mountains*. On the one hand they are dangerous:

> It is not good to live by mountains. They demand human sacrifice. Every year somebody must die.

187

But their presence cannot be denied and closing his essay, Thomas transmutes the tough facts of Snowdonia:

> It is to this that men return, in thought, in reality, seeking for something unnameable, a lost Eden, a lost childhood; for fulfilment, for escape, for refuge, for conquest of themselves, for peace, for adventure. The list is endless. The hills have all this to give and more.

It would seem indeed that Abercuawg is there for the seeking. But if I am to maintain the analogy with Dafydd ap Gwilym and Henry Vaughan, the argument from the domain of nature has to be seen in relation to the theological search. The introduction to the *Penguin Book of Religious Verse* declares his affinity with Keats's belief that it is important to maintain the poet's ability to be "in uncertainties, mysteries, doubts, without any irritable reaching after fact and reason." Indeed Thomas had already declared in the preface that "the ability to be in hell is a spiritual prerogative." It would seem from such self-testimony as 'A Priest to his People' that, as parish-priest he found it difficult to communicate with his people. Here I should interpose a 'domestic' incident. I had known Ronald Thomas and Elsie for many years, and, at one period fellow-priests in Wales, we had shared the same dilemmas; I had indeed accepted his intellectual and spiritual problems as he saw them. But one day I was driving through his first parish of Manafon and stopped for a purchase in the village. When it was transacted, I asked the shop-keeper if she remembered the Revd R.S. Thomas; "The Rector!" she cried, "what a wonderful man and *what* a preacher!" Now of course, it may have been the rhetorical passion she had responded to but I only partly believe that. Further conversation indicated a deeper, perhaps instinctive understanding of what "the Rector" had been proclaiming. Be that as it may, it is clear from the poetry that there is a very equivocal poise between belief and a concerned agnosticism in his thinking. 'Pisces' uneasily acknowledges God's creation of the 'roses/in the delicate flesh/And the tooth that bruises', and it takes the silence of an empty church to reveal to the kneeling priest 'love in a dark crown/of thorns blazing'.

188

'No Iago Prytherch? No Cynddylan on his tractor?' The questions are proper but those inhabitants of R.S. Thomas's poetry have spoken long and eloquently enough, and I wish much more strongly to stress the exploration which, for me, comes to its climax in the volume *Frequencies* (1978). The poems now have attained a new tranquillity, though the search is at least as strenuous as before. Where Henry Vaughan 'saw Eternity the other night' so R.S. Thomas is content now to stare

> over into the eternal
> silence that is the repose of God.

He must be content now to be poised 'somewhere between faith and doubt' and to explore the mystic's language of negatives, in which 'Godhead

> is the colonisation by mind
> of untenanted space.

It is a vast quest and R.S. Thomas, whether he is pursuing truth in the concerns of Wales or searching for Godhead in the spaces between the stars, has never flinched from consequences, in thought or action.

*

We were seated at the hearth in Llanddewi, the morning after his most moving reading of his verse in the Festival. It had been a good visit for him, for he had seen two of my parishioners whom he greatly valued—a pair of red kites. Now we were quietly talking, of ministry, of Wales, of poetry in English and Welsh. I had told him of the curious fact for me that, with increasing skills in sculpture, I found the writing of poetry make more urgent demands on me. He was quiet for a while and speech when it came was a clear command: "Sit back now, Moelwyn. Masticate your experience and spit out what poems you can."

*

189

To visit Aberdaron on the tip of the Lleyn Pennisula, looking out to sea and Enlli was a very different experience. He took me to his church, Eglwys Hywyn Sant, pointed out the pilgrim route but confessed to me that it was not the Christian remains in that most holy place that most fully held him but the geology and the archaeology which revealed the depths and structure of the place.

Back in the Vicarage I entered another world—another two worlds. For his wife, Elsie (Muriel Eldridge, the painter), invited me to her sitting-room and studio. 'Two worlds' and yet related. Everywhere were the cherished fragments of natural life, bird-skulls, vertebrae, wing-feathers, all the fragments that, closely observed were the substance of her minutely detailed drawings which became such desirable postcards. From these microcosms there was an almost disconcerting shift of scale to the large landscapes she was then painting. I felt they were paintings of atmosphere, of the mood of landscape and yet the precision was there, the justice of observation which made, in her smaller works every butterfly-wing identifiable, every feather a signature of the bird's particular being. Duns Scotus would have approved the *haecceitas* of this art!

Mildred Eldridge (Mrs R. S. Thomas) *Hill Sheep, Corris*

190

6

CARVING AND CASTING

There seemed always to be fine rain or mist and accurate direction was difficult, while the coarse heather whipped cruelly at bare young legs. So, much of the climb up Mynydd Margam to 'The Dewless Mound' (Y Twmpath Di-wlith) was on my father's shoulders. Then, after a seemingly endless climb, came the object, "There it is; there's the Bodvoc stone!"

It was my first vivid encounter with sculpture; and it was with sculpture as the enshrining of history; for this stone, standing a little crookedly but of greater than human height for my less than ten years, was incised with the mystery of death and memory:

BODVOCI HIC IACIT
FILIUS CATOGIRNI
PRONEPUS ETERNALIS VEDOMAVI

(The Stone of Bodvoc. Here he lies
the son of Catogirnus
and great-grandson of Eternalis Vedomavus).

My possessive pride in the Bodvoc Stone led me to assent eagerly some years later, when my father suggested that he lead a party of my friends from the County School across the mountain to the site which I remembered from my younger days. We set out, about a dozen of us, on a fine Saturday afternoon and made good time up the flank of Mynydd Margam. But when we had reached the shallower slopes towards the top of the mountain, a thick mist came down and my father had to decide whether to return or risk pressing on. His decision appealed to our schoolboy sense of adventurous exploration. Taking the middle place and stretching us out in a line on either side of him, he directed us to move forward, never for a moment to be out of sight and sound of the two people on each side of us. We went on slowly, calling to each other

191

by name (in fact our laughter would have kept the necessary contact) and, to my very great pride, my father's navigation was justified and again there was the cry: "Here it is—the Bodvoc Stone." The group was gathered together to admire the site and the inscription and, now in a close-knit bunch of boys, we turned for home, getting below the mist in good time before dusk.

*

There were to be other experiences of early sculpture: the stone 'PVMPEIVS CARANTORIVS' down Water Street past Eglwys Nunydd farm and on towards the drowned city of Kenfig; this somewhat falsely stimulated both sight and sound, as it echoed (in my imagination) to the feet of the Legions marching the coastal road, Via Maritima; but this was also of the sixth century and carried the added mystery of Ogam script. And there was the crowning glory of my young knowledge of sculpture, the Cross of Conbelin within the abbey precincts in Margam Park. Here was both mystery and beauty, a work over seven feet high in the local pennant sandstone, intricately carved in Celtic strapwork and knots and so strangely uniting the sacred and secular: a symbolic crucifixion on the front and a spirited hunting scene on the back.

Margam, then, had become a sculpture shrine for the small boy for whom the Park was a place of enchantment to be explored as often as possible—but entered with awe and rather breathlessly, for many men had made their mark here, legionaries, monks, Tudor landowners and their heirs. They had made their mark in stone.

*

Finding the stone with the Pumpeius Carantorius inscription and the further adventure of exploring the buried city of Kenfig, the mysterious pool, the drowned church from which the fortunate listener could hear (as from *la cathédrale engloutie*) the pealing of bells, the remaining fragment of the castle, drearily emerging from the sand-hills, all these required transportation. My friends at school had rather splendid bicycles, with elaborate cable-brakes and three-speed fitments. My mount was a humbler and, to their eyes, bizarre object, an ancient racing bicycle (ancient even in about 1925-6) which seemed to be nothing but a light frame, two wheels, a narrow racing saddle, and handle-bars. There were no gears and—to their amusement and my almost permanent alarm—*no brakes*. You slowed down and, hopefully, stopped the 'bike' by peddling *backwards*. If your chain held, as well as your nerve, this caused some kind of gripping action on the back hub. If it didn't, you jumped for it to the nearest grassy verge. But it was light and it *was* a racing bicycle, faster than the posher versions of any friends. And the final pay-off for me came at river fords or the Stepping Stones at Merthyr Mawr, when I simply slung the 'bike' on to my right shoulder and went across as if unburdened, while they struggled with their more elaborate machines.

*

Margam was indeed an ambiguous place for me—of enchantment, yes, but also as familiar as home. For my father worked in the Estate Office, at the house called Twyn-yr-Hudd (near the present entrance to the Margam Leisure and Sculpture Park). He often took me as a boy to explore the grounds, especially around the Orangery (one of the most beautiful buildings in the country) and the ruins of the Chapter House. My father knew the whole estate and district intimately, for he had been born in nearby Groes, had joined the staff of the Estate while scarcely out of his 'teens and, working under the kindly agent, Mr Lipscombe, eventually took charge of the Estate terrier and rent-roll, a formidable responsibility when the estate compassed rich farms, woodland, the Port Talbot docks and the expanding industry of the busy town (important enough, under its parliamentary title of Aberavon to have Ramsay Macdonald as its M.P.).

The Scottish connection was strong, for Andrew Fletcher of Saltoun inherited from his aunt, Emily Charlotte Talbot, the Margam Estate to add to the Saltoun lands. Margam then became his home during the shooting seasons for deer, pheasant and grouse, while Scotland was for salmon and trout. The staff at Margam received generous gifts of fish from the Saltoun fishing and of course venison and birds from the shoots at Margam. We were by no means 'well-to-do' but I remember my mother's exasperated amusement when I protested at one Sunday lunch, "Oh no! not pheasant again!"

All this meant that there was a real sense of home-coming when, at the founding of the Welsh Sculpture Trust, my iron sculpture, 'The Helmet', found its site near the Chapter House and Orangery where I had played as a child and within sight of the Abbey Church where, in 1938, my wife and I were married.

But much was to happen before 'The Helmet', ten-feet of formidable cast-iron, was in place.

*

The development of sculpture parks in England, Scotland and Wales has a long history. For before the Welsh Sculpture Trust was even a tentative thought, Margam had been for centuries a sculpture park of the Welsh spirit. The direct simplicity of a 'Roman Stone', marking a route or a burial, the Latin so mysteriously complicated with Ogam; the intricate low-relief of a Celtic Cross; the austere moulding of a Norman arch; the decayed glory of the Cistercian Chapter House; the alabaster tombs of the Tudor Mansels, still grave and stately; the balanced splendour of the Orangery, the largest and finest in Britain, built not solely to grow orange trees but to contain Thomas Mansel Talbot's library and the collection of sculptures he had bought on his Grand Tour; the nostalgic antiquarianism of Christopher Rice Mansel Talbot's castle (built between 1830 and 1835) now the burnt-out shell at the heart of the estate. All this centuries-long accumulation of living stone seemed poised, waiting for a new step forward into the confusions of the industrial age.

And of course it was not denied. It isn't always easy to recognise and acknowledge the 'sculptural' objects in our industrial environment but Port Talbot, with its neighbouring towns and villages, has them in plenty. Pit-head winding-gear silhouetted above the hilly skyline; the grouping of elegant cooling-towers at a power-station; some of the concrete motorway bridges; the delicate pylons striding like modern legionaries across the valleys, we have learned in the past twenty or thirty years to look at these structures

194

of the machine age with new eyes, to see them not as scars and debris scattered over a romantic landscape to its grave loss, but rather as having power, stress and balance, their own valid integrity and beauty. And in the shadow of these structures, all those sculptors from Gonzalez and Picasso to Reg Butler, Anthony Caro, Phillip King and their many followers, who have cast, moulded, torn, rivetted and welded iron, steel, aluminium, in their search for new sculptural forms, they have not simply enriched our sensibility with new artefacts; they have extended our vision to accept and adopt forms which we never recognised as sculptural, to see objects of industry and utility as potentially objects of art.

In this long and complex history the Welsh Sculpture Trust now plays a significant part. When the West Glamorgan County Council so imaginatively bought the Margam Estate, it provided its large populace with a varied terrain, both sophisticated and wild, for countless individual and social activities. When they adopted the Welsh Sculpture Trust as collaborators in this venture, the way was open for showing sculpture in a greater variety of settings than anywhere else in Great Britain. The Margam Country Park itself brings the former private estate once more into active relationship with the town, the docks, the industries, which the Mansels, the Talbots and the Fletchers had done so much to bring into being. Now, with the essential support of industry, commerce and of the Welsh Arts Council, sculpture is brought to the notice, indeed before the very feet and eyes of those who have come to the Park for their leisure and entertainment. A living community at Groes and Margam, with its ancient church and 'Round Chapel', links these activities to Port Talbot at this critical time of industrial tragedy; it is a community in dire need of leisure, recreation, creativity, a breathing-space in which to consider its future. The dry, unemotional phrase, 'economic recession', masks a pattern of human tragedy in which the creative arts tend to be shoved aside as irrelevant. A Welsh Sculpture Park is a modest but, we hope, a potent declaration that the arts have a statement to make, an atmosphere to assert, in which re-creation in the fullest sense can be maintained with assurance.

The Sculpture Trust comes into being at a time of some exciting ferment in the world of sculpture. The Kroller-Müller complex at

Otterlo in the Netherlands has, for a generation, declared the relevant union of sculpture and the natural environment, with sophisticated parkland and a more open countryside; in this admirable setting our pioneer generation of innovative sculptors in Britain and in particular Henry Moore and Barbara Hepworth came richly into their own. In 1977 the Yorkshire Sculpture Park, with similar natural surroundings, brought sculpture into another relationship, with the lively educational context of Bretton Hall. Within a year the Scottish Sculpture Trust had established an exciting 'sculpture trail' at Carrbridge in Invernesshire, in collaboration with the Landmark Tourist Centre and the Scottish Arts Council. Here one 'discovers' successive works on something analogous to a Nature Trail and they appear to emerge out of the thickets, sometimes seeming to be completely at home there, others asserting a sharp 'manufactured' contrast. All of them, 'natives' and 'intruders' do much to justify Timothy Neat's claim in the introduction to *The Landmark Sculpture Park* that "most sculpture looks at its best out-of-doors, amidst the changing light of nature." Even more wittily than at Landmark, the Scottish Sculpture Trust set up in Glenshee, the skiing centre near Braemar, a number of works (Kempsell, Laing, Mylius, Pye and Robertson) which calculatedly asserted their intrusive human quality in the natural landscape—including two old persons in fibreglass "who sit and tirelessly enjoy the landscape, like tourists in a lay-by." And all this enterprise was underpinned by the National Gallery of Modern Art, in the Botanical Gardens where Epstein, Moore, and Hepworth, looked out over the Edinburgh skyline, and now that the former John Watson's School has become the Gallery of Modern Art, space is even more generous.

Already, then many of the practical issues had been faced and the initial problems mastered. Peter Murray, in the foreword to the handbook of the Yorkshire Sculpture Park pinpoints the major problem:

'For sculpture to cope with the dramatic vistas which landscape can provide, it must be powerful. This is not to do with size, but with the internalised character and strong 'sculptural sufficiency' of the work.'

196

William Pye, at Glenshee, had welcomed this challenge: "Public places are ideal; they extend the imagination. Gardens, too, and mountains"; and Henry Moore, from magisterial experience in siting sculpture indoors and out, in cities and parks or on the wide expanses of Sir William Keswick's estate at Glenkiln in Dumfriesshire, writes of the placing of sculpture as though, many years ago, he had been anticipating the rich diversity of Margam Park:

> Some Sculpture finds it best setting on a stretch of lawn or beside a pool. Others might be more effective, more poignant, set against the rhythm and raggedness of trees. Some of these might look best against oaks and others against elms. Yet others need the secret glade, a patch of grass enclosed by high bushes to give a sense of privacy.

Much of this variety in setting and in the sculptures themselves the visitor will find in Margam. In it, too, he will find a great variety of aim and purpose; some works represent Barbara Hepworth's concern for 'man in his landscape', a preoccupation splendidly realised in her late work, 'The Family of Man' (now striding up the hillside at Bretton Hall); others react most sympathetically to the abstractions, the mathematical tensions of a scientific age; techniques and materials range from the traditional wood, stone, bronze to a greater attachment to iron, steel and synthetics of all kinds; yet all maintain the integrity of the artists' exploration into the phenomena, the tensions, the revelations, and the agonies of our day. Artists tend not to be over portentous and sculptors have mankind's full quota of relaxed gaiety—but there is an equal gravity in their endeavours. Herbert Read, examining twentieth-century artists' debt to primitive and exotic sculpture, attempted to define the explorations with which sculptors have been engaged since the creation of the early work of Brancusi and Picasso:

> 'Modern man has been in search of a new language of form to satisfy new longings and aspirations—longings for mental appeasement, aspirations to unity, harmony, serenity—an end to his alienation from nature.'

197

These are high endeavours and their urgency may be judged by contrasting two attitudes, in two quotations. Anthony Caro has succinctly and with the direct simplicity of an artist's conviction, given, if unconsciously, an answer to one of the abiding nightmares of our time. A radio commentator, at the end of last year, speaking of the dangers in the increasing international traffic in arms, said chillingly: "The Cost of Killing has risen faster than the Cost of Living." Anthony Caro some years ago gave the artist's true response:

> Art, music and poetry are about what it is like to be alive . . .
> The value of an art work lies in its depth of introspection and emotional content.

That is no mean aspiration for the artist, to assert the values of life in a bleak world.

*

The year 1967 saw a sudden change of direction in my work which led a very few years later to my resigning my English chair in Exeter in order to become more wholly a sculptor and to have time for more poetry (which seemed to be released by my working in stone and bronze). I suppose there had been many hints, positive and negative, for some years that a change was inevitable. Writing *Shakespeare and the Artist* had pushed me towards art history and more into the company of artists than of academics. I had become physically and emotionally weary of academic life, with its many failures of creativity even in those who professed 'the arts'; just at this point a happy accident brought me into contact with Barbara Hepworth and—quite swiftly—to one of those very few friendships which wholly transform lives. The University of Exeter had determined to give Dame Barbara the honorary degree of D.Litt. and I was asked to meet her in St Ives to discuss details of the award and the degree ceremony. This led to many visits and conversations in her studio and when, eventually, she invited me to consider sculpture as at least in part my way of life, I knew that there was already in my background a great deal which impelled me to assent.

The conviction that the creative artist had something crucial to say to the academic mind had sustained me in many years of university teaching, as my conviction steadily strengthened that critical analyses of other men's creativity left the critic on a sterile promontory unless he himself engaged in creative work at the same time. It has always seemed to me an amazing effrontery that university teachers in my discipline should presume to examine works by Shakespeare, Jane Austen, Ted Hughes, in the presence of their undergraduates while never having undergone the creative travail in any medium, verbal or otherwise, themselves.

Before I met Barbara Hepworth, friendship with Josef Herman and John Piper had of course told me a great deal not only about the artist's insights but much more, the tough struggle with materials while an idea seized upon by the imagination is roughed out, shaped and wholly realised. During these years also my setting up in the university 'joint honours' degrees with the arts of music, drama and fine art, had taught me about their related and differing insights; for these were 'joint-honours' degrees with a difference: it was possible to read 'English and Art History' in a number of universities; my department was, I believe, the first to share the Honours degree between English and the Diploma in Art and Design (the Dip.A.D. in Exeter College of Art). In turn, we on the English side demanded poetry, plays or a novel as an integral part of that half of the degree.

Contact with Dame Barbara meant, however, an initiation into a pattern of discipline different from that of the painter. For the sculptor is to a substantial degree indebted to the skills of the studio assistants who undertake much of the arduous work in the early and middle stages, as a piece of sculpture presses towards realisation. I learnt a great deal from contact in those days with her 'boys' as she called her mature and highly competent assistants.

For some months I had delighted in the new insights in St Ives, in the studio of an artist who had lived and fought through the struggles which this century had seen, to establish a valid sculptural tradition in this country. With Gabo and Ben Nicholson and a handful of others, Barbara Hepworth had inherited and enlarged the scope and modes of the sculptural tradition from Rodin and Brancusi and which burst into its first and perhaps fullest creative life in this country in her work and in Henry Moore's.

All this was vibrant about me in the studio at St Ives, in the stone-yard with its partially prepared blocks of marble and in the splendid maze of the garden, where one passed from sculpture to sculpture and then, returning to the studio, saw work in progress, creation in its toughest stages.

One of these visits was to see how she was progressing after a fracture of her hip, which our friend, Norman Capener, consultant orthopaedic surgeon at Exeter, had set for her. (He was the subject of her splendid series of drawings in the operating theatre, drawings which were remarkably sculpturesque in their masked and robed anonymity.) The administration of the department at Exeter, the work of Chancellor in the Cathedral at Salisbury and my regular visits to the University of Chicago had sapped my energies and after a pause in our mutual concerns, Barbara said sharply:

"You live too much from here to here", moving her forefinger across the width of her forehead; "You're all thought! Let's see if you have a pair of hands."

Barbara Hepworth, Garden of Trewyn Studio

Barbara Hepworth, *Three Obliques (Walk-in)*

She trundled her wheel-chair across the studio and began moving about her sculpting tools. I was interested especially in one set of gestures: she picked up a substantial sculptor's hammer, looked across at me as she hefted it in her small hand, slightly shook her head (clearly I could not be expected to handle a tool as heavy as her customary working instrument!) and came back to my chair with a large set of sculpting tools—mallet, hammer, chisels, claws, rifflers—and placed them before me. Some of them were marked with the red adhesive tape which distinguished her tools from those of her 'boys' and these are still treasured. Without explaining their use she left them and went across to the telephone, called the Delabole State Quarry and asked them to put some of their best slate ("the quality you give me") into the boot of my car as I passed on my return to Exeter.

202

"Now I want a piece of sculpture in a month's time." Dame Barbara was not one to be argued with lightly. For some three years I went back again and again to St Ives, for the finest teaching imaginable. After one visit to Scotland, to the bay of Portsoy on the Banffshire coast, I brought back to Exeter several pieces of the local serpentine ('Portsoy marble') and carved my first 'male torso'. I took it down for her comment and it was placed between us on her glass-topped table. She prodded and rotated it to see it in the round:

"Yes; that'll do. But I think that the top curve should be lowered by about an eighth of an inch."

It was the most treasured accolade I had ever received!

*

In 1967 I was invited by R.T. ('Peter') Brooks of the B.B.C. Religious Department to prepare a film on Barbara Hepworth in the 'Viewpoint' series and I was delighted to do so. Preparations were in hand for the eventual installation of her 'Construction (Crucifixion)' in the Close in Salisbury after my installation as Chancellor of the Cathedral. We had therefore talked a great deal together about the nature of 'religious art' and on 11 December 1966 she wrote to me with her customary direct clarity:

As regards the religious works—I have rarely dared to give them religious titles. There are a few earlier which were, I hope, a true act of praise but it seemed to me wrong to label them when the form itself should evoke the response. I speak now of the 'group'; 'Oval Sculpture', 'Trevalgan' etc. In the same way I called the drawings and paintings for the 'Crucifixion' construction 1, 2 & 3 etc.

In this way I think I am left free for further guidance towards the realisation . . . I may need lots of help when I get to the realisation in three dimensions. And it is a strength to me that you are there.

Earlier, (21 November 1966) while the initial drawings were in hand, she wrote:

To me it is important to be in a state of grace to do a Crucifixion.
. . . In envisaging a faceless Christ I seek only to portray eternity
and the mood in which to accept christianity.

Maybe I will be well enough to carry it out.

I felt sure that this was the moment to push forward our discussions
of these matters, with the added spur of a T.V. programme to meet.
Indeed, by the time we came to preparing and in part filming the
programme, work was well advanced on 'Crucifixion' and the
Morris Singer foundry had made preliminary maquettes and a
prototype available for filming at Basingstoke and it was
determined that the 'framework' of the programme, its opening
and closing sequences should be the quite early 'Oval Sculpture'
and 'Crucifixion'.

On the former work she spoke in the programme itself:

This oval sculpture which I carved in 1943 was, I think one of my
most religious sculptures . . . It was made at a time of very deep
despair and trouble when one of my children was gravely ill and
I thought and thought what I could do which was helpful or
useful and decided the only thing I could do would be to make
as affirmative a sculpture as I could and as perfect as possible as
a gift, no matter what happened . . . I realised that eventually I
would find a way of speaking within these terms in my own work
about my own particular feeling and religion.

The central theme of the programme thus became the sculptor's
translation of her own creed into visible terms in a large bronze
structure:

I very much wanted to make a Crucifixion which enabled one to
recognise the figure of Christ on the Cross and the rudimentary
forms to the left and the right, to make spaces where one could
enter and to bring one to one's knees. But to do it in a way which
entirely fitted the development of my own calligraphy and to be
at home on a hillside, or in an old cathedral or a new, and to be
valid in all respects two thousand years hence.

204

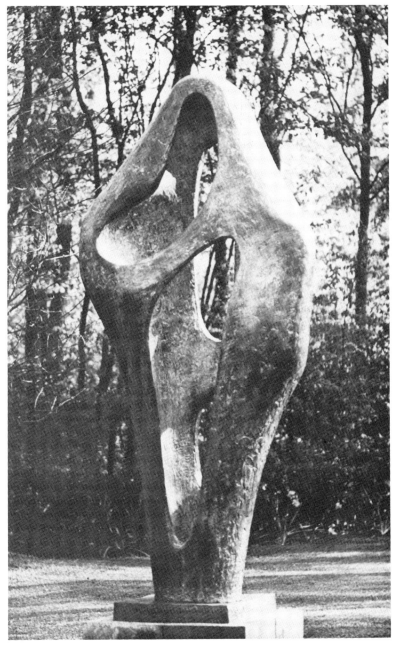

Barbara Hepworth, *Figure in a Landscape*, in the grounds of the University of Exeter

Barbara Hepworth, *Single Form*; a memorial to Dag Hammarskjöld
at the United Nations Building, New York

206

Some weeks before the recording was to take place in St Ives, she asked me for an outline of what I wanted to ask her and I hedged. Then, the day before the recording she demanded a rehearsal and a list of my questions—which she knew I had prepared. Risking her wrath—which descended!—I refused both requests, saying that they would kill the spontaneity of our conversation on camera. I knew the acuteness of her mind and her articulacy, whether in speech or writing and after a while she agreed.

As I had known, the camera-work and the talk went perfectly, as I knew they would; there was never a stumble in her answers and we all, director, crew and I, learned more about sculpture that morning than we thought possible. I hope the recording survives.

*

There were golden days in Cornwall; that day when she, Ben Nicholson and Bernard Leach were given the freedom of St Ives; or the wonderful birthday parties, at one of which John Williams played a superb guitar recital, or the degree ceremony at Exeter—I was too ill to attend—when she was given the university's doctorate.

But there was one series of events which showed most clearly the quality of the artist. 'Crucifixion' was ready at the Basingstoke foundry and prepared for transport to Salisbury Close. There had been much excited talk, with the Dean and Chapter and with Barbara herself about the best site for the work. She told me that her original conception had not included an open-air site and she hoped we would place it westward in the Cathedral—"I never really created it for outside although it did look very good with the sky and clouds behind it in St Ives; but the Cathedral would be the sky in this case." But measurement showed us that it could not be got through the west door in its completed form and we decided on a position to the north of the nave in the spacious green of the Close.

The Dean and all the canons were enthusiastic and many parish clergy in the diocese wrote to commend the gift and our good fortune in receiving it.

But there were mutterings. This 'modern artist' was somehow deemed to sully the mediaeval beauty of Salisbury Close; abstraction in some way obscured the profound reverence of this work, where the three intersecting crosses threw the nature of that tragedy on Golgotha into a new perspective. There were agitated happenings and to our astonishment Wiltshire County Council became involved and I felt I should write to Sir Geoffrey Tritton to lay before him and the County authorities, the nature of the problem which had so astonishingly arisen.

Barbara Hepworth, *Construction* (Crucifixion); formerly in the Close, Salisbury, soon to be at Portsmouth Cathedral

Barbara Hepworth, *Construction 2*; a drawing towards the bronze crucifixion

"You will realise that both in private correspondence and in newspapers, I have kept wholly silent about the Hepworth *Crucifixion*, despite the fact that I was intimately concerned with its coming into the possession of the Close Chapter. It seems now that a great deal might be gained by my putting to you, in private, certain considerations which may modify your opinion, as we gather it.

It seems exceedingly unlikely that any adverse judgement would be seriously made at this point in her career on any major work of Dame Barbara's. Her sculptures appear in all major collections in all continents and she has been honoured not only by our Crown but by innumerable bodies, including the United Nations, and universities in England, Europe and America. Nonetheless, to the public, however nicely we may judge legal rights on either side of this matter, the rejection of planning permission by Wiltshire can only be read as adverse judgement on one of the two most distinguished living sculptors, and is bound to make the Close Chapter appear ridiculous in the eyes of those concerned with the relation of the church and the arts, to say nothing of the wider world of art and scholarship. It therefore seems to me to be the merest act of prudence (and the Close Chapter, whether formally or privately, has taken these prudent steps) that Wiltshire should also consult bodies whose judgements in these matters is universally recognised. If this were done, the whole County Council would be able, properly and objectively, to assess the very considerable strength of feeling that this rejection by the committee has produced in the country, and especially among the highest authorities in the world of art. It is possible that the views expressed to members of the Close Chapter, by members of the Fine Art Commission, of the National and Tate Galleries and many others, have not been drawn to your attention. I beg you not to under-estimate their strength.

I have hesitated for many days before putting the final consideration to you and I do this with full understanding of the difficulty of my communicating it to you. I have all too good reason to know the pain, both spiritual and physical, that this matter has caused to Dame Barbara, and I would simply ask you to be quite certain in your mind that you are right in your judgement before inflicting further and crucial pain on an honourable and generous woman. If it were a wrong decision to leave the *Crucifixion* in the Close, it is an error that could easily be reversed in an hour or two; on the other hand if you were to be wrong in wishing for its removal and succeed in your desire, the critical hurt personally to her, would be irreversible, as would the damage to the reputation of the Chapter and its desire to fulfil a very necessary pastoral activity.

Barbara Hepworth, *Cantate Domino*

211

I am very conscious of the fact that it is impossible for the Chancellor of the Cathedral to write in a wholly private capacity, nor can I separate from the contents of this letter my own deep involvement with the arts in general and with the work of Dame Barbara during this period. You will, I feel sure, understand the spirit in which this letter has been written and my very strong desire that relations should be harmoniously restored between the religious and secular authorities over this work. You will already know, from the vote of the Diocesan Synod, of the whole-hearted support the Diocese gives us. We must most heartily hope that the rift between the Church in this Diocese and the County Council is not unnecessarily perpetuated.

In all this unseemly pother, Dame Barbara remained unruffled: on 10 October 1970 she wrote to me:

Please do not grieve. I can't help thinking that this blow-up is one of anger and it will blow itself out.

Those of us, however, in the Cathedral Chapter who knew that this entry of a great work into the Church was a high moment of insight, could not but feel ashamed that authority could so mistake its role though it did withdraw its objection. Nor has the subsequent history of the work in Salisbury Close made us any happier.

*

Fairly soon after this I determined to resign my chair at Exeter and return to Wales to seek my language again, to minister in a country parish of distinguished history and pursue more freely my work in sculpture and writing. I had not been long settled in Llanddewibrefi vicarage when Barbara's daughter, Sarah Bowness telephoned one evening to say that her mother had died tragically the previous day in a fire at her studio. She had left requests concerning her burial and asked that I should officiate at the Committal at the graveside. It was a sad and proud office to perform.

*

Barbara Hepworth's influence on my work extended long after our friendship was broken by her death. I had shown her one of my earliest versions of 'Growing Form' some ten inches high. The next day, 18 June 1973, she wrote to me:

> Thank you for showing me the new work. I really do think that you would get a great kick out of developing this piece to six or seven feet. It need not cost much, but it would give you such a joy to see the way these forms would develop.
>
> I look forward to hearing that you have acquired a place in which to do it, and I hope that we can meet again before long.

Over the next ten years 'Growing Form' amply lived up to its name. I made two more bronze versions about fifteen inches high, an aluminium cast about twenty-four inches high, now in the Whitworth Art Gallery in Manchester, and, making a considerable leap upwards, when the Burton-on-Trent Art Committee were able to commission a large piece of sculpture for the bank of the Trent outside their Library, with a grant from the Arts Council; 'Growing Form' in seven hundred pounds of cast aluminium on a concrete plinth, stood over nine feet tall.

A new departure for me was to work with a sheet-steel craftsman, Eddie Carter of Spa Sheet Metal. With an armature of steel rods clad with sheets of steel, the form now grew with a new lightness and grace. It was once more over ten feet in height and when I had devised an almost bark-like finish with 'sculptured' Isopon, it grew with a new propriety out of the ling and heather of the Scottish Sculpture Park at Carrbridge in Inverness-shire and surrounded by the pines of the ancient Caledonian Forest.

These all owe their existence to those years of unobtrusive learning, in conversation with Barbara Hepworth and the asides she dropped into talk in the studio or in subsequent letters, asides which always contained the seeds of new forms to pursue. I wish she could have seen 'Growing Form' in its Scottish setting.

*

It has always seemed to me to be unfair that some of our finest artists have been the most elegantly and forcefully articulate in

213

·writing of their life in art. Josef Herman's *Related Twilights* gathers uniquely the aftermath, tragic and noble, of the artist in European Jewry as Hitler pursued his ends; John Piper's explorations into architecture, expertly distilled in brief articles; Henry Moore's essays in the varying aspects of classical European painting and the growth of sculpture in the present century; most ultimately moving for me, Kyffin Williams's *Across the Straits* chronicles the life and background of an ancient family, part of the *bonedd* of Wales, that landed-aristocracy which struggled to preserve the culture of our country; all these writers would have given us a sufficiency of literary grace and power without the even greater gift of their work in stone or paint.

Barbara Hepworth was notably of their company. In one of her essays on the nature of sculpture she wrote also most powerfully of her 'philosophy' of art in the making:

> The consciousness and understanding of volume and mass, laws of gravity, contour of the earth under our feet, thrusts and stresses of internal structure, space displaced and space volume, the relation of man to a mountain and man's eye to the horizon, and all laws of movement and equilibrium. These are surely the very essence of life, the principles and laws which are the vitalisation of our experience, and sculpture a vehicle for projecting our sensibility to the whole of existence.

*

Barbara Hepworth's sculpture worked itself through to its final maturity when pure abstraction was giving way once more to the significance of the human form. Alan Bowness (*Modern Sculpture*, 1965) has succinctly placed this critical development of her art:

> She has written: 'I hope to discover some absolute essence in sculptural terms giving the quality of human relationship.' She was able in the 1930s, under the influence of Brancusi, to create pure abstract forms that existed in their own right without reference to anything outside themselves. They were neither extreme simplifications of parts of the body, as with Brancusi,

214

nor were they the kind of organic forms that we find in Arp's sculpture. They possessed a cool mathematical purity . . . At the same time the human reference was not far away. This is something almost inescapable, however abstract in intention the sculpture may be . . . Slowly in Hepworth's case the three basic

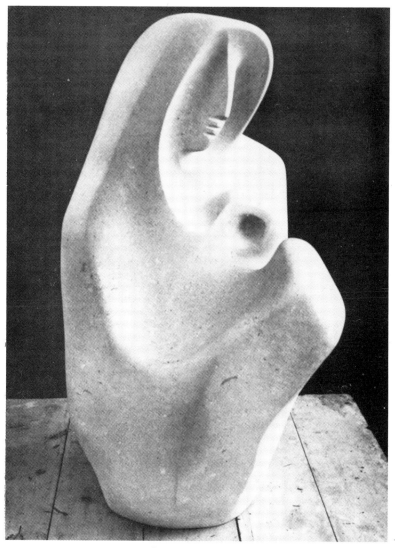

Barbara Hepworth, *Eocene*

215

Barbara Hepworth, *Mother and Child*; memorial to her son Paul in St. Ives Parish Church

216

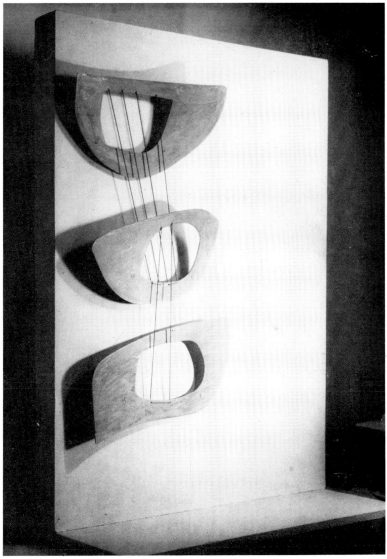

Barbara Hepworth, *Three Forms in Echelon*; coll. the author

forms of her sculpture crystallised. She has described their human significance. 'The forms which have had special meaning for me since childhood have been the standing form (which is the translation of my feeling towards the human being standing in a landscape); the two forms (which is the tender relationship of one living thing beside another); and the closed form . . . which translates for me the association and meaning of gesture in landscape; in the repose of a mother and child, or the feeling of the embrace of living things, either in nature or the human spirit.'

The objectivity within this personal statement was characteristic of her. Though austerity was, for many people the first impression conveyed by both her work and her personality, among her friends her generosity, warmth and immediate response to another's joy or sorrow is the most vivid memory. And there was always fun, from wit and satire to the frank enjoyment of the happy or ludicrous aspects of those around her. Apart from her many kindnesses to me, two occasions in particular moved me deeply. The first was when she took me to see 'Mother and Child' in the church at St Ives, a chaste expression of her grief at the death of her son Paul, flying in the Korean war. The second related to my own son, Paul—it sometimes seemed to me that the great affection she showed him owed something to his name. She certainly showed the greatest possible generosity, when his first substantial book of poems, *Stones*, was published by the Rougemont Press, in preparing two lithographs to be included in the book, in supervising the preparation of the plates and proofing the prints.

There were also the public and semi-public occasions, her unaffected happiness in her friend Bernard Leach's Freedom of St Ives; her look of intense pleasure at her sixty-seventh birthday party at the Tregenna Castle Hotel as John Williams spoke eloquently for us all in his guitar recital. This largeness of spirit was heard by us:

The dignity and kindliness of colliers, mill hands, steel workers —all the people who made up that great industrial area (of Yorkshire) gave me a lasting belief in the unity of man with nature—the nature of hills and dales beyond the towns. It is upon this unity that our continued existence depends.

The concept of a sculpture park in Margam had been realised with some success in the Exhibition of Sculpture Maquettes in 1981. In the following year the park was truly launched with a full-scale exhibition. Among the distinguished artists who had lent their names as patrons of the enterprise, Dame Elisabeth Frink added her vivid presence to the exhibition, no small or nominal gesture from an artist at the height of her creativity.

When lunch was over she asked me if I would take her to see my sculpture, 'The Helmet' and I crossed the open space between the Orangery and the cast-iron piece with some trepidation, for I knew that its conception owed a great deal to her aggressive figures and made a similar protest; it was natural therefore that I should be anxious about her judgment. Its ten feet of rough metal, the arrogant Etruscan helmet and the absence of any suggestion of compassion were intended as a protest against the mindlessness of mere power and I knew too that my instinctive malforming of the head to its predatory beak-form had been an unconscious reference back to her hawk and eagle sculptures. She stood some distance from it and then walked about it to see every angle and then quietly spoke of her satisfaction with it. I felt taken back to that moment, nearly twenty years earlier in St Ives, when Barbara Hepworth had told me that my Portsoy 'Torso' "would do"!

It was a particular pleasure for me that the splendid ascent through the park to the castle at its highest point, should have given Elisabeth Frink's noble heads such an opportunity to make their heroic statement, their unassertive declaration of steadfast opposition to cruelty and oppression.

Two further exhibitions confirmed me in my belief that here was the work that properly succeeded Moore and Hepworth as the richest expression of an individual vision in sculpture in our day. The first was the massive retrospective exhibition in the Royal Academy in 1985. With a quiet absence of rhetoric, this present-ation of her latest work left one breathless with both the cruelty of the 'Goggle-Heads' and the simple dignity of those enduring figures, the 'In Memoriam' of 1983 and the 'Tribute Heads' of 1975. I have to confess that, so overwhelming was the pressure exerted on me by this collection of her sculpture, I had only the

Elisabeth Frink, Altar Cross, Liverpool Metropolitan Cathedral

least resilience left for a swift walk through the Chagall exhibition in the neighbouring galleries of the Academy.

The second exhibition was at the other extreme of presentation: two small Frink bronzes of horses, in the Kingfisher Gallery, tucked away in a side-street of Edinburgh's New Town. Resting on their plinths, these two bronzes had shed the dignity of 'equestrian statue' and invited (and received) the handling to which so much fine sculpture impels the onlooker. Here was the Elisabeth Frink who wrote to me after the Royal Academy exhibition: "I have got back to some sort of normal life down in lovely Dorset and back to work again; what a relief." This seems to me to be the heart of her work: the powerful creative tension between her perception of nobility and compassion in the human and natural world, and her conviction that these qualities are flawed and endangered by the cruelty and aggression which man shares with the predators. Hers is an exhilarating and a disquieting vision.

*

In the *Catalogue Raisonné* of Dame Elisabeth's sculpture, published by the Harpvale Press in 1984, Bryan Robertson writes of her work:

> Just as the lyrical (or romantic or obsessive) flow of feeling in Frink's work finds the form organically from within . . . so also does the puritan thrust, the ethical scrupulousness, almost, of Elisabeth Frink's vision reject stylistic tricks . . .

The terms here are chosen and deployed with exact precision: 'lyrical flow of feeling'; 'the puritan thrust, the ethical scrupulousness'. The tense and deliberate ambiguity of her work could scarcely be stated more comprehensively. It can be tested against her sculptures in 1962 and 1965. In the former year she was commissioned to create a lectern for the new cathedral at Coventry and at first viewing this appears to follow the traditional eagle-form with some remembrance of the symbol for St John the Evangelist. Closer scrutiny reveals a latent power in the bird's posture and the thrust of its head, a power that can signify spirituality or a controlled aggression. Her eagle cannot deny its fierce nobility.

Three years later we have the very disquieting 'Standards'. These shafts, which appear so decorous, are crowned by eagles which unambiguously recall the ruthless power of Roman legions with their insignia. Once more, without rhetorical over-stress, the ambivalence of the eagle's strength becomes powerful art.

Within this same decade an even more powerful ambiguity is seen in the image of man. In 1964 Elisabeth Frink explored the posture of 'First Man'. He stands nobly, poised and erect but clearly, in the

221

Elisabeth Frink, *Walking Madonna*, the Cathedral Close, Salisbury

questing look of his face and head and the half-defensive gesture of his arm, he reveals his bewildered loneliness. This is no idealised, paradisal Adam but man first set in a possibly fruitful, possibly alien environment. His strength and his vulnerability complement each other in a very moving piece of sculpture.

But this is, of course, the beginning of the story; there now follow 'Warriors', 'Sentinel', 'Assassins', 'Goggle-heads', all in their various ways developing the theme of aggressive brutality.

During the same period and in the years following, there are the related figures of nobility, 'Tribute', 'In Memoriam' and the many renderings of man in his transcending power over suffering and cruelty.

Here it is perhaps pertinent to contrast Elisabeth Frink's vision with that of Francis Bacon. His dignitaries screaming in the confinement of their glass cages, or the appalling pun of crucified slabs of meat in a parody-triptych, are searing insights into one state of modern man—and the tortured Cardinal extends this insight back into history. But Bacon's images are unremitting, where Frink's have a more tragic intensity, in the identity of so many of the cruel heads with the calm resignation of those who suffer. Some of the predatory men have jaws and neck muscles which are a travesty of human dignity but some of them have features in which a glint of compassion would identify them with their victims. This is most powerfully seen in the strong patience of the recent 'Head of Christ', shown in Salisbury Cathedral. This conviction that aggressor and victim are of one human flesh, is one of the most powerfully moving in our contemporary art.

Here we must confront the sculpture, 'Judas', which I find the most confounding of all her works. Again, at first sight, it appears to be a direct—even uncomplicated—rendering of evil treachery. The brutality of torso and trunk poised precariously on malformed legs appears to denote its affinity with the brutalised soldiery (for it was sculpted in 1963 and is a 'fore-runner' of the predatory men). But is this too swift a judgment? In so many details it is one with the cruel heads and the very brutality of the bronze surface enhances this affinity. But in the averted, searching gaze and the agony that transfigures the brutal features, this work is far more subtly complex than a direct rendering of treachery. There *is* betrayal (the artist herself, with powerful simplicity, declares that "Judas *is* Judas") but there is the passionate aftermath of betrayal, the suicidal remorse, which extends the treachery into a still more lasting tragedy.

*

An 'aside' is needed here. In the interview with Bryan Robertson, so deftly conducted by him with questions that go to the heart of the

223

Elisabeth Frink, *Judas*

matter, Elisabeth Frink makes an important statement on her attitude to the worship which she inherited from her home and schooling.

224

I used to enjoy the Mass as it was sung in my youth: that is in Latin, which I understood perfectly well as I did Latin at school, and in any case the English translation was always on the other side of the page. It seems to me that the Mass then was universal, in the sense that it was the same all over the world, in whatever church you went to in whatever country. The Mass means far less to me now that it is spoken or rewritten in what I consider very bad English. It has no sense now of dignity or ancient mystery.

Elisabeth Frink, *Tribute Head*

225

All my sense of deprivation cries 'Yes!' to that statement as I deplore the act of naked theft that the 'liturgists' have perpetrated on the Anglican *Book of Common Prayer*. But more significant than my indignation is the tone of the artist. Here must be one of the springs of her sensibility as she created, constantly over the years, the images of the sufferings of the crucified Christ.

It is useful to begin however with her 'Walking Madonna' and the contrast between the preliminary maquette and the finished sculpture. (Nos. 262-63 in the *Catalogue Raisonné*). If we had only the maquette, we might suppose, from the posture and the gestures of arms and hands, that here was a refined version of a 'traditional' Madonna; the final work is very different, a vigorous, almost aggressive figure, marching with purpose into undefined territory. but this is again to simplify the work. Seen (as sculpture should be) from more than one perspective, we have the union of two visions of the Blessed Virgin; the one has the tenderness of the mother who has relinquished her son; the other has the striding purpose of a woman who is more than 'handmaid', submissive to another will—the tough outline of the head in profile declares 'Magnificat' rather than docility. This is 'religious art' which goes far beyond cliché and convention.

Her 'Shepherd and Sheep' (or 'Paternoster') has similar resonances. Set in Paternoster Square, under the shadow of St Paul's, this is a rendering of the twenty-third Psalm and the concept of Christ as the Good Shepherd. But in the total range of Elisabeth Frink's work it reflects still further her exploration of the nature of masculinity. I attempted to define my reading of the sculptured group in a poem, which I thought a concise way of relating the nature of 'maleness' in the animal and human world:

> Gentle maleness; the ram
> tentatively leads,
> the four.ewes, gathered
> in mild confusion.
> A loin-cloth delicately
> defines the shepherd's hips;
> in his left hand
> the crook is scarcely grasped;

his right arm's gesture encloses
defines a space for
his erratic flock.

Once again it is the understatement in the sculpture that is so impressive. It might be a simple countryside scene; yet without stress, it gathers in centuries-old images with their religious overtones.

Equally temperate is Elisabeth Frink's handling over many years of the most potent Christian image, the Crucifixion. From the very early (1950) 'Christ at the Pillar' with its acute perception of suffering, to the austere 'Christ' at Basingstoke in 1983, there is a steady and unsentimental reverence in this examination of Golgotha. The two versions I find most moving are those intended for liturgical use; in 1964 she created the very spare, eight-foot high 'Crucifixion' for St Bernadette's Roman Catholic Church in Belfast and in 1966 the Altar Cross for the Metropolitan Cathedral in Liverpool. In the latter the unusually slender beams of the cross carry a body that is emaciated almost to a geometric form, while at the same time dramatically enclosing the viewer in its wide-armed gesture. In the same year she cast 'Risen Christ' for the church of

Elisabeth Frink, *Paternoster (Shepherd)*, Paternoster Square, London

227

Our Lady of the Wayside in Solihull and it is in this sculpture that I believe we have the most potent relationship of Christ's humanity to those other massive statements of heroic suffering and endurance.

*

Appended to the *Catalogue Raisonné* of Elisabeth Frink's work are two personal estimates. The first, by Brian Phelan, sets the cruelty which she explores within its proper context, her compassion.

> Looking at Frink's goggle man . . . I thought of Lucky in *Waiting for Godot* and his fear of Pozzo. I thought of the scream of terror and pain in *Guernica*.

Yet, despite the horror, Phelan's wider estimate relates to the Salisbury 'Madonna':

> which is for me a powerful expression of human strength and purpose. She affirms life.

At the end of the book, Alex Herbage makes 'A personal comment':

> Elisabeth Frink's work expresses her compassion for humanity against the dark and shuttered eyes of evil . . . Most important of all it gives some hope for the future.

This is indeed just and true; but I think we can go further: 'secular' struggle in her work, man against man, man against predatory aggression, is seen both in contemporary history and *sub specie aeternitatis*. This it is that gives such frightening dimension to her silent declaration that it is the same flesh and blood which participates in good and evil, that the 'goggle-heads' and the heroes of endurance share a common humanity even with the incarnate Christ. Bronze can scarcely be profounder in its affirmations.

JACOB EPSTEIN

"Ce sauvage Americain"
(Paris judgment, 1902)
"Epstein is raising modern
sculpture from the dead"
(Eric Gill, 1908)
"It is a tonic to see
something so abounding in raw
life and vigour, so careless of
good taste and intellectual
respectability."
(John Russell Taylor
in 1987, reviewing in the *The Times*
the Whitechapel Gallery
retrospective)

It was difficult, even in the 'twenties and 'thirties to avoid the impact of Jacob Epstein. Reverberations of the public's response to the British Medical Association statues were still sounding when 'Rock-Drill' shattered academic assumptions of the nature of sculpture in 1915, and I was one year into my university studies when the storm broke over his 'Genesis' in 1931. But it was not until 'Lazarus' was seen in the late 'fourties and then placed in New College, Oxford, that I realised that here was an artist I could not escape. Indeed, 'Lazarus', swathed in his grave-clothes, and with his tilted head agonised in its turn to the grave from which he has been drawn, haunted me until I was able to work it through in my novel, *Jeshua*. It was clear then, and it became still clearer as we saw Depositions, Pietas, Angels and repeated interpretations of Christ, that here was an unique vision, of relevance to Christian art, not so much because Epstein brought a Jewish insight to these sculptures but more, because his Judaic vision was centred in a still wider passion for those artefacts we call 'primitive art'.

Closer contact came for me when George Pace constructed the great arch in the restored Llandaff Cathedral and he and the Dean, Glyn Simon (later Archbishop of Wales) had the vision to invite Epstein to create his 'Majestas', poised on this massive arch and dominating the whole vista of the nave. I believe I was one of the

Jacob Epstein, *Christ in Majesty*, Llandaff Cathedral

first to preach, at Passiontide, under the looming presence of this great work, which had been unveiled, in Epstein's seventy-seventh year, in April 1957. Just before this, we had seen the tender posture of 'Madonna and Christ' at the Convent of the Holy Child Jesus, in Cavendish Square; and we were soon to see the controlled violence of 'St Michael' at the restored Coventry Cathedral. But it was this

Jacob Epstein, *Lazarus,* New College, Oxford

Llandaff 'Christ in Majesty' which was for me to unite with 'Lazarus' as a final definition of religious art in our day. The experience of attempting to preach 'the Passion of Christ' in its presence was like no other in any church or cathedral.

A different and more personal involvement with Jacob Epstein occurred in 1959. The Vicar of Selby wished to see Epstein's 'Ecce Homo' placed in Selby Abbey, the massive pillars of which presented one of the few church-sites which could cope with this massive statue. There was a protest from 434 Selby residents (only 34 of the objectors worshipped at the abbey) and the Chancellor of York Diocese, Mr Walter Wigglesworth convened a Consistory Court on 11 June 1959 and four of the witnesses invited to speak for the Vicar and Churchwardens were Canon Purvis of York Minster, Miss Cooper-Abbs of Northallerton, Professor E J Tinsley of the University of Hull, (later Bishop of Bristol) and myself—invited, presumably, because of my experience at Llandaff. *The Times* testified that "we regarded the statue as a major work of art and supported its installation in the abbey."

The hearing at the Consistory Court was fascinating. One of the objectors, Miss Hatty Robinson, condemned it with a striking if unconscious vision of the truth: "by its size and ugliness it puts one in mind of a heathen idol." It is, of course, large, six tons of Italian marble and eleven feet high. The suggestion in 'heathen idol' reflected that union with Jewish and Christian vision of alien insights from primitive works which so dominated Epstein's collecting. It was a union that I was to find so deeply confirmed in the work of Mircea Eliade and later in my son Paul's studies in Shamanism.

More conventional was the objection, "we consider the statue too modernistic and quite out of keeping with the ancient and wonderful beauty of the abbey", a sentiment which pursued us in Salisbury Close over the Hepworth 'Crucifixion' and which frustrates that inclusiveness of taste which marked all previous ages in church patronage.

The vicar, the very sensitive author of the Pitkin Guide to Selby Abbey, said in evidence that he "had realised that strength alone was a small part of its measure and there was an amazing sense of peace and beauty"—a judgment fully realised when 'Ecce Homo'

Jacob Epstein, *Ecce Homo,* Coventry Cathedral

found its place in the bombed ruin of St Michael's in Coventry and as it gazed across at the new cathedral with Epstein's 'St Michael' on its outside wall.

Even sadder than the objections to modernity was the concern of the last witness for the objectors who "feared for the effect the statue might have on the minds of children who came face to face with it after being shown the traditional pictorial image of Christ in their Sunday school books." One would have thought that that hidden but devastating judgment on 'pictorial images in Sunday school books' would have settled the judgment. To our astonishment, the Chancellor found against the Vicar and Church wardens and for the objectors, not the first time that ecclesiastical authority has frozen the vitality of patronage.

*

When I was invited to be a witness at this Selby hearing, I asked if I might visit Epstein's studio and home in London, for I knew 'Ecce Homo' only from photographs and wished not to be questioned on judgments to be made, without my having seen the original work. My request was greeted warmly and my visit began in the large studio where the sculpture stood. In this enclosed space, smaller than the site proposed, in the south aisle of the abbey, the work was overwhelming: helpless majesty, a defiance of pain and ultimate tragedy and an inclusion, within its vision of humanity, of the sufferings of those races which we now call 'the third world'; crucifixion, I felt as I stood beside it, could scarcely do more than seal the image with its 'Consummatum est'. While we were in the studio we spoke very little, except about my experience of the Llandaff 'Majestas'. There was a calm stillness in Epstein's look and carriage and I looked forward to the refreshment and conversation to which he now invited me. As we passed from the working area to his home proper, I was confronted, as I walked in, by a glorious bronze of a young woman's head and shoulders. My exclamation was quite spontaneous, "How beautiful!" and his reply took me a little aback, "Yes, isn't she?" For this was Jewish parenthood at its warmest, and where I admired the inanimate bronze, it was for him simply his daughter. This led to his close

234

questioning about my children. I told him a little about Paul, then coming to the end of his time at St George's, and said that I had a photograph of Christina. It's a very good photograph of a happy young girl about to become a beautiful woman; Epstein looked at it in complete silence and then said quite simply, "When can you bring her up to London? I should like a bronze of her head—lovely bone!"

Christina was naturally delighted but it was some months before a school term, university teaching and Epstein's increasing illness, allowed us to fix a time for the first sitting. Then just a week before we were due in Hyde Park Gate, we opened *The Times,* to find that Sir Jacob Epstein had died.

*

The years increased my knowledge and with it my admiration for Epstein's work but an enigma remained at the heart of it: why was it that Jewish artists seemed to have this powerful vision of Jesus Christ? I knew Chagall's versions, in painting, lithograph and stained glass, some of it overwhelming in its visionary intensity. Then came drawings by another Jewish artist, which 'rounded off' the enigma. The publisher of *Jeshua* invited Josef Herman to draw designs for its jacket. Josef asked me what incidents I wished him to recall for the preliminary drawings. Remembering his drawings of labourers pruning vines and Jesus's constant image of the Kingdom as Vineyard, I asked if it were possible to have Jeshua brooding over such a vineyard. An alternative in my mind was the entry on Palm Sunday to Jerusalem, the humble ride on a donkey.

Josef responded with two splendid drawings. I liked 'The Vineyard' marginally the better, but Josef and Christopher Davies preferred 'The Entry to Jerusalem' and I was glad to assent.

But this prompted the question still more urgently: why this consistent Jewish insight? Josef replied to my question:

The iconography and the presentation of Jesus in the works of Jewish artists is indeed a fascinating subject. Chagall is not the only artist who worked on the image of Christ. Being Chagall, he represented him with a body and festures recognisably Russian-

Jewish. But other artists of Jewish descent treated Christ differently. Epstein's Christ is more primitive, without Jewish racial characteristics; in fact his Christ has all the stark nobility of Tribal Art. There are also Christ figures by Jacques Lipschitz, by Ossip Zadkine and a legion of others, and all of them are part of different artistic traditions. Most Jewish artists would share your own view as you expressed it in *Jeshua*, that Christ is not outside but a coherent part of ancient Jewry. There is also another characteristic of the Christ representations in Jewish artists' works: he has never been represented as an outcast, nor as a rebel, nor as a king, earthly or heavenly; most of the time he is an ordinary man even when on the cross—there may be exceptions of which I don't know.

Even a confirmed Judaist—neither Lipschitz nor Epstein come into this category—like Benno Schotz has made one of the finest studies of the crucifixion, which is at present with me. He took me to see the large-scale work in some church in Scotland which I profoundly disliked and told him so—when we came back to his studio he gave me the study with his modest words, "You may be right."

All this shows that the presentation of Christ is not unique to the imagination of Chagall.— This will have to do for the moment.—More when we meet . . .

This, for all its splendid length, is very tantalising. There is so much more for Josef to say: about the *variety* in the Epstein representations; about Chagall and the contrast between his glass and other renderings of Christ; and most teasing of all, those two versions by Benno Schotz, whom Josef knew so well. I hope I can soon persuade him to a full-length book on this fascinating question.

*

236

As I look back over twenty years of sculpting I can see that any development that I made depended on two very different things. The first was my need. with this new medium literally to my hand, to express concepts that would have seemed very different in words. The second was a constant matter of wonder: the entry into the world of craftsmen, as I learnt to practise—or at least to understand—a great diversity of crafts, most of them related to heavy industry.

The first growth in my new awareness of matters that had a fresh definition in this new activity, was in clarifying ideas that had always troubled and often exhilarated me. Thomas Hardy speaks of our life as a "tremulous stay". Physically, for me, this expressed itself now in a new awareness of man's insecure balance as he stands erect. I say 'man's' advisedly, for the female stance has always seemed to me so much more secure on its curved and broad-hipped 'armature'. Man, standing erect, has a triangular torso poised on an elongated triangle from narrow hips to heel. The result was that my 'male torsos', poised on a point and dowelled to a heavy base, pursued every material I acquired or craft that I learnt.

Countering this sense of insecurity was my pleasure in any aspect of plant growth and again I tried to translate this into stone and metal, in some twenty to thirty variants of 'Growing Form'.

Then there was the more teasing matter of spiritual belief. A painter or a renaissance sculptor can take over the great ikons of the past and render them in a manner which freezes a powerful moment in scripture or in vision. Chichester Cathedral, Chartres in dramatic sculpture, glass at the Ste Chapelle or Canterbury, the engravings of Dürer and the paintings of Rembrandt, they still speak eloquently in a century that so 'tremulously' holds its beliefs. Artists in this age, however, find it difficult to initiate such ikonic references to faith; the incidents of past belief are now more elusive and, whatever our private belief, its public expression communicates more indirectly with our fellows. We speak more freely of awe and less freely of biblical happening. This involved for me the most difficult exploration. The crucifix was of course central but after some three attempts, for the church at Exminster, the

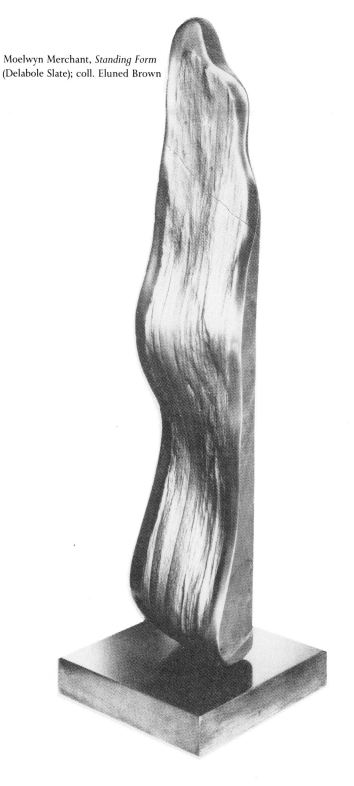

Moelwyn Merchant, *Standing Form*
(Delabole Slate); coll. Eluned Brown

University Chapel at Exeter and for a version now in St Michael's College, Llandaff, I gave up the attempt to render the classical crucifix and explored the crucifixion itself more closely—more of that later.

Relations with craftsmen were freer because they were humane. They began only a week or two after Barbara Hepworth had challenged me to find my hands in sculpture. I had returned to the Delabole Slate Quarry and the Managing Director, Mr Setchell, walked me around their waste tips, for he sensed that the fractured surfaces of slate, torn by tons of pressure, might be interesting to me. Indeed they were and I saw one piece very soon that looked like a wide double throne. "What a start that would be for a pair of thrones, if it could be split vertically." "Of course it can and here are the tools." He put into my hands a broad-bladed chisel and a mallet. Tentatively I asked him if he would offer the necessary cleaving point and obeying his demand that I "strike hard and firmly" I did so and to my astonishment the two forms fell apart and my 'Thrones' were half made. I realised that my sculpting on them now, mainly with fine rasp and abrasive cloths, had the opportunity of developing a natural form within them, that the male and female forms could inhere in the thrones themselves which demanded no occupants.

At a later visit I found an even nobler form, again torn across the laminations of slate in a wave pattern like flowing hair. To frame these striations in a highly polished edging of the slate gave me, I believe, my best slate sculpture, 'Standing Form'.

Soon I felt the need for a material that was more responsive to direct carving and less controlled by geological forces. I was lecturing for Frank Owen at Westham House in Barford, near Stratford-on-Avon and, in casual conversation about local stone, was advised to drive over to Yelvertoft in Northamptonshire, where marble in great variety and the alabaster with which churches had already made me familiar could be bought. There I met Nigel Owen, who not only sold me some fine alabaster, from the purest white to the banded brick-colour of the softer stone, but also taught me its texture and handling. It bruises more easily than marble and once the rough shape has been reached, demands the most delicate of handling to maintain the surface finish.

239

Moelwyn Merchant, *Thrones* (Delabole Slate), coll. Paul Merchant

A Bronze version in the National Museum of Wales, Cardiff
An Aluminium version in the Wakefield City Art Gallery

This was in 1965 and Nigel is now assisted by his son Michael Owen. He has become most knowledgeable in the sources of alabaster now so rapidly declining and I have learned in these last years, since finding in Scotland the stone of Glen Tilt, Portsoy and the Coreen Hills, that I can take a boulder to Yelvertoft and know that Michael's intuitive knowledge of cleavage, fracture, 'shakes' to be avoided and planes to be followed means, that in a detailed conversation between us, a sculpture reveals its abstract form; I know also something of the relationship that I saw in St Ives between Barbara Hepworth and her 'boys', skilled craft at the disposal of the sculptor's conception.

It had always been my assumption that casting in metal was beyond both my skill and my purse. Then I had the year in Salisbury Close and there was the entry of Barbara Hepworth's 'Crucifixion' to be sited there. It was accompanied from Basingstoke by the director of the Morris Singer Foundry and over lunch in our flat he remarked that some of my small stone pieces would cast well in bronze. Would we like to see one made at Basingstoke? It was soon to be Dame Barbara's birthday and I thought this might provide a suitable gift. It was a fascinating introduction to the new craft and when we returned to Exeter, I asked at the College of Art where their casts were made. I found that Mr Sercombe, in charge of the foundry at the local engineering works, was expert and sensitive to their requirements and for a year or two, until we moved to Llanddewi, I was happy to take my patterns to him.

It now seemed time for tentative exhibiting and in 1972 and 1974 the University put on shows of my work in stone and bronze that gave me a new confidence. Then in 1975-76 Alan Cotton, a painter friend and I put on a travelling exhibition which showed in five centres in the South-West, from the City Art Gallery in Plymouth to the Nuffield Gallery in Southampton. This was my farewell to Devon and Cornwall and our home was now to be Dyfed.

Where then in rural West Wales was I to find craftsmen to match those with whom I had worked? I was to be happily surprised.

My first contact was with a factory in Llanelli, my wife's birthplace, where a foundry was in the charge of Terry Davies, one of the most brilliant full-backs Welsh Rugby had known. Would his foundry skills match those on Cardiff Arms Park? They did; and for two years I drove happily down to Llanelli and, in the intervals of moulding the sand and pouring the metal, we sat over mugs of tea recalling international matches I had seen and many that I hadn't— a grateful confluence of arts.

There had been much talk when I arrived of a unique craftsman in Talsarn, the *woman*-blacksmith, Gwyneth Price, and her brother David who assisted their father in all the crafts with horses and machinery which the rural community demanded. I had brought from Exeter a Christ figure from the edition cast to be mounted on slate for Exminster and the University chapel. Now I wondered if the smithy at Talsarn could fulfil another wish of mine, to mount the darkly patinated third figure on a more brutal cross, an iron sword. They welcomed me gladly; I watched Gwyneth expertly shoe a farm pony and then her father took my drawing of a sword and we discussed the choice of metal and the surface finish I wanted. I was astonished at the speed with which the cross was completed and the figure mounted and I knew that if the bronze and the iron were left to the air for their patina, they would grow to the proper harmony.

Another craft was now to be learnt. A member of my congregation at Llanddewibrefi was Ogwyn Davies, Art and Pottery master at Tregaron County School. He had evening classes in the school in the winter terms and in two years we had become at least knowledgeable and mildly skilful in throwing on the wheel, slabbing and hand-moulding; we knew when the object was properly 'leather-hard' and had an elementary skill in glazing. This gave me advances on two fronts. I could now produce patterns for casting in bronze or aluminium, which foundry-men liked for their lightness and strength; and I could attempt sculptural forms which would be an end in themselves. When, therefore, with Ogwyn Davies's backing, I was able to 'rent' firing-space in the Tregaron Pottery, I developed about half a dozen 'Growing Forms', two of which I felt to match the earlier versions in stone and bronze and on a substantially bigger scale.

Visits to Aberystwyth, to the Drama Department and Alistair Crawford's studio, also allowed me the occasional visit to the church at Llanbadarn Fawr. There one sculpture drew me each

Moelwyn Merchant, *The Helmet* (Cast Iron), Welsh Sculpture Trust, Margam Park, Port Talbot

time, first simply to contemplate its mystery and then to draw it with a view to produce my own sculpture in bronze based on it. It was the Llanbadarn Cross and there was a variety of views on its date and quality. The prevailing view among archaeologists was that it was a primitive failure, a rude attempt, abandoned, to produce a statement of the crucifixion, and dated from the end of the Celtic period or just after. This seemed to me, whatever the dating, an improper judgment. It was worn over a lot of its surface but enough remained to show that this was a slab cross in which the formalised rendering of a human body took on a crucifixion shape. Respecting the undoubted pattern that remained, I attempted in my drawing to restore a greater precision to the incised carving. I then carved the work in wood and had a small edition cast in bronze.

This exploration of an early work was a critical step in my view of the Crucifixion in art. From this time I was determined that every figure of mine that attempted this theme should unite the Cross and the Crucified as one figure and I have made some ten versions in bronze and aluminium and I hope my strength will allow a really large version in sheet-steel.

Alistair Crawford was at this time directing the exhibitions at the Art Centre (Oriel) in the University College and in 1977 put on a substantial showing of my work, including 'Llanbadarn Cross'. It is a splendid thing that Alistair Crawford has now been given a personal chair as the first Professor of Fine Art in the University of Wales.

Scotland had over the years provided me with four or five new kinds of sculpting stone; Glen Tilt, through the friendship of the craftsman Watty Weir of Dunkeld and Birnam, and Portsoy and Coreen through our own explorations. Now a chance advertisement for decorative objects in blown glass roused other expectations. I asked the relevant department of the Scottish Arts Council who, in their opinion, was most likely to collaborate with me in parodying my 'Growing Form' in blown glass. "Try John Deacons at the Jay Glass Works in Crieff." I 'phoned him for an appointment and his soft voice left me quite unprepared for the gentle giant who greeted us—well over six feet and with a back like the side of a house. I had taken a version of 'Growing Form', about twelve inches in height, to show him and asked if it was possible to

244

Moelwyn Merchant, *Growing Form* (Aluminium); Public Library Site, Burton-on-Trent
There are four earlier versions of *Growing Form* in the Eton College collection, in bronze, aluminium, blown glass and ceramic.

245

produce a version in blown glass—and of about the same size as the bronze. He looked at it carefully, while I began to reflect that this would require taking at least two or three pounds of molten glass on his blowing rod, when the average weight for their customary objects would be just a few ounces. He turned to me with a quiet smile and the half-lidded eyes I was to become so used to and said "Ay, no problem!"

I had seen scarcely any work in glass of this kind and John Deacons began by introducing me to the two roaring furnaces with the molten glass and the large annealing furnace where the temperature of the object made would be controlled and reduced. I had then to learn the colour of the molten glass at the working temperatures—for John would be wholly dependent on my shouted commands as the work progressed. I say 'shouted', for the noise of the furnace blasts was deafening. He thought I knew what I was up to and said that when he had blown to the required flask shape, he would have to roll it on his metal stand and then slit the still glowing glass with metal shears, to produce my open, 'growing' form—and, would I remember that if I hesitated, and the glass fell too far below a 'cherry-red', further work would be impossible.

I had not been challenged in this way before not even at the smithy at Talsarn. John gathered his molten glass on the rod, blew the flask shape, fashioned it on the steel and, with glances for my shouted directions, clipped the wall of glowing glass to the shape I wanted. The whole process, from gathering to the final severing of the sculpture to be set for annealing, took about twenty minutes— and I have never known longer. With the great heat and the sound of the blasts, with watching an unfamiliar process in which I was a critical collaborator, I was left exhausted but pleased that it had not so far been a failure.

I returned to Crieff and the new 'Growing Form' the following day—and this time I had seen it grow—was ready and wholly successful. Over the next year or two we produced about ten pieces, not all of them of the same pattern and I was delighted that John and I had been able to push this technique in the direction of valid sculpture. When I saw him and Anne again last autumn he was working happily—"a very good American outlet!"—in a new workshop and I wished I had the strength and breath to start again.

246

Moelwyn Merchant, *Crucifixion*; St Michael's College, Llandaff

Moelwyn Merchant, *Torso* (alabaster); coll. Eton College

248

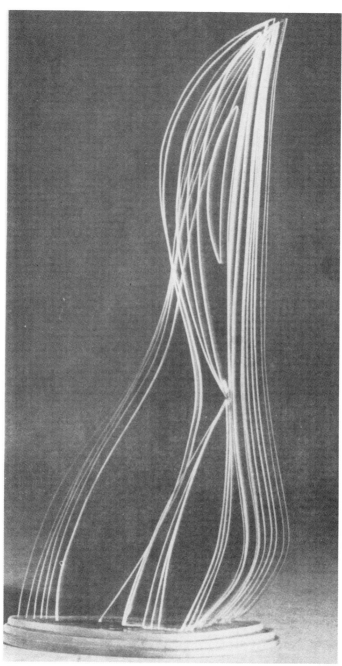

Moelwyn Merchant, *Standing Form* (Sheet glass), coll. Elan Closs Stephens

Moelwyn Merchant, *Isaiah's Vision* (Sheet glass),
Holland House, Cropthorne, Worcester

Moelwyn Merchant, *Golgotha* (Sheet glass), Church House, Westminster

Back in Leamington I had meanwhile to get in touch with a foundry, which would undertake my casting. Ball Brothers at Stratford were prepared to cast in bronze, aluminium or iron and after one trial with Paul Waters in the bronze foundry, I knew I had found the ideal craftsman to work with. His instinct led him immediately to see the problems which my unusual patterns set him—for it was after all an engineering foundry. I even grew not to dread the word 'undercutting' which is the bane of sand-casting, for Paul's skills had devices I hadn't hitherto met and I grew bolder in the patterns I fashioned for his craft. Over the years we produced sculpture which ranged from some three or four pounds of metal, to 'Growing Form' which required seven hundred and fifty pounds of aluminium.

Then came tragedy. Paul was found to have cancer and though he struggled on, one week of hospital treatment and two weeks at the foundry, his death was inevitable. In the weeks before he died, I had had cast small replicas of the Burton 'Growing Form' as remembrances for the craftsmen who had produced the large cast. But Paul, a devout Roman Catholic, had seen a glass cruciform on one visit to my home and asked if he might have that instead. One of our last conversations told of his happiness when their parish priest came to his home to bless it. I have not had the heart to return to the foundry where our friendship had grown.

Burnishing the large pieces I was now making was beyond my time and strength and again I was fortunate. At Nuneaton I found the workshop of two brothers, Bill and Jim Olner, who had established Nuneaton Fine Finishers when they preferred working for themselves after many years at B.L. and Rolls Royce. Here I found the same atmosphere as at Ball Brothers with Paul Waters, and I could stand at the lathe while one of the Olner brothers, usually Jim, allowed me to watch every move in the 'finishing', every grade of abrasive used and the control of those surfaces which were to be left as they had come from the foundry sand. Again it was like possessing four hands and arms.

Work at Crieff had given me a taste for the texture of glass and, finding that a firm had now perfected a glass bond, I wondered whether it would be possible to create structures in laminated sheet glass. In a small workshop in the heart of Leamington I found

251

Michael Bedingfield who seemed to be able to cut glass to any shape, even the extremely difficult concave edges. I explained to him that I wished to build up three-dimensional objects by layering sheets of glass until I had built up a sculptural form. With photographs of some of my 'Torsos' I showed him how I hoped to abstract their shape in 'float glass'. He agreed that it was possible and after a seminar on 4 and 6 mil. glass in its varying colours, green and 'smokey', and the technique of arrissing—the removal of the fine cutting edge of the glass,—I went away to prepare my first templates in card.

Our first experiment was a small 'Torso' and since it worked well we produced two larger versions. A design problem was this: the glass bond, a true bond and not an adhesive, had a refractive index very close to that of glass, but not quite the same; therefore, though it could be applied in very small dots, a close look revealed it. If therefore the 'smokey' glass could be used judiciously in the design, this problem almost disappeared. The real pleasure of using plate glass in this way is that the snapping of the glass when it it cut, gives a multitude of facets along the edges and when I was invited to show thirty of my glass sculptures in the Pilkington Glass Museum in St Helen's, I described it as "both sculpture and drawing green lines in air." The largest of the Torsos remains, in the directors' dining room, at Pilkington's.

The union of 'drawing' and three-dimensional sculpture made me determine on larger works. The first was a 'Golgotha' (in the foyer of Church House, Westminster) in which the three crucified are united in the design, which I intended to have overtones of 'My dancing day'. The second was a commission from Peter Middlemiss, warden of Holland House, Cropthorne, the retreat house of Worcester diocese. The plain but exceedingly beautiful chapel has a large, clear-glass east window looking out on the mature trees in the garden. I was taken to the back of the chapel and asked what it lacked. It seemed to me that its barn structure and plain brick had to be treated with great respect but that the bare wall flanking the east window could profitably take a sculptural object and I was asked to provide it. I submitted a drawing, a specification for 'Isaiah's Vision', a six-winged angel which was held within a plain mandorla. They liked it and at the

252

end of 1987 Michael Bedingfield helped instal it in the chapel, where indeed it seems appropriate.

Meanwhile two exhibitions in Scotland gave a further fillip to my work. Cyril Gerber of the Compass Gallery in Glasgow (and brother of my friend, Joseph Gerber) invited me to show with Frances Thwaites, the Edinburgh painter. I was amazed at the success of this show which sold a very substantial proportion of the sculptures and the following year (1981) a much larger one-man show, arranged by Debbie Butler at the MacRobert Gallery in Stirling University was an equal success. I rather ruefully wondered why Scotland should be so conspicuously more generous in its appraisal and patronage than either England or Wales.

Under the stimulus of these exhibitions and with an Arts Council commission under the 'Sculpture in Open Spaces' scheme for a large work on the river bank at Burton-on-Trent, I began to work in larger scale but on the old themes. Thus the Burton sculpture was the largest version, until that time, of 'Growing Form' and it seemed to me that sheet-metal would give me the opportunity of still greater height of working. Bob Catchpole at Eton had introduced me to welded steel armatures and it took little searching in Leamington to find Eddie Waters and his lively firm, Spa Sheet Metal. This was collaboration as exciting as any and by cladding the armature with metal cut to my templates, we constructed 'Growing Form' at a height of nearly eleven feet. Experiments with welding-metal, gunned on to the surface of the steel, produced a bark-like texture and finishing the whole with black Hammerite with silver brushed sparingly over the 'bark' produced a final form which now 'grows' from the ling and heather of the Scottish Sculpture Park at Carrbridge in Inverness-shire; it borrows nobility from the acres of Caledonian Forest, pines that have grown and seeded there for centuries, which enclose the sculptures in the park.

So much of this complicated work would have been impossible but for the help and advice of a natural craftsman, so different in background and instincts from my friends in the factories. David Walters, a university teacher of acoustics in Aston University, had trained as an architect and practised—still practises—as a consultant. I suspect his even greater devotion is to music: he has built and gives recitals on a chamber organ and a harpsichord both of which travel with him to the concerts in which he plays continuo. In his workshop his skills are wholly at my disposal—for a tricky piece of dowelling in a fragile stone; or advice, and hard work, on the structure of a plinth for a large sculpture. The additional pleasure is that, over coffee when the job is finished there is animated discussion of the latest baroque 'releases', the last or the next recital of his, or that performance which he will conduct in our parish church or the Cathedral of St James in Birmingham. A man, quietly and wittily, after my own heart.

The story of this work of mine came to a happy stage when Gordon Young, the highly inventive sculptor, and director of the Welsh Sculpture Park, invited me to show in their first full-scale exhibition at Margam in 1983. This naturally gave me the greatest possible pleasure, for the setting of the exhibition was Margam Abbey the Orangery and the Castle, in the grounds of which so much of my childhood had been spent. In the event, my sculpture was sited just opposite the Orangery and therefore within sight of the beautiful Chapter House; it faced one of Barbara Hepworth's finest pieces and I felt that my work had come full circle. Gordon Young, now successfully creating very massive works ('Heavy Stuff' as his 1985 exhibition at Plymouth was called) with a remarkable group at Bradford, witty, humane and 'available' to the onlooker, was a generous promoter of the Margam show. He looked over the maquettes and small bronzes I had to hand and asked me if I could enlarge an 'Etruscan' figure of mine to about ten feet in height. I decided that cast-iron was the appropriate material and looked around for a foundry.

It happened that I had worked in Westham House, Barford alongside Eric Griffiths, the sculpture director of Royal Doulton and talking over my problem with him I found that his brother Bill owned and worked an iron foundry in Stafford. Arrangements were made, I prepared the massive pattern in three sections and the cast was successfully made. Bill supervised the transport to Margam and a thirty-foot crane swung it into place where it menaces the peace of the Cistercian foundation. For in a way, 'The Helmet' is my one protest against violence; the face has, in profile, the aggression of a bird of prey, surmounted by the flaunting helmet, representative of all mindless command; the torso is hollow,

254

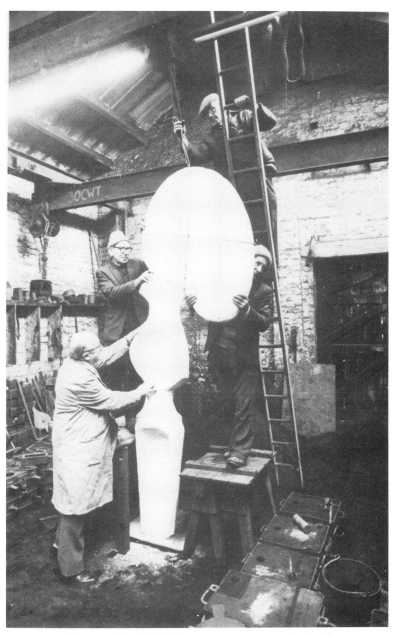

Moelwyn Merchant, *The Helmet*; preparing to cast at the foundry

without heart or viscera and the iron is itself a metal declaration of abhorrence. The child who played on that grass some seventy years ago would scarcely recognise the sculpture's origins.

A chance conversation during a lunch interval when, with Professor Walford Davies, I was lecturing to a large gathering of Clwyd teenagers, led to one of the most exciting of exhibitions. I had been speaking of Scottish ventures and hinting rather broadly that I wished I could show in Wales. Mrs Marion Roberts, vigorous both in Library operations in Wrexham and in promoting art in North Wales, said at once that this disparity must be remedied! Within days I had heard from Steve Brake, Exhibition Officer in the County Library Services and very soon he was in Leamington, selecting some fifty of my pieces and preparing a tour of exhibitions which went to five centres: Margam, at the Sculpture Park; The Turner House Gallery of the National Museum; Theatr Clwyd; the National Library in Aberystwyth and ending at the new gallery in the former Archbishop's Palace at Abergwili, Carmarthen. It was a sweep around all the places which had enclosed my life in Wales. With great generosity, Clwyd and the Welsh Arts Council published an elaborate booklet, *A Life's Work : Gwaith Oes*, with an introduction by Josef Herman and a survey—with twenty illustrations—of my work, sculpture and publications. The touring exhibition finished late in 1985 and since it was my seventy-second year, the slight flavour of the valedictory in the title of the booklet was appropriate.

It was good to know that my work had come home.

Friendship alone led to the last stages in my sculpting. Josef Herman, when his Warsaw 'Memory of Memories' came to light, was asked to show a selection of the drawings at the Ben Uri Gallery in Soho and he invited me to show some sculptures in the same exhibition. With the moving genius of Josef's drawings it couldn't fail to be a success and we were invited to transfer it to the Manor House Centre for Judaism in Finchley. Here there was an unexpected reward for me, in the friendship of Rabbi Tony Bayfield at the time when my novel *Jeshua* was reaching a critical stage; this was not the least of my many boons at the hands of Josef Herman.

When, therefore, I felt last year, that my sculpture had perhaps worked through to some kind of conclusion and that I should now

256

give myself almost entirely once more to writing, it seemed appropriate that my last exhibition should again be with Josef, and at no great distance from Edinburgh. The village of Stenton shelters in the southern slopes of the Lammermuirs and there, some years ago, Angus and Gwenda Macaulay bought the village inn, the Royal Oak. Two years later they had built a long gallery alongside a bar which had been converted to a small dining-room. It is a superb little setting for exhibitions of Scottish art; the food is excellent and discreetly accompanied by Mozart. Since I had shown there in some mixed exhibitions, it was a happy thought of Angus Macaulay's that I should show more extensively, to accompany a collection of the Herman drawings in the Highlands and especially around Skye, Mallaig and Arisaig. Josef agreed and added a group of the Welsh miners. It was a happy conclusion to work which had begun in that studio in St Ives, so many years ago.

*

It was like a grounded vision. The previous afternoon, twelve foundrymen at Ball Brothers, led by Paul Waters, had placed the large mould from the pattern of 'Growing Form'—for the riverside site at Burton-on-Trent—within heaving distance of the pots of molten aluminium. We had expected that the cast would take about four hundred pounds of metal but at the first pouring it was obvious that it would need a great deal more and two more furnaces were brought into commission.

The foundrymen kept their drilled precision as, two by two, they swung the pots of glowing metal over the entry to the cast but, since it was necessary to complete the pouring swiftly, to preserve the cast in a homogeneous mass, there was now a greater urgency than usual, even a degree of hurry in their movements. In the event they poured seven hundred and fifty pounds of metal, until the swaying circle of aluminium appeared, brilliant at the sand vent.

Then the waiting, twenty-four hours to allow the metal to cool before the mould could safely be opened. I was at the foundry with an hour to spare, anxious for the condition of the cast—would it be without blemish after all the hurried anxiety of the pouring? would the surface be perfect enough for its burnishing and patination?

would we indeed be able to handle a piece of sculpture which, without its plinth, was nearly twice the weight we had anticipated?

In my nervous state I was wandering around the foundry floor, waiting for Paul Waters to supervise the opening of the sand mould. I took a turn past the pits where the pots of metal had reached their melting-and pouring-point, the route which the foundrymen had traversed the previous day. There, in the debris of the floor, was a large splash of aluminium, dropped from one of the pots, swung to the pouring. This large spilled piece of metal had the form—body and two battered wings—of an angel that had somehow crashed in flight; one of those angels indeed had, back before time was.

I picked up the battered fragment and here, held in the hand, the resemblance was more striking. There were the wings, torn and spread from the body, the marks of the uncontrolled flight to earth and hell, and in that moment of handling, a sculpture was already forming in my mind, It was to be *Confrontation of Angels*. Paul Waters was able to cast a head on to the broken body and a few weeks later I took him a pattern—balsawood, sheet metal and plaster—for a more dignified winged figure, a St Michael whose stance was to confront the fallen Lucifer and curb any attempt to regain angelic power.

Mounted on two pieces of Hornton Stone, they now confront each other in Eluned Brown's home in Gloucester Place in Edinburgh; a cast from the two original figures had also been mounted on a 'hill' of Hornton Stone and they are now in Chelsea at the home of our friends, Hans and Jo Marcus.

And still I felt the 'Confrontation' demanded larger scale. Central Television were engaged in filming a range of my work in a variety of media and the director of the film, Ronald Lello, suggested that the latter half of the programme could appropriately be occupied by shooting each stage of the sculpture: preparing the two large angel patterns (twice the height of the original figures); casting in the foundry; 'fine-finishing' and patinating; and finally mounting on a large 'hill' again of Hornton Stone and standing just within the entrance to Leamington Parish Church.

Moelwyn Merchant, *Confrontation of Angels* (Aluminium on Hornton Stone); All Saints Church, Leamington Spa

Byre, pigsty, stable and long-house
stand cheek by jowl,
a round of labour
centred on the midden.

For the rest, the warmth
of the gracious world
centres on the altar.

One sleepless night
in the troubled small hours
the farm rose, floated
above the village,
descended and enveloped the church;
the altar was stripped,
the sanctuary clear as crystal;

and the animal warmth, manure-reek
became curiously translated,
a gift of sensual nature.

Moelwyn Merchant THE VISION OF MRS TOMOS GODRE'R PANT Drawing by Seren Thorpe

A poster-poem printed by Paul Merchant at the Windmill Hill Press, Leamington Spa

7

THE MUSIC-MAKERS

The greatest excitement at home on a Saturday afternoon occurred when my father felt he could afford a yellow-label H.M.V. record; this was rare, for his purchases were usually red-label but one yellow-label (it still sounds excellent) records Galli-Curci and Caruso in opera.

But of course our tradition in South Wales was almost entirely choral. Every year my parents sang in the chorus, in *Elijah, Messiah, St Paul*, at which performances I sold programmes. My father had a fine low-baritone voice and when a double-quartet was needed in the oratorio, he was invariably the second bass as they supplemented the professionals. After one such performance he returned home radiant: Norman Allin had suggested, after he had sung alongside my father, that he too should become a professional singer!

There were, it's true, the occasional non-vocal records—his Peer Gynt suite and the William Tell Overture still survive in my collection. Then, when we went on a holiday to Llandudno, my father bought a family-ticket for the whole fortnight, so that every night in the Pier Pavilion we heard an orchestra conducted by the young and almost unknown Malcolm Sargent. I owe him almost all my introduction to classical music.

It was my first undergraduate year at Cardiff that gave me my first strenuous insight into live performance. In those days (the early 'thirties) the Welsh National Orchestra performed at lunch-times in the Museum, just two hundred yards from the entrance to University College. Warwick Braithwaite was the conductor and this was my earliest experience of brass at full strength and in the reverberant hall of the Museum, Wagner resounded like the Last Trump.

More muted but even more revealing were the Wednesday evening performances by the college Chamber Players in the Reardon Smith Lecture Theatre. Here for the first time I knew the intellectual and emotional power of the string quartet and my conviction grew that even if there were other music to be attended to, string quartets were my choice for a desert island.

Dr David Evans, our professor of Music was that rare person in the Wales of his day, an enthusiast for the music of Bach—Handel reigned supreme in the 'twenties and 'thirties—and I was fortunate in my first year to sing in the performance he conducted of the *Mass in B Minor*, to be followed later in the year by Elgar's *Music Makers*.

*

ALUN HODDINOTT

Some twenty years after my first contact with the Department of Music in Cardiff, Alun Hoddinott was one of our undergraduates in English. He studied with us for only two years, for his central interest was music. Born in Bargoed in 1929, he began to learn the violin at the age of four and wrote a good deal of music before he entered the university.

It was obvious to me, from conversations in the senior common room that the academic musicians were nonplussed by the development of his compositions; he had absorbed all they wished of classical structures and techniques and was now launched on atonality—"he spatters the notes down at random" as one of my colleagues complained to me. But bewildered or not by this disconcerting young man, they could not deny both his vigour and his accomplishment and, after a period of teaching in the Cardiff College of Music and Drama, he returned to University College as a lecturer and is now about to retire early from the Chair of Music.

Llandaff Cathedral, sorely stricken by bombing in the war, was by 1961 restored and the Llandaff Festival had been founded. Alun Hoddinott was commissioned to produce a large-scale work and asked me for a libretto. I devised for him *The Race of Adam*, conflating scenes from the mediaeval drama cycles, from Adam to the Resurrection. George Pace had fashioned the massive concrete arch at the cathedral crossing, on which was poised Epstein's *Majestas* and beneath it, the four-fold span of the arch defined a rectangular space which became the setting for our performance, John Piper having designed for us a very noble swag curtain as a background to the 'stage'.

There were some small-scale works for which Alun asked for libretti, the most successful being, I suppose, *Puer Natus*, my translation of an early German carol. Then, just as I was about to go to live briefly in the Close at Salisbury after my time in hospital, the Three Choirs Festival at Gloucester commissioned another large work from him and again he asked me for a libretto. This was a more elaborate and, I believe, more original text for him to set. *The Tree of Life* was based on the mediaeval *Legenda Aurea*: the dying Adam asks his son Seth to fetch three seeds from the Tree of Life at the centre of Paradise and to place them beneath his tongue at his burial. Three trees grew from Adam's grave, and when they had united in one massive trunk, were destined to be the main beam in Solomon's Temple. But however hewn, it would not fit the building and, rejected, dammed a stream which became the Pool of Siloam. When an upright was needed for the cross of Christ, the beam floated in the Pool of Siloam and the Tree of Life had become the Cross of Crucifixion. Finally, it flourished and was fruitful in the garden of the New Jerusalem.

Collaborating with the composer in this work was a rich education in the creativity of a musician. I realised from the first, the instinctive knowledge of the composer for the single word or the rhythmic order of words which would be the proper foundation for his composition; and I knew that when words of mine were impossible for him to set, even though on the written page they had been true and harmonious enough, there was nothing to do but re-write them.

I was in Vancouver when the first performance took place but later I heard the Cardiff University Choir give a very fine performance, conducted by Clifford Bunford. The work, to my mind, contains some of Alun's finest music and I get the most intense pleasure from the movement, 'The Pool of Siloam'.

The only other long work I have written for him is *The Bells of Paradise* first performed two years ago at the new St David's Hall in Cardiff. Of much greater pride for me was my son Paul's libretto for Alun Hoddinott's *St Paul at Malta*, commissioned for the Silver Jubilee of the Stroud Festival. It was first performed there on 14 October 1971. It is a chastening but happy experience to find your son do everything better than you can!

Hoddinott's work is of great diversity, with concertos, sonatas, quartets, symphonies and oratorios and there have been splendid performances on gramophone records; my favourite of these is Gervase de Peyer's performance of the clarinet sonata but—naturally—the one that gives me greatest pride is the Fifth Symphony which is generously dedicated to me.

It is, however, his setting of words to which one constantly returns. These range from his early composition of Welsh Carols, arranged and translated by his wife, Rhiannon, to the full-length opera, *The Beach of Falesa*, with a libretto by Glyn Jones based on a

Alan Richards, one of a series of prints based on the Hoddinott/Merchant *Tree of Life*

265

short story by R.L. Stevenson and performed by the Welsh National Opera Company in March 1964. Much of his work is poised between great lyricism and the most tragic tension, and two of his compositions show this very dramatically. *Roman Dream*, his opus 54, was based on a narrative poem by the Welsh poet and novelist, Emyr Humphreys. It relates a nightmare endured by one who lives and tries to work under a dictatorship. The music, Hoddinott tells us, is influenced by Bartok's 'Night Music' and the spare scoring, soprano and tenor with piano, harp and percussion, allows the terror to make its full impact (it was recorded in 1972, with Margaret Price, Gerald English—the soloists of *The Tree of Life*—and James Lockhart).

Equally disturbing in its drama is his opus 76, *The Sun the Great Luminary of the Universe* (the Swansea Festival 1970 and recorded in 1973 by the London Symphony Orchestra). This is based on a long visionary passage from James Joyce's *Portrait of the Artist*:

> The last day had come . . . The stars of heaven were falling upon the earth like the figs cast by the fig-tree which the wind has shaken. The sun, the great luminary of the universe had become a sackcloth of hair. The moon was blood red. The firmament was as a scroll rolled away. The archangel Michael, the prince of the heavenly host, appeared glorious and terrible against the sky . . . Time is, time was, but time shall be no more.

The deeply disturbing music follows the tragic tensions of Joyce's words but not 'programatically' and we are not surprised that Bach's 'Es ist genug' informs some of the music's statement and 'Dies Irae' closes the work.

We may return more tranquilly to his opus 86, *Landscapes* based on the poem by T.H. Parry-Williams, *Eryri*, (Snowdon), in which snow, blood and the power of the sun mingle to transfigure the mountain landscape.

A composer of massive achievement, with still a promise of change and revelation.

*

Moelwyn Merchant, *Triad* (Delabole Slate), Department of Music, University College, Cardiff

Alun Hoddinott's intensely personal compositions are under-pinned by an extremely active public life: building a flourishing department at Cardiff, work in the Welsh Arts Council and the jury of the Young Musicians competition; conducting in Europe and the United States and Canada and—most taxing of all, founding and directing the Cardiff Festival of Music; in the twenty years of its programmes it is difficult to detect the absence of any composer or performer of note. Its commissions numbered seventy and there were first performances of other works not specially commissioned by the Festival itself—a massive and exhilarating achievement.

His literary interests are manifestly wide and varied but he has also enriched the Festival and his department by exhibitions of sculpture and painting. The cover of the scholarly journal *Soundings* reproduces a photograph of Barbara Hepworth's bronze Triptych which is sited outside the Music Department. I have especial reason to be grateful to him not simply for the constant requests for libretti but also for inviting me to share the first exhibition of art in the department and then for commissioning my first large sculpture, a seven-foot piece in Delabole slate for the foyer of the department's concert halt; since it consisted of three substantial pillars and was constantly within the sound of music, we happily called it *Triad*.

*

There have been many attempts to fashion Shakespeare's plays into operas and Verdi's *Otello* is, for me, the most successful in the nineteenth century. Boito's libretto is spare and economical, and, understanding the simplification that is sometimes needed if the words are to penetrate the music, he made an occasional adaptation that was striking in performance. So, in Bochum in 1964, Iago's 'soliloquy', 'I believe in a cruel God' dramatically shifted the emphasis of his character; no 'unmotivated evil' now but a 'Credo' of passionate intensity.

That method of interpretation was not the intention of Benjamin Britten and Peter Pears as they prepared *A Midsummer Night's Dream* for Aldeburgh. Britten wrote in *The Observer* (5 June 1960):

> Peter Pears and I had endless trouble with the references and proportions of the play. We stuck faithfully to Shakespeare's words, adding only one line, 'Compelling thee to marry with Demetrius.'

Using for their abridgment mainly the First Folio text, they were able to use about one-half the original play.

I had always found *A Midsummer Night's Dream* an ambiguous play. The accepted opinion was that it was a kind of dramatic epithalamium, "for some courtly marriage." But what of Puck who (like the Eumenides) was given an emollient nickname, 'Robin Goodfellow' but who, at his crucial final entrance declares a disquieting allegiance:

> And we fairies that do run
>   By the triple Hecate's team,
> From the presence of the sun,
>   Following darkness like a dream . . .

'Triple Hecate', 'from . . . the sun', 'following darkness'—the implications are clear, that this is a good deal more than a 'friendly sprite', that he and those like him, are governed by the *diva triformis*, Hecate, who broods over Macbeth and is invoked in a curse by Lear and whose quality of ill-omen Blake had the insight to render.

Moreover, the play opens with a ravishment disguised in the oblique courtesy, 'I wooed thee with my sword', while the quarrel of Titania and Oberon opens with the startling recriminations of knowledgeable lust:

My credit with Hippolita . . . thy love to Theseus . . .

Benjamin Britten was aware of this darker side of the play from the beginning:

The fairies are very different from the innocent nothings that often appear in productions of Shakespeare.

and 'the kind of sharpness' which he found in them is echoed in John Piper's exceedingly beautiful but often disquieting sets. They had a dark, almost sub-marine quality, with a disconcerting trick of shifting scale and proportion; a flower suddenly takes on the giant dimensions of a tree, so that lovers and rustics are dwarfed by a dandelion head; fairies at a turn of lighting are momentarily revealed as of oak-like proportions. As gauze after gauze was drawn, plane after plane of the visionary world came into focus and then receded; the whole production, in music and setting had at once the frightening clarity of a nightmare and the blurred edges of a dream. At the same time Britten wittily glances at other composers and Mendelssohn, Verdi and *Tristan* make their momentary entries.

All this virtuosity comes to its most moving climax in the reconciliation of the lovers. In a Shakespeare production on stage the highly charged lines,

> And I have seen Demetrius like a jewel,
> Mine own and not mine own

are liable to slide by, with no stress on their profound statement of love, its possessiveness and courteous restraint. Britten allowed no such error. The words 'mine own and not mine own' were given to each lover in turn until all four were united, hands clasped at stage-centre, in a rapturous fugue.

John Piper had suggested to Benjamin Britten that I be invited to lecture on the morning after the first performance on 11 June 1960, on the stage-history of *The Dream*. I had been so overwhelmed by the performance that I spent a worried night, trying to see how I could have the effrontery to give such a lecture after such a performance. I arrived at the hall to be confronted by a large audience which included Britten, Pears and the whole body of musicians. I went to the lectern and said, "I'm sorry but after that superlative performance last night, I cannot give you the lecture I've prepared." There was substantial consternation but I went on, "I shall, if you'll let me, give my impressions of the performance and its illumination of Shakespeare's play for me." I spoke for about an hour and I believe that hour made for me two of my most valued friends. At lunch at the Red House they invited me back for the Festival the following year and it was arranged that I preach at the Festival Service. Later that day I listened to the *St John Passion* in the same church and it was, I believe, the last time that Peter Pears sang the role of the Evangelist.

Aldeburgh has a very special atmosphere and personality of its own. I remember with particular happiness sitting with Julian Bream for a quiet chat before the evening performance. He was in his characteristic relaxed mood and told me how the guitar had become for him as loved as the lute. One evening he had been playing quietly for his own pleasure in a corner of a Spanish inn. After he had played for a while he realised that the inn was quite silent and when he had finished all the drinkers burst out with "Ole, Ole." I felt sure that those words were as sweet for him as any applause in the Wigmore Hall or even at the Maltings.

*

Two performances of Britten's *Dream* have kept the opera and that first performance alive for me. The first was at the Welsh National Opera's performance at Theatr Clwyd, the intimacy of which took me back to the atmosphere of Aldeburgh.

The second was at Glyndebourne in 1984. Our friend Helmut Rothenberg had gathered a party from England and the Continent to see the opera and invited us to join them, I to give a talk on

271

'Shakespeare and Britten' before the performance. We stayed overnight with Hans and Jo Marcus in London and they drove us down to Glyndebourne the following morning. Here again was an atmosphere wholly different from Aldeburgh and Theatr Clwyd and again the opera glowed in full splendour.

*

RE-CREATION

In one of the introductory essays to *The Operas of Benjamin Britten* (edited by David Herbert, 1979) Dame Janet Baker writes very movingly of the experience of rehearsing with Britten and performing his work.

> I have always believed that the creative person inhabits a world unknown to others. The gulf which exists between his world and that of the re-creative artist is wide indeed. Even at their most sublime, performers are still only able to go as far as the entrance and look from afar towards the land where the composer is perfectly at home. The suffering such a homeland exacts from an individual as the price he must pay for the original ideas he brings back to us is unimaginable. And yet, while there is no doubt that the composer wants no other country, it must be frighteningly lonely there.

That is a *very* remarkable statement. In its humility it speaks eloquently of Dame Janet herself, one of the greatest interpretative artists of this generation. She knows precisely where she, the performer, stands, looking with admiring wonder into the creator's world. At the same time she knows in all humility that performers can indeed be 'at their most sublime'—indeed she would not be the highly intelligent singer that she is, if she did not realise that performance after performance, recording after recording of hers have truly reached sublimity.

A year or two ago I was fortunate to sit, at a Glyndebourne performance of Britten's *Midsummer Night's Dream,* immediately behind Dame Janet and her husband and it was a lesson in generous understanding to see the warm smile she gave to him when the

272

performance on stage especially moved her. About a year later I saw precisely the same generous warmth when, again in a fortunate seat, I could see Elizabeth Schwarzkopf's understanding response to a performance by the Amadeus Quartet. *Si sic omnes.*

The passage I have quoted from Janet Baker's essay is, however, even more eloquent of her understanding of the creator's, the composer's realm. Few could have found that realm more intimately accessible than she; and yet her judgment, after years of performance is that she stands at the frontier, "looks from afar towards the land" which the composer inhabits. This judgment is the more moving—the more astonishing in its humility—when we remember that Britten composed his *Phaedra* for her. Had she been an actress of the Edwardian school she would properly have claimed that she 'created' *Phaedra*—as I once heard a member of Frank Benson's company say to me, "Yes, I created Juliet for Sir Frank" and the dismaying claim was made with no hint of conscious arrogance. Not so Dame Janet. Before she gives her account of rehearsing *Phaedra* with Britten for its first performance, she has already discussed the performer's claim to be as important as the composer because of "bringing the work to life." For her, a performance, however distinguished is not on the same level as that process which seized an inspired idea and shaped it into concrete form.

This credo of Janet Baker's raises one of the profoundest questions in our modern artistic scene. This is not simply the question that by 'the Arts', most people—including government ministers—mean 'the performing arts' and it would be a disconcerting exercise to compare the sums of public money devoted simply to Covent Garden, the National Theatre and the Royal Shakespeare Company with the *total sum* received by the creative artists, the composers, the painters, the poets, the novelists, the sculptors, the dramatists. This is a deeply disquieting question and we may well be impoverishing the creativity of our society by this unseemly imbalance.

But—to set aside this vulgar aspect of our current dilemmas— there are more teasing matters to face. To put it personally and concretely, I have seen performances of Shakespeare where the insights—often the most exploratory and scholarly insights—of an actor have revealed meanings which years of my reading have not shown me. Michael Redgrave's Lear, at the moment when he spoke to Cordelia of his penitential renewal:

I'll kneel and ask of thee forgiveness,

a scene that had before deeply exercised my mind now leapt straight to the heart. And these moments in the theatre have not been rare. But there have been those ugly moments—and they too not rare—where the arrogant assertions of a director have taken Shakespeare's text and manipulated it to satisfy his tiny ego, when the wonder of the Shakespearean vision has, for those three hours, been effectively obliterated. I am ashamed—and not on my own behalf—when I have found it difficult to see a performance through to its end in our most 'prestigious' Shakespeare Theatre.

All this is far from the private world which Dame Janet Baker inhabits. I have no doubt that, like so many singers and actors of distinction, she has met other performers, directors and conductors who have caught much foggier glimpses of the composer's country than she. But this has not blunted the insight which was the source of her remarkable essay.

The truth, I suppose, as always remains elusive. To employ the original terms, 'creative artist' and 're-creative artist', the one has the travail of the vision grasped, shaped and finished; the other has the duty to understand, to reveal what might otherwise elude an audience or a reader. We may reflect that there was truth and no irony whatever in T.S. Eliot's writing to a critic who had given a rich account of *The Four* Quartets, that the book had revealed matters in the poems of which he, Eliot the creator of them, had not known. It would seem that in this complex matter of the arts, even critics have their function.

*

And the interpretation of actors. We have had splendid readings of Shakespeare roles in our generation and a great deal of *Shakespeare and the Artist* would have been the poorer without the illumination which came from close discussion with actors of their interpretations on stage.

Two of these stage artists gave me unusual opportunities for discussion extending over the years. The first of these was Siân Phillips.

Her performance in *I, Claudius* had a chilling perfection, the cool assertion of perverted authority which was a triumph of *acting technique*. I use this ambiguous phrase which might be deemed to be muted praise—but is not—because I had known her for many years and understood many of the springs of her acting. For she was an undergraduate at Cardiff when I taught there and I was her tutor in her third year. She already had a very mature beauty and presence, and her voice, whether she spoke English or her flexible South-Welsh, was low and controlled. She came to me at the beginning of the long vacation before her final honours year:

"The Union Dramatic Society has asked me to play Desdemona and Hermione next year. Are you willing that I should play both?"

"If you play one of them you have a very good chance of taking a 'first' in your degree; if you play both, it must almost certainly be a 'second'."

"That's clear then;" was her confident reply, "I play both!"

She did. They were deeply moving performances with an almost unbelievable delicacy of insight, which made it difficult to believe that she was only a little over twenty years old. Before going to R.A.D.A. she had the wisdom to join B.B.C. Wales, primarily as an announcer and news-reader in English and Welsh, and played in performances by the small but very competent drama company in the Cardiff studios.

Unhappily I missed her 'college-leaving' performance as Hedda Gabler in R.A.D.A. (I believe the gold-medal performance of her year) but then saw her at the Bristol Old Vic performance of a play by my friend John Hall.

Still later I saw her performance in *The Shrew* in the same season that Dame Peggy Ashcroft was playing the role in Stratford. Though I regard Dame Peggy as the queen of actresses in our day, I found it difficult to say which of them the more potently revealed Shakespeare for me.

Siân Phillips has the complete versatility of the accomplished professional. Whether speaking Welsh verse in film in the Welsh countryside, singing in musical comedy in the witty European tradition, playing the great tragic roles of our classical theatre she moves from one world to another with assured ease—a rare talent to admire.

*

One of the privileges of being an academic in the Shakespearian field has been the opportunity of talking over at some length his roles with Peter O'Toole. He would come to stay with us for a day or two before the season started and over the years this has meant the fascinating exploration of Hamlet, Shylock, Macbeth, Thersites and Petruchio, with a very considerable increase in my own insights as a result.

The first of these visits—nearly a week because it preceded the season at Stratford where he was to play Shylock, Thersites and Petruchio—was to our house in Exeter. He arrived in his chauffeur-driven Rolls, to be greeted at the door by my daughter Christina and her friend Annabel. Before he had even entered or properly greeted us, he had asked Christina whether the two of them would like the Rolls for a while, to be driven around Cornwall, and away they went like trainee duchesses in the back of the Silver Cloud.

We got down to the text at once. Peter's first question recognised professionally his youth for the part of Shylock: "How young can I play him?" We had to set aside the stage traditions from the eighteenth century, through Edmund Kean and Irving and after a long discussion of the text, the result was Peter's choice of an early middle-aged figure of great dignity and of austere spirituality; (when the play opened in Stratford Peter employed the minutes just off-stage before each entrance, repeating Hebrew prayers taught him by a Jewish member of the company). This had to be for him an almost wholly sympathetic Shylock, a contrast with the shoddy Christians by whom he was surrounded and subdued.

It was also a Shylock who played with the scriptural traditions of his race, moving among them with witty knowledge. He was delighted when I told him the irony within Shylock's speech to Antonio during their talk of usury. Shylock cites Jacob and his device for breeding parti-coloured lambs as a justification of 'interest', 'increase' or 'usury' and went on to define Jacob's place

276

among the patriarchs—"from our father Abraham the third possessor." Now Jacob was not the third in succession from Abraham, for Esau, the dispossessed, was the legitimate third. Without a pause, Peter took 'centre stage' in our drawing-room and the pause between "the third possessor" and "aye, he was the third", was occupied in a silent mime of counting, with a wry smile: Abraham—Isaac—Esau—Jacob. I imagine that few in the audience followed the mischievous implication but it gave Peter great satisfaction and, with similar detail, filled out a rich interpretation. Dorothy Tutin played Portia and he told me that at his broken exit, up-stage, when he stumbled and fell as the Christians crowded in upon him like hounds, "Dotty lifted me up by the hand and as I looked at her, her eyes were full of tears."

When the season was over we decided to have a record of this performance and at his home in Hampstead we sat on a rug before the fire to make a tape of it. I played all the parts except Shylock, even, heaven help me!—Portia! It was a strange experience but there came a moment which halted the recording. I was reading Tubal in the harrowing scene where Shylock's emotions of dereliction and hatred are played upon. I gave Peter the line in which Jessica has sold his turquoise ring "for a monkey." Shylock bursts out, "I had it of Leah when I was a bachelor" and at the words, "I would not have sold it for a wilderness of monkeys," Peter's voice broke on 'wilderness' and we had to stop while he recovered his poise. Indeed, whether he was in Hampstead, in the desert with Lawrence, at Massada with Roman officers or on stage at Stratford, the frontier for Peter O'Toole between tragic life and the craft of acting was very delicately held.

Robert Morgan, *Miners* (lino-cut)

MEN IN BLACK

The men in black with pit faces
Of skin tight over tough bones
Stand under a grey-loaded sky
In the shade of a black mountain.
Words of David fall on their ears
And bend them with fear and mystery.
The reader in white, unmoved and neutral,
Breaks the last link between them
And the young man in the earth of Wales.
When the black cars sneak away
The yard settles to its cold silence
With a new sleeper from Cynon Pit.

Robert Morgan was a coal miner for twelve years and, after college training in Birmingham and Bognor Regis, became a teacher in Portsmouth. His first volume of poetry, *The Night's Prison*, was published by Rupert Hart-Davis in 1967 and in that same year a verse-play was broadcast on the Third Programme of the B.B.C. *Exeter Books 16* was devoted to his verse and he was one of the readers in the first Llanddewibrefi Festival.

8

ANGLICANA ECCLESIA

My last years in Exeter were full of confused decision and I felt that I was probably moving away from academic life or that academic life was moving away from me. I knew that the Department of English was now safely on its feet and was making on its own a more than adequate statement of my assumption, that criticism without creativity was sterile. I had seen the vigour with which criticism had been renewed when my teachers wrote their own admirable verse and accepted that the verse written by their undergraduates was a valid, indeed essential part of their discipline. This is by no means a universal assumption in our universities and just this year I have learned of one Department of English which does not allow volumes of verse published by the senior members to appear in the annual report of the university—but only 'serious critical work.' There are many ways of destroying creativity.

But all this had been said at Exeter and accepted as normal. For myself I had already responded to Barbara Hepworth's tuition in sculpture and I was now prepared to be shaken from my academic security.

A signal of change was a complex thrombosis which threatened my leg, my pleura and my left lung. When I came out of hospital the university generously gave me a year free of teaching and the Bishop of Salisbury gave us a flat in the Close—a thirteenth-century flat.

Joseph Fison had come to Salisbury after a life already of rich variety; Jerusalem, Truro, Rochester, they had all known his scholarship, sanctity and almost boyish wit. Then came the University Church at Cambridge. My friendship with Howard Root, then Dean of Emmanuel College, took me regularly on visits to Cambridge and I got to know Joe Fison quite intimately. It was obvious that he was going to make a remarkable success of his ministry at Great St Mary's but I was more than a little dismayed to realise that he had periods when he sounded overborne by his predecessor, Mervyn Stockwood, who had become Bishop of Southwark, whose great gifts were of a different order from Joe's. These were great days at Cambridge with Robert Runcie at Trinity Hall and a circle of young theologians with Howard Root at their centre, and Donald Davie to keep poetry and criticism in fine shape.

To preach for Joe at Great St Mary's was to experience the vitality he had injected into the large undergraduate congregation and the discussions after the services were among the best I had experienced. One summer he asked me to take over the University Church while he had his month's holiday. It was an exhilarating time as I inherited—in the only slightly subdued atmosphere of vacation—the quality of liturgical life he had established.

It was therefore with mixed feelings that we heard of his enthronement at Salisbury. The Sarum Rite, the heart of English catholic worship; would his fiery evangelical temperament be quenched at this centre of the Establishment?

We maintained our close friendship and he invited me to be one of his examining chaplains. Then came a morning when I was conducting a research seminar in my room and my secretary knew I was not to be disturbed during these hours. The bell rang and she said: "I think you'd better take this; it's the Bishop of Salisbury." The conversation was brief: "Moelwyn, I want you to become a canon here at Salisbury." "Just like that?" "Yes, just like that; come over on Sunday morning." Only great saints can be so clear and economical.

I drove across on the Sunday morning and after the service, with scarcely a word of discussion, he said, "And your stall will be this one, next to my *cathedra.*" I must have looked surprised for he went on: "Yes, by the way, I want you to be Chancellor of the cathedral." We went across to his home in the South Canonry for lunch and over the meal he explained some of his hopes for the cathedral and diocese and his hope that I could combine, at least for a while, the two posts at Exeter and Sarum until I was clearer about my future. So for three years, I drove the two-hundred-mile round trip once, twice and sometimes three times every week. I had not realised that the office of Chancellor involved a kind of visiting inspectorate (in a very mild way) of the Public Schools in the diocese—and Salisbury has more than most. More seriously I was responsible for the post-ordination training of the young clergymen—and Salisbury was wide-spread. But it was all most interesting, a good foil to my work in Exeter and my almost annual visits to the University of Chicago.

Then came the thrombosis and the year in the Close at Salisbury. It had all the variety of action and atmosphere I had not expected! In purely personal terms it was as happy as any year I had known: long and intimate talks with the bishop in his study in the South Canonry, (I never came away from these visits without feeling an exhilarating sense of purpose in his guidance of the diocese); the Dean, Kenneth Howarth, reserved and scholarly, open to any suggestion for intellectual excitement in our work (it was characteristic of him—as I observed—that he didn't need the Psalter in the Offices—he knew all one hundred and fifty psalms); the Precentor, Cyril Taylor, gentle, ironical but warm in conversation and, as a former Principal of the Royal School of Church Music, vastly knowledgeable in liturgical music; the Archdeacon, Basil Wingfield-Digby, wise and experienced in church affairs; and the Principal of the Theological College, Harold Wilson, who established a pattern of theological training which welcomed our collaboration in the Close. All this meant that the Daily Offices and the Eucharist on Sunday, with the historical backing of the Sarum Rite in all its complexity and beauty of vestments, the most elaborate in Christendom (with the lovely extravagance of rose for the one Sunday of Mid-Lent) were a constant happiness. For myself there was the occasional opportunity of preaching in the cathedral, the regular lecturing in the College in programmes which Harold Wilson had drawn up with unique insight into the young clergyman's needs in the arts of communication.

The Dean also gave me his amused blessing for Friday afternoon lectures in the Cathedral on Shakespeare to which all sixth forms in Salisbury had been invited. The second (I believe on *Lear*) was attended by over one hundred and thirty young people and some thirty teachers. It was affectionately called 'Merchant's Free University in the North Transept' and I was sorry when it came to an end.

There *were* shadows; the rejection by some of Barbara Hepworth's 'Crucifixion—Construction' and the further unhappiness over the Close Chapter's sponsorship of the Southern Arts' exhibition of contemporary sculpture. My year in the Close was coming to an end, when I should return to Exeter. It was time to determine the direction of my future and, since Kenneth Howarth had announced his impending retirement, the bishop asked me if I would agree to his desire to nominate me as Dean to succeed Kenneth. It is of course not an episcopal appointment but I felt I had to tell Joe how my mind was moving after this year in the Close. Though I was by no means sure that I should long continue in academic life, I was quite sure that I was not fitted by temperament to be a significant figure in the Anglican Establishment, as the Dean of Salisbury would certainly be. I am wholly devoted to the liturgy, the devotion and the history of the Anglican communion but I had many doubts about the Establishment itself; for I knew that the disestablishment of the Anglican Church in Wales in the 'twenties had produced a renaissance in the church in Wales which, to many of us, went back to the seventeenth-century flowering in the poetry of Henry Vaughan and his fellows and back beyond that century to the age of the Celtic saints. We knew that Bishop Morgan's Bible had the significance for Wales of Luther's for Germany. With this Welsh experience in my blood, I knew that I had to ask Bishop Fison not to nominate me and I believe this also became his decision. I left Salisbury with great regret and was glad to be invited to retain my contact with the cathedral by becoming a canon-emeritus.

*

To return to Wales, to become vicar of Llanddewibrefi in Dyfed, was in so many diverse ways to come full circle. The first and most potent reason for leaving academic life and 'retiring' to the country was to give me more time for sculpture and writing. I had no idea, when I first made the decision to retire from the University, that I should go to a parish; on the contrary, we were intent on 'a small cottage' in Wales, where roots could be struck again, the language spoken more regularly and leisure to find oneself.

282

It happened during my last term at Exeter that some senior members of the University were host to a large group of visiting clergymen at a conference. One of the party for which I was responsible was an old friend from our first days in the priesthood, Eric Roberts, Bishop of St Davids. He told me that he thought a country living in his diocese would meet so many of my needs and made me, among other parishes, the irresistible offer of Llan-ddewibrefi. I say 'irresistible' for wasn't this 'St Davids-on-Brefi-Stream', the holy place where St David had summoned all the Celtic bishops and abbots to the 'Synod of Brefi' in the early sixth century to meet and to counter the heresy of Pelagius? Wasn't this the place where he preached to them, on a field still called 'Dôl y Saint', 'The Meadow of the Saints'? And wasn't this meadow the place where, in response to the cry that he couldn't be heard by the multitude, that he placed a kerchief on the ground and, as he stood on it, the ground rose to a hillock beneath his feet and a dove on his shoulder whispered the truths into his ear? And doesn't the church today stand on that same hillock, attesting the truth of the miracle—even if geologists don't agree?

Llanddewibrefi had a notable religious history after the days of Dewi Sant. In the chancel and tower are inscribed (Ogam) and carved stones from the seventh to the tenth centuries. By the twelfth century the church, with its powerful, fortress-like tower, had much of its present character and a poet, Gwynfardd Brych-einiog, speaks of its bishop, presiding over "the five altars of Brefi." In the next century, Bishop Beck of St Davids replaced the 'Clas' of married clergy with a College of Canons—a precentor and twelve prebendaries, to sing the daily Offices and Mass—a provision as rich as a twentieth-century cathedral. There was much to live up to, with the depleted resources of our day, a solitary priest to maintain the praises.

But it was 'irresistible' also on other grounds, for as I began to explore the parish I found the fragments of other ancient beliefs. At one little house at the southern edge of Llanddewi, and still carrying the name of the saint, he was said to have stopped for refreshment—at least a drink of water,—for was he not 'Dewi Dyfrwr', 'David the Waterdrinker'?—and at his request a spring of water rose at his feet. I suppose I must have looked sceptical, for my hostess led me to the hearth where a log-fire burnt vigorously and, at the hearth's side she pulled at a stone lid and revealed there a well from which they still drew their water. Fire and water at the same hearth—the elemental signs took me back in memory to the bread and wine of that meal in the Campagna—and I assented to the name of that little home—'Dewi's Well'.

The parish was vast—I was told it was over eighty miles in circumference and one of the most extensive in Great Britain but with only five hundred inhabitants all concentrated, except for some scattered upland farms, within the little village itself. I was also vicar to nineteen pairs of red kites, at that time the sole survivors of the breed; I hear that they are now about twenty-nine pairs and some of them have nested quite a distance from the parish.

It was, however, not until the sensational 'Operation Julie' that I learnt that I was also vicar to the largest group of cannabis growers and distributors, with intensive operations both in Llanddewi and neighbouring Tregaron, with purveyor trails all the way to London. Many of them I knew—and found them disarmingly engaging. I imagine most if not all of them have now served their prison sentences.

*

The sense of 'full circle' dominated the first months in Llan-ddewibrefi. It was first a return after four generations to my Dyfed roots; for my mother's father was born, as his forbears had been, on the Cardiganshire coast at Llangrannog and my great-great-uncle had been the village carpenter (his photograph, with his two dour sisters, still lies in the drawer of the fine oak kitchen cupboard and chest which he made) and I suppose all this tends to account for the change of heart of my parishioners after they first heard me speak. For there had been a considerable dismay among them when they first heard that the bishop had appointed a Professor of English (and called 'Merchant') to be the vicar of this almost monoglot Welsh parish. My admirable young church-warden, Arwyn Roberts and the aging Edward Davies, had loyally kept from their friends the fact that they had met and spoken to me—and in the language of the Bible and of heaven! Arwyn asked me at the 'welcoming tea' "to say a few words"; I did so and the whispers came back to me clearly: "Ein hiaith ni!" "a'r un acen hefyd!"—"our language, and in the same accent too!" Indeed I owe much to Arwyn and old Edward Davies. Arwyn was a young officer of the Forestry Commission and a passionate soccer referee; with his gentle wife Beti and the two girls, he was able to keep me wholly in touch with the 'younger element'. Edward Davies, a prosperous retired farmer, and like Arwyn of a Llanddewi family, was wise, learned in the ways of the country and deeply devoted to the church. But in his speech there was a spicing of sardonic wit that made every visit to his home a delight. Funerals were important in the country community and if the death was of a reputedly wealthy farmer, the question of his possessions was a lively one. Edward was one day attending the funeral of a close friend and another farmer asked the inevitable question:

"How much did he leave?"

"Everything," said Edward and the conversation closed.

*

My four years at Llanddewi were full of the most intense activity (did the bishop really say "leisure to think"?) but now it is the memory of individual members of my congregation that remains. Ithwen Davies, who scrupulously kept the church clean and spent every Wednesday morning and lunchtime in the Vicarage—one of the remarkable and perhaps unsung saints, a widow, with a large and talented family to whom every kind of human ill came to assail them. Yet, like her daughter Mary, who died so tragically, there was never a word of complaint but a smiling, patient acceptance of all that tried to break her spirit. Equally warm was the welcome at the house on the square, below the church and opposite the Foelallt Inn; here Ben and Ray Davies were always ready with their advice if 'Ficer bach' seemed to over-reach himself and though Ben was in enforced retirement from the coalfield, his wit and the acuteness of his comment on his extremely wide reading made me question some of my academic assumptions.

And, of course, the austere dignity of Jack Jones. Having left school quite young to go 'on the line', he rose, by the time he retired to be station-master of nearby Llanio halt. No great position, you will think but wait: Jack became a magistrate and in this very squirearchical society of rural Dyfed became Chairman of the Bench. For me he was an encyclopaedia of local knowledge and at least once a week we drove to some outlying spot and on the way he would point out every farm and its history.

Strangely, each week he would quietly refuse to return to the Vicarage for a meal; then one day we refrained from inviting him but drove instead past his home and up our drive. Tea was in the large sitting room which the parish had fashioned for me out of two smaller rooms. Above the fire was a large Piper oil of 'Garn Fawr'; near it were two Herman lithographs, the Ceri Richards 'Do Not Go Gentle' and Barbara Hepworth's severe bronze, 'Forms on a Wall'. Jack Jones sat before the fire and I remained quite silent opposite him. He looked intently at every object in the room and his only comment was a breathed out "Wel, wel" at intervals. At last he seemed to gather himself to meet my questioning silence and he spoke quietly in his very precise Welsh: "Vicar, during the last five months we have become intimate friends; now in the last five minutes an abyss has opened between us." I knew exactly what he meant and, believe me, 'abyss' sounds more cruel in Welsh than it does in English. I didn't contradict him but said simply, "Come here like this every week and see what these things mean to me and the abyss will close." He came and both in the Vicarage and his home we had many hours of talk and his grave wisdom opened to embrace the art and the literature which was so much of my life.

There were others too but Wil Bach, the gentlest of christian gentlemen, must stand for them all. His smile irradiated every meeting with him; he never missed a service at the church and his solitary life in his scrupulously-kept cottage was the very essence of rural patience and honest work.

Many of the farmers were Methodist but again I found that not only was it the Vicar's duty to visit them on every occasion, sad or joyful, the welcome was as unaffected as from my own people of the altar, and there were others within the village itself: Jenkin Jones, 'pwyllog' and urbane as we talked about parish affairs and his wife Megan, a harpist, who died so tragically young, soon after I left Llanddewi. All these friends collaborated in my work in the village, whether these affairs were secular or ecumenical.

There was however a problem. A small proportion of our congregations throughout the year spoke only English. One of these families, Mr and Mrs John Scott had retired to live in Llanddewi permanently and they were valuable members of the community in every way and were busy learning Welsh. Mrs Scott was the daughter of an Edinburgh Professor of Mathematics and John Scott, a novelist and a friend of Richard Hughes, had newly retired from the editorship of the I.M.F. journal in Washington. Then there were Catherine and Freddie Varney who came every summer to their home on the hill and whose daughter Cherryl had been an undergraduate at Exeter. And finally our most intimate friends, John Griffiths, a consultant at Bart's and his wife Rosemary, a vicar's daughter and their so competent family, had bought the farm in the valley, Cwm Dulas. This meant a regular English addition to our worshippers of between six and twenty people, with John Griffiths, a Welsh speaker from Llanelli, a mediator among us. (Now that he lives at Hailey Manor, we see at least as much of him and his family.)

I had, in the first few months, come to realise that the village valued its Welsh heritage but felt nothing but welcome for the new friends. I had made the Eucharist the main service on Sunday morning and the ringing of the bell for Mattins and Evensong each day drew some to worship but was welcomed even by the non-conformists—"It's so good to know, Vicar, when we hear it, that there's someone praying for us."

Then in early autumn I asked them if there was anything they missed from the old customs of the parish. "Oh, yes, *Plygain,*" they said. Now *plygain* was familiar to me from my childhood, the dawn-service of Christmas morning, taken over by Methodism from the first Eucharist of the Nativity. "What time was it held?" "At six o'clock, giving us time after it for the milking." So, six it was to be. At about half-past five we set out from the Vicarage the half mile to church. There was not a glimmer of light anywhere and as I let myself into the church and the vestry, I reconciled myself to a very modest service. There was still not a sound from the nave but when I vested and went into the church, there they were, a full and expectantly silent congregation, Anglicans, Methodists, Independents, all waiting for the Christmas dawn. From my experience that day I invited them all again to a Maundy Thursday evening Communion and because some of them, not confirmed Anglicans, had hesitated to respond to my invitation to the altar, I introduced them to the Eastern Orthodox custom of 'blessed bread' and after the service we all moved about the nave and chancel, eating the plain bread which seemed to make us one.

*

But those English friends? They themselves were wholly content with the excellent bi-lingual prayer-book of the Church in Wales and were rapidly making the responses in Welsh. But I was not content; and here I made the only liturgical reform I have ever been responsible for: I preached *twice*, in Welsh, on the Epistle, before the Creed and in English, on the Gospel after the Creed. Because the sermons were about five minutes each in length, the English could wait upon the Welsh address, tuning in to some sentences, while the Welsh, all of whom understood English, however diffidently some might speak it, had therefore 'two for the price of one.' Indeed, one eve of our feast day of St David I went a step further. The Aberystwyth University choir came across to sing the full service, Byrd's Five-part Mass, in Latin. With my sermons this may well have been one of the rare tri-lingual services in Wales.

I was of course aware that in other towns and villages in West and North Wales there was unease and even hostility at the buying up of small Welsh homes by well-to-do English people from the Midlands and that they often came to their 'holiday homes' with their cars loaded with provisions, so that not only were the houses put beyond the reach of young people but the shops also were impoverished. There were two reactions to this invasion by those whom the Scottish Highlands call 'White Settlers': the first was the physical attack on 'second homes' burning many of them, and in addition making the countryside uncomfortable, with graffiti besmirching beauty-spots and sign-posts destroyed or simply turned in the wrong direction.

The other reaction, while no less deploring the erosion of 'Welshness' and the loss of the language, was to shrug it off, as all the British have always shrugged off and then assimilated invaders.

A story which went the rounds of the Dyfed vicarages and manses at that time, illustrates this attitude:

A vicar heard some of his boys playing a ball-tamping game while reciting to its rhythm the chant:

> Bloody English, second homes,
> Bloody English, second homes.

The vicar protested that this was not a nice sentiment and told them to try a new rhyme the following day. This time he heard the chant:

> Jesus Christ, born in a stable,
> Jesus Christ, born in a stable.

"Now that's very much better, boys, very, very good! Now tell me, why was Jesus Christ born in a stable?" The reply was firm:

> "Bloody English, second homes."

Both reactions, bitterness and laughter, are wholly understandable and I find it all the more painful from seeing the even more complex situation in Scotland. Gaelic is quietly disappearing and to my question to a waitress or shop-assistant in the old Gaelic areas, "Do you speak the Gaelic?" there almost always comes the sad reply, "No, but my mother does" and the soft voice has all the pathos of someone reconciled to an irresistible force. Hugh MacDiarmid's language for almost half his poetry, though heard in recitals or dramatic performances, is also losing its contest. And yet—and yet, somehow the Scot keeps his proud identity, a vigorous literature, painting and sculpture which at least holds its own with that of England and music which has fostered composers who have international repute. The death of a language, Welsh or Gaelic, is more than a tragedy for the Welsh or the Scots; it is a tragedy for European culture. But there are other vehicles of national identity and culture which go beyond language, and pride demands their fostering.

*

When I arrived at Llanddewibrefi there was no minister at Methodist Bethesda or its Manse. Then came word that the redoubtable T.J. Davies was being sent to look after the Methodists. Everyone told me that he was abrasive and would give me a bad time! But I had read his weekly column in the local paper and had realised that here was one man, a Welsh scholar, who understood the necessity for demotic Welsh; his column sounded (and I mean 'sounded') exactly as if every vowel and consonant was taken down as *spoken*. Here was clearly a man who knew the sociology of language; what else? I wondered.

It happened that T.J. was ill and in hospital in Aberystwyth at the time he should have begun his ministry with us and I believe he was rather startled that almost his first visitor there was 'the Vicar'. At once we became friends and rarely, for the next three years, did we miss our morning coffee once each week at the Manse or the Vicarage, to chat about the parish, Welsh affairs and literature. Out of this came our valuable religious experiment. I suggested that on the last three Sunday evenings each month, we all three, ourselves, Methodists and Independents, went to evening service as 'guests', taking no public part but savouring our several traditions of worship and preaching. It was, I truly believe, a wholly satisfying experiment and I equally firmly believe that this is the kind of way that ecumenical understanding should follow.

*

It has always been a matter of regret—even of resentment—for me that the fine arts have become the possession of the great metropolitan centres, with London absorbing the greater bulk of funding and the valuable festivals on the whole confined to cities and towns that were already 'show places'. I determined that my little parish of five hundred souls (and a hinterland, if you span the triangle Aberystwyth—Tregaron—Lampeter, of fewer than twenty thousand) should have for four days each year a Festival that in quality would rival any in Britain. Indeed I told the committee I brought together that nothing should appear, in music, poetry or art, in the Llanddewibrefi Festival that could not be transferred without change to the Edinburgh Festival. And we succeeded!

290

It was fortunate that at this time I was a member of the Welsh Arts Council and its Music and Fine Arts panels and also of the West Wales Arts Association, and was able to get a small but adequate grant. The committee needed gentling along. "It will be sacred music, won't it?" asked one lady. "Not if I can help it" I replied and so we worked at it. Our organist, Irene Thomas, had already shown us what could be done with the excellent chamber organ that Edward Davies had given the church; perfect for baroque music, it also turned out to be an excellent 'continuo' and in the hands of Richard Elfyn Jones (who had been playing the massive Albert Hall organ just the previous week) it gave us Bach, his predecessors and contemporaries, to our immense pleasure.

We were among the first to engage Peter Pears and Ossian Ellis in their joint recital, though Peter Pears went down with a throat infection the weekend before, with Ossian Ellis giving us a solo performance of major harp works, a history of the instrument and his own *penillion* singing. Delme Bryn-Jones, Ann Griffiths, Rhisiart Arwel, Kenneth Bowen and Helen Field were among our soloists. Poetry had equal distinction, with R.S. Thomas, Euros Bowen, Jeremy Hooker, Robert Morgan, Ruth Bidgood and Pennar Davies giving recitals and, on one notable day, we were the first to invite to Wales the 'poet-laureate' of Gaelic poetry, Sorley Maclean, who read his poetry in Gaelic and English, while in the same recital my old friend Alun Llywelyn-Williams read his poetry in Welsh and English.

We were fortunate that Alun Hoddinott and John Piper agreed from the start to be watchdogs over our music and fine art. This meant original compositions from Alun and the introduction of fine classical performances.

John Piper drew two studies of the church and village which became the lithographed covers of the first and third souvenir programmes and Kyffin Williams did the same for the second souvenir. Each festival had an art exhibition and again the artists gave us distinction: John Piper, Kyffin Williams, Josef Herman, Ceri Richards, John Petts, Jonah Jones, David Tinker and Ogwyn Davies.

You will see that we had reason to be proud of our venture and I haven't tired you with an account of the Llandewibrefi Lecture, the preachers at the Sunday Eucharist, the exhibitions of crafts, the

Kyffin Williams

LLANDDEWIBREFI

The battlemented tower
lords confidently over the valley,
the cottages huddled in the shadow
in manorial dependence.

Within the battlements a watch-tower,
a keep, last line of defence,
stands alert towards the pass in the hills;
kite and buzzard wheel
where wolves once howled,
disturbing the manor's peace.

No dawn-smoke rises
from these cold hearths;
the sheep huddle, hidden
beyond those bare folds;
the scree of cottages at the crag fo
of the fortress-church
teems with sleeping man.

Moelwyn Merchant

Kyffin Williams, a poster-poem based on his drawing for the brochure of the
Llanddewibrefi Festival

292

'Gymanfa' with which each festival closed, and even the minute 'fringe' which began in our second year.

One social question hovered in my mind during those fruitful years. I knew from Arts Council figures that for the annual cost of the Welsh National Eisteddfod, I could mount two hundred and fifty versions of the Llanddewi Festival; that is to say that in exchange for the six days of the National Eisteddfod, we could give Wales a thousand days of the arts at the highest level; or to put it in another way, in each week of the year, in four or perhaps even five centres spanning Wales, we could have such festivals in towns and villages. It gave me 'furiously to think', as it should other people. Just think what that would do for our poets, artists, dramatists, musicians, what it would do for the colleges and university colleges in Wales, what it would do for performers and above all, what it would do for the sensibility of our people. Will *someone* please think about it?

*

It was the greatest pleasure for me that I was not wholly cut off from academic life while parochial affairs were so absorbing. On the traditional Monday 'free day' for parsons, I went regularly to the National Library in Aberystwyth to find conditions not unlike the generous conditions for research at the Folger or Newberry Libraries in the United States. Here I worked mainly on the background for poems on the invasion of Wales by Edward I and the poems of Dafydd ap Gwilym and his burial at Ystrad Fflur.

In the afternoon I went across to the Drama Department to conduct a series of seminars on Shakespeare. John Edmunds, the head of the department, had the appropriate background for founding a most lively department—an actor and television newsreader with what must be, in his profession, the unique distinction of a Ph.D. at the Birmingham Shakespeare Institute in French classical drama. He had gathered about him a brilliant group of colleagues: Elan Closs Stephens, as articulately stimulating in Welsh as in English and now, with Dr Edmunds's departure for the British Council, head of the department; my former student from Cardiff days, Hazel Davies, wife of Walford Davies, head of

293

the Department of Extra-mural studies, and the ebullient Ioan Williams, a young colleague of mine in Exeter, who left for Warwick and then found the compulsion of Wales irresistible. The team was completed by the professionally experienced Emily Davies, in charge of the practical production-side and carrying both Welsh and English productions to splendid performances. It was exciting to find, either in their studio theatre or in the more lavish Arts Centre on the hill, productions of Brecht and of Saunders Lewis, of the Theatre of the Absurd and Shakespeare, all making their own impact on a department which also pursued the critical exploration of theatre history. It was a heartening reflection of work at Exeter and I was gratefully happy when I was invited to be an honorary professor in the department.

ALISTAIR CRAWFORD

These were the days when I first met Alistair Crawford, in charge of graphics in the Department of Fine Art. I already knew some of his work from exhibitions and, from reports to the Art Panel of the Welsh Arts Council, I knew of his growing authority in the field of British, European and American photography. Now I was to see some of the results of his researches in exhibitions of Elio Ciol and John Thomas—each of these a revelation of a new world for me— and it was good to read—and to see—the definitive and lavish catalogue of the work of Carlo Bevilacqua ('Il Maestro'). It was therefore an especial pleasure to be involved in the Welsh Arts Council's first 'Major Printmaking Award' in 1977 which enabled him to work with the resources and craftsmen of Editions Alecto.

It was a complex world of creativity within which I met him in his studios, in the University and at his home in Bow Street. A strange, mysterious and ordinary world—this paradox is at the centre of Alistair Crawford's art. Landscape is factual, recognisable, even identifiable, yet visionary, sometimes disturbingly so. We are not wholly surprised to find a foreground dominated by a large ceramic pot, as big as two fields, and yet merging into the structural significance of the landscape itself. His paradoxical view of landscape lies both within the romantic tradition and remains astringently outside it. Samuel Palmer flooded his lush world with

294

the mystery of profusion; Crawford defines his landscape sparely almost puritanically—no 'boscage', no piled cumulus, but a pattern of hieroglyphs which suggest the object (or its essence) with minimal strokes—bird-flight like an animated circumflex, a cloud or pine-grove as deft as an oriental brush-stroke.

I should expect an artist named Crawford, born in Aberdeenshire, to be both astringent and intellectual. He is both. As sparing in his prose style as in his drawing or printmaking techniques, he can define with merciless precision an art which he is determined not to pursue:

> I used to go round galleries and all I could see was 'look at me. I am avant garde and Big' but then I discovered that small was not only beautiful but also extremely quiet.
> —Interview with A P Jones 1979

That last word, 'quiet', both unexpected and characteristic, places his paintings and prints in their predominant mood; they invite your attention not with rhetoric but with the gentlest of gestures— 'gentlest' until, having submitted yourself to them, they hold you very firmly. Talk at the Vicarage and his Bow Street home was always 'professional.' His wife, Joan, was neither English nor Scottish but Yorkshire, a quite other country, and our talk was always spiced by her perceptive irony. Very soon Alistair told me that some of my poems written at Llanddewibrefi made him wish to produce a series of paintings which he would call 'Dyfed Landscapes'. So began the four paintings which, with their interlocking mountain background, constituted one extended frieze in which the four poems, 'Ann Williams', 'There are certain things you cannot say about a stone', 'Revealing a Skull' and 'Miracles at Llanddewibrefi' triggered the imagery but left the paintings to their own painterly integrity.

This didn't go far enough for Alistair. He now determined on four etching/aquatints which would relate in the same way and have my four poems lithographed alongside the prints. Then he asked me to react to the four images with a poem which would then become the fifth print and I responded with 'Envoi'. It all seemed, to my prejudiced eye, extremely successful and I was delighted when the National Library purchased the drawings and the engraved series.

MS
ANN WILLIA
OF PANT Y BLAWD
DIED 10TH JULY 1808
AGED 56

THOUGH THE ACRES TEEMED,
LIFE WAS STUNTED, BITTER, CONFINED

DEATH LED TO A NARROW GRAVE
CRAMMED AT THE PATH'S EDGE
THE STONE NOT WIDE ENOUGH
TO TAKE HER NAME WITH GRACE

Alistair Crawford, *The Dyfed Landscapes* 1980
(1) *Ann Williams* (oil crayon/pencil);

REVEALING A SKULL

THE SHEEP DIES;
LYING ON ITS SIDE,
THE HEATHER TOO YIELDING,
IT STRUGGLES BRIEFLY,
BLEATS ITS SURRENDER.

THE BUZZARD SEVERS THE VERTEBRAE,
CLAWING THE TISSUE FROM THE BONE

CROW BUZZARD AND KITE CIRCLE
IN WATCHFUL ORDER,
UNGRACIOUSLY CONCEDING PRECEDENCE
AND IN SUCCESSION
DELICATELY PICK THE SHREDS.

THE SUN DRIES THE REMNANT TISSUE.

WINTER SNAPS AWAY THE FRAGMENTS,
THE SKULL REVEALED, WHITE AND EMPTY.

SPORES AND DAMP AIR ADD THEIR GREEN FLUSH,
THE ILLUSION OF LIFE.

(2) *Revealing a Skull* (oil crayon/pencil)

297

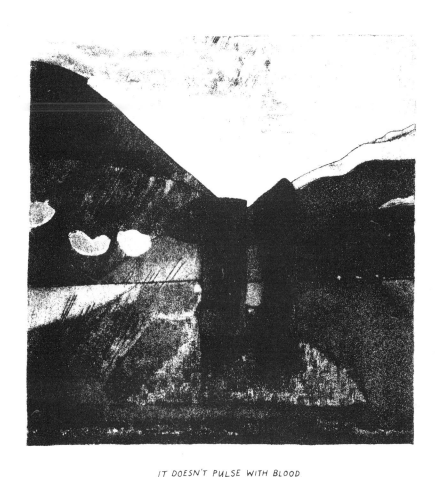

IT DOESN'T PULSE WITH BLOOD,
LEAVES NO LOOP OR WHORL OF PRINT,
THE SOFT IMPRESS OF FLESH;

IT HAS NO RESILIENCE LIKE STEEL
NOR TENSE PLANGENCY OF WIRE,
NOR HUMILIATION OF RUST.

IT BLOOMS WITH NO FLOWER
NOR LEAF WITH SAP RISING;
IT STRIKES NO ROOT IN EARTH.

BUT IT WEATHERS TO A TEXTURE
LIKE FLESH VEINED AND SCARRED,
IT FRACTURES TO CRYSTAL

AND FOUND OR CARVED,
WEATHERED OR TOOLED WITH CARE,
STONE IS A STILL POINT,
A MOMENT OF AWE.

(3) *There are certain things you cannot say about a stone* (oil crayon/pencil)

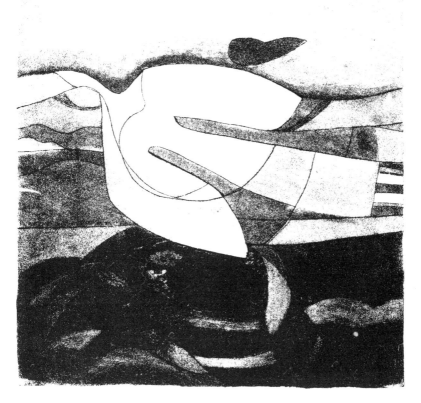

MIRACLES AT LLANDDEWIBREFI

GEOLOGY IS NEVER SIMPLE,
NOR, FOR THAT MATTER, VERY CONVENIENT.

THE BISHOPS GATHERED AT DOL-Y-SAINT
WITH A SPRINKLING OF ABBOTS,
A MITIGATION OF LAYMEN;
THEIR PURPOSE : TO TELL PELAGIUS
THAT BOOTSTRAPS ARE NOT FOR LIFTING,
THAT GRACE IS HUMBLER GEAR.

BUT WHEN DEWI PREACHED THE TRUTH
(SIX FOOT AND MORE AND A GOOD VOICE)
THEY SAID THEY COULD NOT HEAR.

THE DOVE AND THE EARTH BETWEEN THEM
GAVE THE APPROPRIATE ANSWER :
THE DOVE WHISPERED THE TRUMPET WORDS
AND THE EARTH ROSE, A PULPIT ELEVATION

AND GEOLOGISTS CALL IT
A TERMINAL MORAIN.

(4) *Miracles at Llanddewibrefi* (oil crayon/pencil)

299

What I found remarkable was that the drawings and prints appeared totally independent of the poems and at the same time, both individually and collectively gave the poems a significance well beyond their original inspiration.

*

These years in Dyfed had given great happiness but it became obvious to me and my family that I could no longer sustain the pressures of a parish, of sculpture and writing and my permanent craving to teach. We therefore began to look around for a house, away from the parish as was only seemly, despite our many friendships, but still if possible within Dyfed. Then Paul and Grace intervened and suggested that they would be much happier if we shared a home with them.

Paul was teaching in the Department of English in Warwick and Grace taught ceramics at the Mid-Warwickshire College. They looked for a house which would be large enough to convert into two flats and within a month had found one, already converted. This led to ten rich years: sculpture (with some of my ceramic patterns for bronze fired by Grace), writing, with Paul's kindly ruthlessness in scrutiny; and a press in the basement which Paul elevated to 'The Windmill Press' with some excellent publications of his own and other poems.

Now, sadly, Paul and Grace have gone to America (Grace is 'Southern' and a graduate of 'Old Miss'); I miss Paul's astringency but his last book of poems has been a massive compensation; for *Bone from a Stag's Heart* was a Poetry Book Society recommendation.

*

Royal Leamington Spa is a handsome town, still substantially Georgian, with some fine crescents and terraces; at the same time it manifestly 'earns its living', with industrial estates and the palpable impact on its life and atmosphere of Ford, B.L., Borg Clutches and the like. Above all, from my selfish viewpoint, the industries of the Midlands ensured for the solitary sculptor a supply of highly skilled and friendly craftsmen who were glad to put their expertise at my disposal. All this meant an immediate and very diverse expansion in my sculpting, with new forms and greatly increased dimensions for older conceptions now made possible. It astonished me once more that a craftsman whose life experience had perhaps been wholly in heavy industry, could look at a small maquette of mine and see immediately not only the concept but also the problems and solutions involved in translating the work into another medium or transforming it from a 'domestic' size to a monumental, outdoor form. My respect grew at each visit to their factory or workshop for the articulacy of their finger-tips. Never once did I encounter in all these craftsmen the bewildered, often cynical, rejection of an abstract form, as they handled one of my pieces; there was never the ironic question, "What does it mean? What does it stand for?" which more 'sophisticated people' utter. There grew then a relationship between artist and craftsman as deep and as fully creative as that other fellowship of the literate, the poets, novelists and dramatists. I was glad that the chances of life had led me to this experience before it was too late.

*

Very soon I was involved in two other associations. The parish church of All Saints, cathedral-like in its dimensions and with all the borrowed beauty of a late 'Tractarian' church on an old foundation, now recollected French Gothic in its Spa setting. It has always had a seemly tradition of worship and the vicar, Ian Campbell, has a tolerant vision which seizes on any creative idea which enhances the worship of the congregation. It was a pleasure to find a worshipping community which welcomed a great variety of organ recitals and concerts—there is ample space for a large orchestra and choir for large-scale works—and which welcomed art exhibitions in the church and refrained from demanding that they be religious artefacts.

In the day to day world of the artists I was delighted to be invited to join a group of painters and sculptors, the 76 Group, which was formed within a few months of our coming to Leamington. Our shows, one or two each year, spanned the Midlands, from the new gallery at Stoke-on-Trent to small private galleries in our hinterland. It was a professional association, expert but unpretentious and though it has now dissolved—as is proper for such groups when the original intention and impulse have fulfilled themselves—our friendship and creative criticism remain.

*

However desirable it may be that such groups as these dissolve when their purpose and impetus have been realised, friendships and professional relations extend beyond the life of the groups. Three friendships I particularly value: with Mary Riley, a painter whose vitality and gusto of creation has transcended illness; with Colin Saxton, Head of Art at the Lanchester Polytechnic, whose drawings towards an oil portrait of me, compassed eight leisurely Saturday mornings punctuated by Beethoven and Schubert; and Tim Threlfall, sculptor and art critic (also at the Lanchester Polytechnic) whose work on Noguchi demands immediate publication; all three a grateful extension of years of exhibition together.

*

Now that Paul, Grace and Luke have moved to Portland, Oregon, where Paul has begun a new life, directing a small poetry-publishing house, and Grace pursues her studio pottery, we found our joint home too large for just the two of us. We therefore sold it and moved to this present eyrie, a first-floor flat nearby. To move home is a strange experience, especially if one is no longer young. Familiar objects take on unfamiliar stances, books have become elusive and seem mysteriously to have bred innumerable offspring. Most disconcertingly, a change of context seems to involve a change of personality, as though a great part of the truth of our being was a relationship between our living selves and our inanimate surroundings. This transformation is deeply disturbing and we adopt tactics to counter the trauma. In the early days of our move, I took the two volumes of Hugh MacDiarmid's *Complete Works* and read steadily through them without intermission. By this immersion in the lifetime's work of a loved and distinguished poet, I could hear the voice again, saw on the page the words that had so moved me, "This is the kind of poetry I want." By thus consciously setting a third person between the two persons I now seemed to find in myself, the former inhabitant of the old familiar home and the new who had as yet to find his whole being, I suppose I was formulating my own 'Rites of Passage'. These rites are essential if we are safely to move from one being to another. They are deeply disturbing, for they involve being in doubts and distractions. I don't think I'm exaggerating this dislocation and I'm beginning to be assured that it is not entirely to our detriment. Some apparently trivial matters may explain what I mean:

I am now writing in a window-space which overlooks three handsome Georgian houses and beyond them, through the leafless branches of tall trees, I see the hills which contain Leamington on its eastern side. The picture, framed in the window, unites the unostentatious beauty of our finest domestic architecture with its natural setting.

Then, these windows on our first-floor elevation—we lived on the ground floor in our previous home—give a remarkable and quite unexpected vision of cloud landscapes, in their infinite variety of form and colour from dawn to sunset. This is no small treasury to inherit from the migration.

The pictures and sculptures about me as I write are not simply 'works of art'; they are the living presence of friendships. Now, as I pause in writing, I see one wall wholly devoted to Josef Herman, while Alistair Crawford's work and a small watercolour by Dorothy Pound look across at the Hermans. As I move to follow the sun, two paintings by John Piper enclose a bronze by Barbara Hepworth, while Kyffin Williams again brings Llanddewibrefi before my eyes. This is a context created by friends and shaped anew by me. In it I can relax in the tranquillity of recollecting; for the moment it seems quite pleasant to be in the late seventies.

*

This must be an attempt to be coherent about belief, that most elusive part of one's being. It is a stream; it has got unity, from its infant source in some upland until it is merged in 'the sea of faith',

303

one hopes at the flood. But its course is erratic; it is lost to sight, superficially in reeds, sometimes deeply in caverns but for the most part consciously *there.*

It was in so many ways fortunate that I was born into a devout South Welsh Methodist family whose intentions for me were manifest from my baptism. I was named William for my father but Moelwyn was to be the name of daily use, a daily reminder that I was intended to follow in the footsteps of one of the greatest preachers of that generation, Moelwyn Hughes. It was perhaps not without significance that he was named after the Moelwyn Mountains, the sturdy southern rampart of Snowdonia; there was to be a slatey, granitic toughness perhaps in some substratum of my being!

A child in my environment had a certain toughness in his training. From infancy I had to learn longer and longer passages from the Bible for recitation before the elders every Wednesday evening at *Seiat* and by the age of about eight these passages might be a Psalm in length or even St Paul on charity as he wrote to the Corinthians. One of the intriguing results is that, after years of English, in worship and preaching, my instinctive reference point is the Welsh Bible of the noble Bishop Morgan of Llanrhaedr-ym-Mochnant. So the words come welling up:

> Yr Arglwydd yw fy mugail . . .
> Cofia'n awr dy Greawdwr . . .

and a hundred other loved passages.

My parents told me (and they were truthful people) that at the age of five or six, I would turn the massive arm-chair around, kneel on its seat and, using the curved back as a kind of lectern, preach to my 'congregation', the assembled family. The sermon they remembered best was on the troubles of the people of Moses as they fled between Piahiroth and Baalzephon—little wonder the graver Jacobean dramatists became my later concern.

For my first seventeen years I heard, I suppose much of the greatest preaching of that age; Cynddylan, Brynsiencyn, Philip Jones of Porth-cawl and the delightfully spare preacher who limited his sermons to twenty minutes (a half or one third of the usual length) and was therefore known not by his name but as Y Pregethwr-ugain-munud—The Twenty-minute-Preacher. And there were always the sweet tones of Talfan Davies to be cherished. These sermons remain fast in the memory—indeed I have preached many of them!—but one (the name of the preacher forgotten) is perhaps the most vividly recalled. The text was: 'Lord, teach us to pray' and the structure—the invariable rhetoric of Introduction: Three Topics: Conclusion, was this:

> Every man prays
> Every prayer is answered
> Be careful how you pray.

It was scholarly, undemonstrative and unforgetable.

This was the atmosphere of all the years until my seventeenth, when on the threshold of university, my wisely perceptive father took me aside and said, in substance: "You are moving away from Methodism and you must not prepare for the ministry. Study English and History and become a teacher until you know your real mind." It was generous and a true release.

In Cardiff one of my closest friends was Alun Llywelyn-Williams, whose father was the City medical officer. Their kindness and warm hospitality held me for a while in their Welsh Methodist place of worship in Crwys Road but gradually Eglwys Dewi Sant and St John's at the centre of the city drew me ever more strongly.

The final thrust was, in a basic sense of the word, a 'vocation'. After graduation, I had been lecturing in an adult education class at Usk, for a few weeks, my topic mediaeval history. The vicar of Usk, Billy Davies, a rugged catholic who, before his marriage, had been a Bush Brother in Australia, took me back to the vicarage as usual and spoke bluntly: "You tell me you're a Methodist but you lecture like a Catholic. You will come up next Monday an hour earlier to begin your preparation for confirmation." In the same tones a year later the saintly Dr Joyce, our bishop and Archbishop of Wales, told me, "I want you to be ordained and you will be taught by Pusey House and the Cowley Fathers." This assuredness of command I suppose prepared me for Joe Fison, the bishop of Salisbury some decades later.

305

Meanwhile, as I have written earlier, I had listened to and read Karl Barth and his fellow theologians and had learned the rigours of theological argument so different from the Biblical study of my youth, yet so strongly based on the same sources. Now I was ready for further discipline and it came, through Frederic Hood and the Cowley Fathers.

Pusey House in Canon Hood's day was a centre for catholic worship at Oxford and for exact scholarship, notably in Patristic Theology with F.L. Cross at its heart and in Church History, in which the young priest, Eric Kemp specialised (he is now Bishop of Chichester).

The house of the Cowley Fathers was the greater shock and stimulus at that time. The plainchant of the liturgy, with a beauty and flexible precision which I was later to associate with Solesmes, was controlled by a Canadian, Father Rose, while my personal training was supervised by the gentle and saintly Father Pridham. I was particularly struck by their grave austerity (the food was no temptation to the flesh) and their ready laughter as they listened to the less sombre lections at meal-time. This spilled over into their instructions as, in my deacon's year, I prepared for my priesting. One of the younger fathers had detected that I was fearful of hearing my first confessions. "Take it quietly," he said "and remember the story of the young priest who asked his old confessor to listen to his first morning of penitents. 'How did I do, father?' the young man asked anxiously; 'Very well, my son but perhaps in future, when you hear their sins, there should in your response, be more 'Tut! Tut!' and a little less 'Phew!'" I was convinced from that day onwards that there must be a great deal of loud laughter in heaven!

And so the break was made. One of my greatest fears for the Church, which we call the body of Christ, is schism, the tearing of it asunder. Our instinctive desire to assert ourselves, the aggressive maintaining that every little quirk of belief is *the core* of the faith, has through the ages caused these rents and rifts which are a scandal both to believer and unbeliever. That there are differences of opinion and stress will be inevitable—a Luther will quite properly assert his ministry of grace and be resounding in condemning corruption—but these convictions can and must be accommodated within that vehicle of charity and compassion, Christ's Body.

This was the source of much of my unhappiness in my early twenties, before my confirmation as an Anglican. I could understand the Calvinism in my Calvinistic Methodism in Port Talbot but I could also sympathise with the unease of eighteenth-century bishops as the Methodist fathers, still Anglican priests to their death, insisted on their right to preach anywhere, even without episcopal licence. This echoed Wesley's declaration, which always caused me to question its propriety: "The world is my parish."

Now, when I had a tiny parish of my own, the little hillock of Llanhenog in Gwent, I knew that the real discipline, the real and lasting devotion, was to preach a hundred sermons every year to the *same* people in the *same* church. There is of course something exhilarating, deeply satisfying, about visiting a strange church, especially a cathedral, and preaching at the very top of one's bent!—the same temptation to glory assails a 'visiting professor'— but the true discipline is to be at home with the people the church has put in our care. We are not St Paul, bringing the unheard faith, the unseen revelation to an alien people; the Church demands stability, a resting-place for the meditation of the people of God.

These pastoral concerns were confirmed in a strange way by an academic discipline. I had learned from two friends the complex relevance of theology to our seemingly 'secular' activities. Gordon Phillips, later to become Chaplain to the University of London, Canon of St Paul's and then Dean of Llandaff, was at the time when I was training for Orders, in his first curacy at St Julian's, Newport and within walking distance of our house in Caerleon. We had a small Broadwood 'grand' and Gordon had no piano—to our great gain. For he came regularly across and taught us how Bach's greatest keyboard works could sound on a modern instrument. After a splendid rendering of the Italian Concerto or an hour of Preludes and Fugues, he would settle down to talk, brilliant talk that was later to capture the London undergraduates. With 'Greats' and Theology, his knowledge of the Latin and Greek Fathers was extensive (it showed in his later writings) but it was his teasing, never malicious, tearing apart of my naiveties that caused a new

307

growth in my thinking. And I knew also that music and painting were to be the vehicles of much thinking about belief.

Friendship with Father Martin Jarrett-Kerr C.R., was to bring similar insights. Here was a monk in one of our 'learned' communities, the Mirfield Fathers, who had devoted all his scholarship to an exploration of the theological implications of recent literature, French and English. It was not surprising, then, that Nathan Scott and Dick Young in Chicago were his friends and that he was the means of my knowing them. He lectured for me at Cardiff but perhaps his most memorable visit was to 'preach Harvest' for me at Llanhenog. As we went by taxi the three miles to church, the car rocked with our laughter as 'Bill' regaled us with anecdotes. As I paid the driver, he said to me in bewilderment, "Was *that* a monk?" "Oh yes, a learned and holy one," I replied; I hope it extended his perception of the church and her priesthood —as Bill certainly did mine.

All this came to inform and enliven a course in which I was involved at Cardiff. It was called 'The History of Ideas' and involved, *inter alia*, lectures on Hooker, Locke and Kant with excursions into Copernicus and Newton (I would not have such effrontery today). But the section of the course which taught me most (whatever it did to the listeners) was a group of lectures on Duns Scotus and St Thomas Aquinas. Thomism had captured me in Pusey House and in the reading assigned me by Canon Hood. By the time I came to speak of it to my students I had begun already to isolate the central topic which was to dominate my thinking from that time until the writing of *Jeshua*, the Incarnation, the nature of the young man at Nazareth, the Son of God.

This central mystery of our faith was greatly relevant to the debate between Thomists and Scotists, and Aquinas and Duns Scotus assumed a towering significance in their conflicting view of the Incarnation—it was indeed the beginning of the debate in my mind as, in Chicago, Thomist and Franciscan, Jesuit and Poor Clare, made their several contributions to the struggle in my mind.

Put in its bare, crudest terms, the two facets of doctrine had these contrasting assumptions: to the Thomist, the coming of the Son of God, to birth, crucifixion and resurrection, was the timeless answer of the Godhead to the Fall, the primal sin of man in Eden; and since this eternal plan brought mankind the inestimable boon of the knowledge of Jesus of Nazareth, the very sin of the Fall was radiant with the compassionate purpose of God. The natural human response was: "O Beata Culpa!", "Oh blessed Fault" that brought to us that Birth.

Duns Scotus found this an unacceptable reading of divine providence: the Incarnation conditional on the sin of man? Christ forced down to earth by man's culpability?—never! The Incarnation was the summit of divine creativity, the greatest boon the Godhead could confer on mankind; only an envious God could deny to man the greatest gift it was possible to make. The birth of the Son of God, the climax in creative revelations, was necessary, was in the inevitable nature of things. Of course it redeemed man from the Fall—but it would have come, from the compulsion of divine love, whether man had sinned or not.

It was a bonny debate! It held me through the years and though for me Aquinas was the greatest theologian, superior even to Augustine and the natural servant of St Paul, Duns Scotus attracted me greatly in this matter of Nazareth.

One happy irony emerged from all this. As I attended Welsh services in Cardiff's Eglwys Dewi Sant and then found my roots again in the church of Llanddewibrefi, I knew that the hymns of my childhood, and especially the glories of William Williams, Pantycelyn and the young saint of Dolwar Fach, Ann Griffiths, had already taught me all this. One hymn in particular, so richly Scotist, now came into its own:

> Cyn llunio'r byd, cyn lledu'r nefoedd wen . . .
> Fe drefnwyd ffordd . . .

which declares without ambiguity that 'Before the earth was shaped and the heaven's spread forth, a plan was conceived' to save 'frail, lost and sinful man.' And if this Scotist theology of Pedr Fardd does not satisfy you, then turn to Ann Griffiths, who in happier times might well have been a Poor Clare. In what is to me her sublimest hymn, which begins:

> Wele'n sefyll rhwng y myrtwydd . . .
> See him standing 'midst the myrtle . . .

she pursues with metaphysical wit the image of the divine lover, which has its origin in the *Song of Songs,* rich source of so much of our imagery. It is so good to find apparently divergent streams unite as tributaries in a greater river.

*

The black congregations of America and especially the heroic sanctity of Martin Luther King and his followers greatly extended the social significance of belief for me. But even greater was the impact of Mircea Eliade and Charles Long in the exploration of 'religious anthropology' and the beliefs of those whom we arrogantly call primitive. I had had some opportunity of seeing African sculpture in Josef Herman's unique collection with its union of realism and mystery, but now I began to realise the ambiguity in much of our religious belief. I had met it quite early among devout people in Wales. Some of them told me that they disliked rabbit or hare for food because the animals were 'vermin.' This manifest absurdity springs, so they tell me, from a quite different source. The two creatures, fertility objects themselves, are sacred to Diana and early priesthood in Wales could never be sure, if they saw them eaten, whether they were satisfying hunger or serving their pre-christian religion. In the same way horse is disliked in England and the Tau cross is rarely seen; both are taboo objects, for the horse is sacred to Odin and the Tau cross resembles Odin's hammer; again the early christian might be ensuring safety within both cults if either was used. Our superstitions often conceal deep and forgotten fears.

When I retired from Exeter and the Bishop of St Davids invited me to serve in his diocese, he offered me two attractive parishes, Llanddewibrefi which I accepted and Ysbyty Cynfyn at Devil's Bridge. The latter, in a picturesque defile below the flank of Plynlimmon, showed the secure judgment of Celtic Christianity in converting pagan sites and monuments to Christian significance; for into the boundary of the churchyard is built a complete and still very impressive stone circle. The church therefore stands in what from pre-christian days was already hallowed ground.

The Dream of the Rood, the most sophisticated poem in Old English, had from student days fascinated me by its complex

310

ambiguity. Here, in dramatic form, with the shifting of speakers within the poem—the poet, the Cross, the young warrior Christ—the Crucifixion is made one with the heroic tradition out of which the Sagas had come. Here the young hero goes to climb and to clasp his rood, self-crucified as the heathen look on. The two traditions have become inseparable and the union is the more remarkable when, in Galloway one sees the Ruthwell Cross, of the mid-eighth century, the crowning glory of Northumbrian Christianity. The great cross shaft has panels with the life of Christ, formalised vine-scrolls and, in runes on the shaft margin, passages from *The Dream of the Rood*; for the meditative gaze of the worshipper, Golgotha is united to the most intricate sculpture and the greatest devotional poem of Anglo-Saxon Britain.

Iona, Whithorn, Lindisfarne, all three in their several ways, with the illuminated manuscripts that enriched our concept of early Celtic Christianity, had very barely paved the way for the confounding obscurity of Pictish art in Scotland. I came upon its superlative beauty almost by accident. I had been looking for raw stone, material for my own sculpting, when I decided to compare the artefacts of early religion, crosses and the like, in Wales and Scotland. High crosses in Wales had been long familiar and the Llanbadarn Cross was a story to itself. But Pictishland, that was quite another story and two substantial visits were devoted to its exploration.

The first, so alien experience was in the quite unlikely setting of the Manse lawn at Glamis. Here the massive dressed stone had a finely-wrought cross of complex interlaced strapwork and within the four spaces defined by the upright and the arms of the cross are figures and symbols wholly obscure to our understanding, while on the undressed stone of the reverse side are engraved equally obscure symbols from the hitherto undeciphered vocabulary of Pictish art. In the churchyard at Aberlemno and at the roadside outside the village are two of the finest of these sculptures, the cross occupying the greater part of the front face, while the reverse sides are richly covered with apparently secular motifs, hunting and battle scenes, domestic objects and cryptic symbols.

To what complexity of religious experience did these early sculptural master-works lead me? The delicate restraint with which

311

the Crucified is no more than suggested, in all of them by the perfection of the abstract ornament at the heart of the cross and, at Aberlemno, by the bowed heads and folded wings of the flanking angels, meditating on the sacrifice before them. All this is quite comprehensible, as is the life of King David so graphically carved on the St Andrews tomb-chest. All these were within the already ancient tradition of Christian iconography—but the symbols? Their very names were mysterious: Crescent and V-rod, Mirror and Comb, Serpent and Z-rod, Double-disc and Z-rod. Equally mysterious in purpose were the more familiar signs: Eagle, Fish, Bull, Bear, Horse, Wolf and Serpent. Were they totems? family emblems? memorial symbols? boundary marks? Were they the determination of some early Pictish Christians, that with their emphatic religious symbol, the Cross reverently carved, there should go memories of earlier cults surfacing to their conscious art as they defined their personalised national identity? But, like the Etruscans, the Picts have no surviving language with which to speak to us. We must be content with these standing stones, magnificent in their isolation in the open and breathing with a vitality that survives the confines of museum collections at Meigle or St Vigeans. It is a rare experience, this sharing of devotion with a whole kingdom that, for our day, is dumb in all but its superlative sculpture.

*

All this is a far cry from the recital of a child's verses from the Bible, the disputation of learned old men, as, a boy in the family pew, I listened with awe to my grandfather. It is a long journey from Cardiff by way of Exeter and Salisbury Cathedrals and the David shrine at Llanddewi, to these mysteries of an earlier religion. One can only trust to memory and the knowledge that every tributary swells the stream.

*

Those of us who value the words of the Liturgy not only for the nobility of their meaning but for the resonances which the words carry, vibrant from the past, have had to endure a great deal at the

312

hands of translators and liturgists in these last years. Someone who can conceive this noble fragment of dialogue:

> The Lord be with you:
> And with thy spirit,

and can render it as

> The Lord be with you,
> And also with you,

has little conception of the overtones of words, the distinction between a casual greeting in a supermarket and the courteous return of a profound aspiration. One liturgist told me that 'with thy spirit' was no longer 'understanded of the people' and was confounded when I asked him if he understood the mind-boggling concept, 'The Lord be with you', and its overwhelming spiritual implications.

On the morning of the Nativity, our congregations are now assailed by a new translation of St John's sublimity. The King James translators gave us

> In the beginning was the Word . . . and
> the Word was God.

The splendid simplicity of that second phrase has now become

> And what God was the Word was.

One would have hoped that such an order of banality was beyond a literate person; it should certainly not sully the liturgy. Translation can reach even further depths when the writer tries hard enough. The awful mystery of evil can be rendered:

> . . . because your adversary the devil,
> as a roaring lion, walketh about,
> seeking whom he may devour,

but the Jerusalem Bible renders this passage from the first Epistle of St Peter:

> Your enemy the devil is prowling
> about like a roaring lion,
> looking for someone to eat.

If we are lacking verbal sense, let us at least have a sense of humour.

Probably the gravest change in our sense of propriety is provided by the omission of 'Thou' and 'Thee' in our address to the Godhead. The trivial answer to any objection is that the words are archaic and their tone misunderstood. This is of course simply not true, for many thousands of our countrymen use the forms without misgiving and if it were true, then English would be the sole European language with this grave deprivation in its vocabulary.

As a Welshman, like my French and German friends, I know precisely when the formal and courteous 'Chwi' may become 'Ti'; 'Vous', 'Sie' have the same delicate transition to 'Tu' and 'Du'. There are no rules, but every acquaintance knows when friendship, valued intimacy has reached its verbal stage.

It is not, of course, a matter of formality as against intimacy. The liturgist puts the case for 'You only are holy' as a matter of reaching out to a familiar friend, the breaking down of formality—though the word 'holy' is something of a stumbling-block in that argument. No!, 'Ti', 'Tu', 'Du' are hard won; true, they imply familiarity, a domestic trust at the hearth, the familiar intimacy of friends and lovers. But in that familiar trust there is also a quality of reverence, of unspoken assumptions about a common experience and a common fidelity. 'Ti' to a friend inclines to the intimate element in the word; 'Ti' in address to the Godhead inclines to the reverential element which is nonetheless present in all friendly discourse.

Martin Buber has made us, surely, fully aware that relationship can be richly expressed in the formula, 'I—Thou' and since relationship, trust, friendships, love, is the highest thing we know in our diurnal communications, it is surely in place to express our eternal conversations. 'Thou only art holy' stands with the overtones we accord to the seemingly alien but so resonant 'Kyrie eleison'. If English liturgists cannot respond to these distinctions then the language is indeed the poorer.

*

The converse to all this may be found in the jarring absurdity of 'sal-vay-see-on' and 'tem-tay-see-on'. Now, this is not to be attributed to sloppy pronunciation such as we have in 'Gloria in Egg-shell-sis'; indeed not, for this is the result of a little fragment of musicology, treasured, I presume, for its rarity. The final single syllable of 'temptation', I'm solemnly told by cathedral organists, is, in Tudor pronunciation, a di-syllable and demands two notes; hence 'she-on'. I naturally knew about Elizabethan pronunciation and offered one cathedral organist the opportunity of teaching his choir to sing the whole of the Lord's Prayer as a Tudor musician would have heard it; (the sound would then be somewhat nearer 'temp-tah-see-ohn') but he thought I was joking. I then suggested that elision was a not infrequent device for singing two notes to one syllable.

The problem is, of course, that this tiny fragment of misused 'scholarship' has now become wholly current and if one cathedral organist has the good sense to sing it with comprehension, he will be jeered at as an ignorant fellow who does not know his Tudors! It's all very sad and those of us who love Byrd and his fellows would wish to hear him without having to wait tensely for 'Sal-vay-see-on' to assail us with all the jarring intensity of a dentist's drill.

*

As I look back over the years, words—teaching, preaching, writing—were all fighting a losing battle, even though I was not aware of it. Ikons—paintings, drawings, sculpture—gradually asserted their place, until I was able to look at the power of words with a new insight. Two verbal objects now came under even closer scrutiny, the lecture and the sermon, and earlier convictions now took on a greater urgency.

Perhaps I can best put it in this way: For many years now— probably since I first left my Welsh environment in my young

315

manhood—I have scarcely heard any sermons at all. I have heard many little essays, written with more or less conviction and grace and read out to a congregation with more or less grace and conviction. These brief essays, some of them elegant enough, theologically sound enough, to merit publication, were *not* sermons, and it is defrauding our congregations to call their delivery preaching. Once written, they are fixed in form, apply not to the real people 'out there' but to a notional congregation, which may be in town or country, at Eucharist or Evensong, of varying need and sophistication—admirable essays—yes, perhaps; but preaching, emphatically no.

The excuse offered by teachers of 'preaching' in our Theological Colleges is that writing a 'sermon' avoids the rambling, unformed discourse; perhaps it does sometimes, but often it does not. Probably those who teach this form of pulpit speech have rarely if ever undertaken the disciplined struggle that preparing a true sermon involves: the careful skeletal structure, the Biblical context and its relevance to a particular congregation, and the quiet mulling over, the day or the hours before preaching. This is no light discipline but it has this overwhelming advantage over the essay: it speaks directly, eye to eye, to every member of the congregation. There is assent or dissent, puzzlement or pleasure on the faces of each person before you, and the preacher can shift his verbal stance, change the stresses to meet each expression. The preacher speaks to *them*; the *kerygma* is trumpeted, declared to them and to them alone.

One cannot plead against this view that there is a literary glory in the published sermons, especially of the seventeenth-century divines, of Donne and his contemporaries. There is abundant evidence that these were generally written *after* delivery at Paul's Cross or elsewhere. These preachers were so skilled—as we should be if we were as 'professional' as they—in the arts of Rhetoric and of Memory, that preparation, delivery, recollection and com-mitting to paper were a continuous series of steps in an unbroken process.

So it is with lecturing. Young lecturers seem to feel that they are cheating their undergraduates if lectures are not scholarly disquisitions, ready at the time of delivery for the learned journals.

There is a curious judgment that rates tutorials, seminars and lectures in a descending order of esteem, forgetting the important fact that they too are a closely related process. Not least among our negative debts to the 'Oxbridge' view of teaching is the strange snobbery of the statement, "We tutor and leave lecturing to the others", which forgets that the union of close tuition—which we all esteem—with the broad and hopefully exciting entry to a subject which the lecture provides, is the true nature of university teaching. To my young teachers at Exeter I always pleaded: "You have only one duty in a lecture—go before your audience with the unspoken plea, 'Look what I've found!' and when they share your excitement they will truly be learning—and your tutorials and their essays, will be the livelier."

To go full circle: to say to a congregation, "Look what I've found: the truth of the raising of Lazarus, the meaning of 'the still small voice', the agony of dereliction on Gethsemane", when we have spoken of all these things over the months and years, we may be able to say the only theological truth that ultimately matters, 'We have found together some of the truth about Jesus of Nazareth, Son of God.'

There will be a further happiness when words are given their proper function; they will be seen in the liturgy, as in secular life, to reach out in vital collaboration to their relatives in art, the abstract riches of music and the so very concrete riches of the visual arts.

*

Lunch in the House of Lords with David Jenkins, Bishop of Durham, was a disturbing and a gracious experience. There was a brief prelude: as I waited for him in the outer hall, Lord Home of the Hirsel passed and smiled, that gentle, assured smile of a man at peace with himself. Why didn't I speak? I wanted to have if only the briefest word with this man whom I regarded as the Prime Minister of most assured integrity in our century. I suppose our smiles were speech enough.

David Jenkins collected me and lunch was very moving—the food indifferent but that didn't matter. For here was tragedy, uttered, analysed with the smiling lightness of another soul at peace with itself. He spoke with charitable regret of those who manipulated brief phrases from his sermons or speeches and twisted them out of context. I thought the most malicious was to take his temperate statement: "we must be careful not to make our speaking of the Resurrection sound like a conjuring trick with bones" which became the newspaper headline of the diametrically opposite sense: 'Bishop says Resurrection a Conjuring Trick with Bones'. The manipulators, whether clergymen or newspaper sub-editors were among those who had never troubled to read his Bampton Lectures, *The Glory of Man* and would perhaps not have had the sensibility to understand them—this was my comment, not his.

The tragedy in all this was not that of the Bishop of Durham but of the church itself. For there are at least two degrees of faith among the faithful. There are those—and Bishops can be among them—for whom the Apostles' and the Nicene Creeds are handrails to be clung to; let the grasp slip, let a knot appear in the wood of the handrail and what catastrophe follows! And there are those who venture out beyond the safety margin, who are in the open and vulnerable. Their climb towards truth may be through foot-hills of scree; they may reach solid rock but their further exploration is to the very frontiers of belief. They are at that frontier with poets, artists, composers, with scientists who break beyond accepted formulae; their vision drives them even beyond the known frontiers, the *Commedia* of whose vision traverses both Purgatorio and Inferno on their way to their Paradiso. This I have seen in the eyes of Josef Herman, as he distilled the final truth for himself out of the Holocaust that left him as the sole remnant of his family, and made of that truth high art; in the focussed words of Ezra Pound, as for decades he pursued his search for law, for charity and equity; in the eyes of Barbara Hepworth as she spoke of sculptured structures: "These things have been our faith"; and the eyes of Trevor Huddleston have shown the struggle beyond the frontiers—and yet filled with light as he spoke of a trumpet given him by 'Satchmo', as Louis Armstrong enabled him to fulfil his dream that his black friends in South Africa should make great and stirring music.

These were some of the things we spoke of, over that lunch. We had our several dreams, knew that some would be fulfilled, some denied. For him the greatest grief was to find the living church regard him and his explorations dangerous heresy. For me it was a like sorrow that at that time, to worthy men—bishops were among them—the ordination of women was an equal menace to the safety of the Church, and were prepared to contemplate the mortal sin of schism, to tear apart the Body of Christ rather than see that Body raised at the altar by hands that were female. In face of such ironies it is sometimes made difficult to believe that 'the gates of Hell shall not prevail'.

It is perhaps fitting to say that those two hours were no sombre interlude and the warmest memory is of the mischievous smile that enlivened any statement of the Bishop's and the spontaneous warmth in the smile of Lord Home as he passed by.

*

Disciplined movement can be a fine thing when it is ordered towards an end which is beauty or reverence. The naively balletic movements of ministers about an altar, celebrant, deacon, sub-deacon moving with grace towards the Word, the censer swung to a rhythm that gives the incense clouds, while the infant 'boat-boy' looks tentatively for his next pace. I knew this movement so economically in Rome when, on a Sunday morning I went from the Torre del Grillo across Hadrian's Forum to one of the baroque churches on the opposite side; one glance from the west door, without my hearing one word of the Latin showed me, from the pattern of the ministers at the altar, exactly where we were in the Mass and one could attach oneself to its rhythm.

They tell me that the same discipline informs the members of a great orchestra. The conductor's beat, their rehearsed knowledge of the score, their own trained competence ensures a well-wrought unity in the performance but—and this is the significant relation to a vested minister at the Eucharist—without wholly subordinating the individual artistry of bow or breath. A friend who is a viola player in one of our great orchestras told me that some performances were 'all technique', a kind of automatic pilot but there were occasions—and, in a smiling aside, Simon Rattle was mentioned—when a performance took fire "and then, though you were one of many dozen players, you took fire too and played like a genius!"

One of the boons of a musical performance on television (and I grant that the sound may not be of the highest quality) is that one participates with greater intimacy than even the front row of the Proms in moments in the performance which you would miss in the concert-hall. One such performance I find unforgetable. Jacqueline Du Pré, Daniel Barenboim and Pinchas Zuckerman were playing one of Beethoven's piano trios. In the slow movement, as the melody was passed from instrument to instrument, it was not the hands or the bow which held my attention but their eyes, the brief smiling glance from player to player as the score wove its tapestry of sound, the individual beauty of tone subdued to perfect harmony by these glances. It was the most perfect intimacy of friendship serving Beethoven's score.

It isn't always so. There was that unhappy evening at the Bolshoi where they were dancing *Romeo and Juliet*. Now here I must declare prejudice and interest. I have had splendid evenings at ballet performances: Kurt Joos and *The Green Table, Petrouschka* both action and staggering music, a Cranko ballet at Covent Garden, or the Polish Ballet in their version of the Faust legend. These were alive, creative steps into the future. But it is a grave pity that 'classical ballet', preserved from the most visually decadent period of the nineteenth-century stage should be the ideal of so many 'balletomanes'. I should happily exchange one performance of *Pineapple Poll* for a season of *Sylphides!* I think that what upsets me is not just the 'tu-tu', it is the frightening precision which only the supreme dancers seem to transcend.

Anyway, there I was at the Bolshoi, and as *Romeo and Juliet* gave its naive copy of Shakespeare's tragedy, so the discipline of the choric dancing seemed to have subdued the dancers to anonymity. At the interval I felt I couldn't bear any more and said to our Cultural Attaché, my host, "I must leave now." He was concerned that I might be ill. "No, I can't stand it; the chorus is like a detachment of the Red Army on manoeuvre." In an agony of concern for the diplomatic niceties he whispered, "For God's sake, keep your voice down!" and I was allowed to return to my hotel alone.

I was to know worse a few years later. As a guest at a Deanery, I was invited to the ceremonial party which was to observe the 'march past' of a military band. We were seated almost on the pavement and in virtual touching distance of the players.

They marched up in silence. Then the lifted baton of the band-master set the music going; after a time the two sections of the band began marching and counter-marching with the dazzling, the appalling precision of all military bands, while the band-master (significant variant from 'conductor', which I'm glad they don't use) struck out his inhuman beat as though mechanically controlled. It was a frightening denial of human dignity, the denial at the core of so much 'military discipline' and a universe removed from the experience of my friend, the young viola player in an orchestra.

"I can't stand this much longer," I whispered.

"Sh!" said the Dean's wife.

*

Preaching in cathedrals is always something of an adventure, even when one is on home territory, in the Welsh cathedrals or Salisbury. There is the regular congregation for whom the noble building is quite simply their parish church, as Exeter was for us for so many years. But then there were the wholly incalculable visitors who might be from any continent or creed. How were they to be met from the pulpit?

I was very aware of this dilemma many years ago when Canon Hood invited me to preach at St Paul's on one of his 'residence Sundays'. I knew from previous visits that this was a huge congregation, most of whose faces would be blurs in the vast spaces of the nave. It happened at that time that 'social awareness' was a general theme in the London theatre and Shelagh Delaney's play, *A Taste of Honey*, was having a good deal of attention and critical acclaim. I thought it might be a good occasion for talking about the moral and theological power of literature and especially dramatic literature. In the course of my closing passages I said something like this:

321

It is indeed more important for priests today, if they are to be sensitive to the spiritual needs of their people, to read *A Taste of Honey* than the meditations of St Teresa of Avila.

The consequences were explosive. I had been told by Frederic Hood that my preacher's fee, a bottle of sherry from, I believe, the Lord Mayor, would be discreetly at the foot of the pulpit steps. Clutching my bottle, I went to unvest, to be confronted by Bishop Wand. Now, I had a great regard for Bishop Wand (as indeed I had for St Teresa) but he was very angry with me for my profound indiscretion. I think he was pacified when I enlarged my argument.

When I returned to Exeter, I found that the sherry was excellent. Some years later I returned to give the St Paul's Lectures in the quiet of the crypt and I made sure each day that I made my way there past the Nicholas Stone effigy of John Donne, the sensitive face so much of his age, and wrapped in his shroud—the very precise mood and devotion of his sonnets on the approach of death.

*

Canterbury was less daunting, for the occasion was the annual service of the Friends of the Cathedral, a more domestic occasion in the choir, with the splendid music more intimately enjoyed. Equally memorable was Victor de Waal's guiding me through the cathedral treasures, which a casual visit would have missed. Then the return to the Deanery for quiet talk at the hearth. It was the period after the Falklands war and Victor, with Alan Webster, the Dean of St Paul's, the Archbishop and Cardinal Hume were deeply disturbed, indeed distressed at the Prime Minister's reluctance to countenance prayers for the Argentinian dead—it was not of course her privilege to say so and the prayers were appropriately said. But it was reported that an ecclesiastic had remarked: "She thinks she's Joan of Arc—and she was burned!" I quietly kept to myself the recollection that Joan was later canonised.

*

After four years of worship in Salisbury and one year spent wholly in residence in the Close, I thought it unlikely that I could fail to judge the temper of the congregation but I'm not sure about the last occasion I preached there. I had returned to Exeter and had resigned my Chancellor's stall and been invited back to preach. It was an unhappy time world-wide: severe conflicts in Africa and not only in the South; bitterness and death rising to their climax in Northern Ireland; a coal-strike which was particularly harrowing in my native South Wales. My text was a favourite quotation of mine: 'Be still then and know that I am God.' I asked the congregation to be very quiet and to listen to three sounds in their inner minds: The sound of weeping in a black farm as their land was devastated; the sound of weeping mothers, Catholic and Protestant in Northern Ireland as they mourned dead sons; most difficult of all for them, would they listen for the creak of timbers in an old coal seam as the tens of thousands of tons of earth bore down on these frail protections for working miners. In the deep silence that followed my plea, I asked for their compassion for all grief.

We processed to the Canons' Vestry and I had just removed my surplice when a tall, very military figure appeared in the doorway.

"How dare you preach a political sermon in this cathedral?"

"How dare I not?" I was as quiet as I could manage, for I hoped I was in the presence not of failed compassion but of the emotion arising from 'invincible ignorance'. I hope I was not mistaken.

*

'The sound of silence' was a new concept for me and I met it for the first time in Fountains Abbey. I had been filming for a religious broadcast and when I thought we had finished, the director, R.T. Brooks shouted, "Quiet everybody" and held a microphone high above his head for a minute. I asked him what he was recording; "The sound of silence," he said, "for those quiet interludes between shots." Then he told me to listen and it was a wonderful silence, so unlike the muffling atmosphere of a studio. There was the distant sound of birds and the bleating of sheep and, within the ruined walls, the almost inaudible breathing of the wind.

Silence had never been quite the same since and when I went to Lichfield Cathedral to preach at the Festival Service, I again used my exhortation, "Be still", I asked for the silence I had known in

323

Fountains Abbey but of course this was quite different: the almost inaudible breathing of the congregation, the faint movements of wood in an ancient building and the almost totally muted sounds of the city outside. I hoped the silence placed a framework about the splendour of the Festival music.

*

After Exeter and Salisbury, and the earlier memories of Llandaff, Manchester Cathedral feels most like 'home', The reasons are many. Manchester and the parish of Salford brought me again in touch with Gwilym Morgan, one of my earliest pupils. When I went to Newport High School I was only a few years older than Gwilym, when he asked me to coach him in logic before he left for the London School of Economics. I don't think I was capable of explaining to him a single syllogism—it wasn't my *métier*—but we became good friends. He graduated, went to Westcott House for ordination training, worked in the Student Christian Movement and then found himself Vicar of Salford, successor to the saintly Peter Green and very soon the friend of L.S. Lowry who had so vividly depicted his parish and its people.

A series at Granada Television brought me still closer to Manchester and to Gwilym and I began to feel that perhaps this was the cultural capital of England. When he became a Canon at the Cathedral, I was invited to preach at the 1971 Arts Festival which celebrated the five hundred and fiftieth anniversary of the Cathedral. I preached a number of times later and was also invited to mount a small exhibition of sculptures in one of the chapels.

This was the background to a piece of work which brought me once more to collaborate with Gwilym Morgan. The Archbishops had set up a Commission to review the Church of England's machinery for Faculty Jurisdiction. A 'Faculty', granted by the Chancellor of a Diocese, or in less important cases, by an Archdeacon, is necessary if a church is to be altered in any way or to have a significant object, furnishing or art, acquired or removed. The Commission had therefore a number of ecclesiastical judges, registrars, Bishops, Deans, Archdeacons and Chairmen of Diocesan Advisory Committees and the number of twenty or so which constituted the final committee included Members of Parliament and learned lay-men.

Canon Gwilym Morgan, Chairman of the Manchester Advisory Committee suggested that I be appointed, not on grounds that I was a priest and an academic but as a sculptor. In the event I was the only member who practised any art. The Bishop of Chichester (Dr Eric Kemp, who brought back for me memories of Pusey House) was our chairman and he steered us through an arduous four years.

There were pressures. Many of the conservation groups disliked the exemption that the Church enjoyed from the controls on secular buildings and we were fortunate in having Marcus Binney co-opted, since he continues to be one of the most powerful and well-informed of the conservationists while Martin Caroe, the architect, Dame Betty Ridley and Patrick Cormack, M.P. ensured another range of expertise. The two lawyers, Judge Michael Goodman and Professor Phillips, Chancellor of Winchester Diocese, kept us to the legal verities, while Ashley Barker of the Historic Buildings Commission, and Peter Burman of the Council for the Care of Churches had the expertise to enable us to weather the onslaught of the conservationists while adopting their appropriate wisdom. It was a fascinating and worthwhile time, of over four years.

But gradually I grew restive. It was all very well to reform and regulate but what, in the sphere of art were we to regulate? And was 'regulation' a creative guide for the Church's attitude to the artist? There were many hours of legal nicety in which I longed to chant Roy Campbell's couplet:

> They use the snaffle and the bit all right,
> But where's the bloody horse?

After I had made a refined version of that protest the Chairman suggested that I set up a sub-committee of artists to explore this relationship of Church and Art. It was, I think, very successful and we produced an Appendix, 'The Church and the Arts' to the report of the Commission, *The Continuing Care of Churches and Cathedrals*. Almost without exception the artists I invited to this committee responded positively and the following attended our discussions:

325

Mark Angus (stained glass artist), Anthony Green, R.A. (painter), Mrs Renate Melinsky (embroidery), Michael Reardon (architect) and Carel Weight, R.A. (painter).

Many of these artists had shown at the exhibition, 'Prophecy and Vision', organised by a committee of Anglicans and Roman Catholics, with the Arnolfini Gallery and the Bristol Municipal Art Galleries. Its catalogue ranged over the wide extent of art devoted to the work of the Church and we were glad to adopt a passage from an essay in that catalogue as a key to our own work on the committee; the Bishop of Bristol, Dr Tinsley wrote:

> 'The best theology is that which points away from itself and in the case of Christian theology this means having the 'signful', indirect, ambiguous, parabolic, ironic tone of the Incarnation itself. And for this, a more adequate theology may well be that expressed in a concrete but non-verbal way in the arts.'

The members of the committee were both realistic in their expectations from these declared aims and expressed some warnings. Anthony Green told us bluntly that he found the contemporary church no longer a serious patron of the arts and we remembered as he spoke that his large 'Crucifixion' was one of the most remarkable works in the 'Prophecy and Vision' exhibition. Carel Weight told us that young artists were perhaps "largely indifferent to the Church institution but with a deep sense of 'the spiritual'" and that we must expect a slow growth of changed attitudes on both sides. It was all very exhilarating and we were quietly optimistic as we faced the Commission with our findings and the surprisingly warm press conference at the publication of the Report. I felt personally heartened that this work endorsed so much that I had long pleaded for.

*

It has been my happy fortune to have worshipped and preached at so many of these great storehouses of beauty 'where prayer has been valid', the cathedrals which have gathered, sometimes with careful deliberation, sometimes seemingly in fits of absent-

326

mindedness, some of the greatest art in our island. Their roll-call is for me so moving; St Davids, St Paul's, Chichester, Chester and Winchester; Portsmouth, Coventry and Llandaff, my 'home'. The casual or even the earnest visitor may think of them as sacred museums or places where Evensong rivals a concert-hall in beauty, and in a way they are right. But my relatively brief time on the Close Chapter at Salisbury taught me that the protection of this divine beauty is a difficult, sometimes tiresome duty. So often we found on our agenda repairs to the Bishop of Sherborne's garden-wall, the concern for the foundations or the spire, with reverberations from William Golding's novel ever in our ears. Deans and Chapters are a special breed—I hope I say that now with proper and objective humility!—and they and the fabric they cherish deserve our concern.

9

SEEKING AN IKON

From the beauty of Eluned Brown's Edinburgh home in Gloucester Place, I learned the peculiar enchantment of the 'New Town', that astonishing architectural project which spanned the width of the city and a century of its history, from Georgian to Victorian—and Gloucester Place is at its centre, linking Royal Circus with the Moray Place complex of development. The spacious rooms and delicate plaster-work make a happy context for art of any time, including our own.

Edinburgh itself is a place in which to find oneself, to gather the verities, from the primitive Salisbury Crags at Arthur's seat, through the subdued menace of the Castle, to the tough grace of the great schools, Royal High School, Heriot's and the others, which speak of a Scottish Enlightenment when English schools and universities had not awakened from their sombre lethargy. And there is a witty incongruity within the Renaissance University that the Arts building takes its name from the sceptical David Hume. 'Athens of the North' Edinburgh may be, but it rests its power on a nationhood of learning which made St Andrews, Aberdeen and Glasgow the appropriate mediaeval forebears of James VI's 'tounis college'.

To a Welshman, though proud of the analogy of our four university colleges spanning Wales and built 'on the pennies of the poor' as English education was just shaking itself out of its Augustan torpor, there is still a profound sadness in the analogy. For the moment after Bosworth, which saw the Welsh dynasty of the Tudors on the English throne, saw also the departure of our aristocracy and a great number of our gentry to London. The enrichment of the English capital by the Cecils (Seisyllt), the Herberts, the Middletons, the Donnes, saw also the impoverishment of patronage in Wales. There were of course splendid exceptions, and Henry Vaughan of Llansantffraed was the seventeenth-century harbinger of the eighteenth-century Welsh enlightenment, led by the squires and the country clergy.

But patronage had indeed been lost, in a way that the accession of 'James the Sixth and First' had not brought about for Scotland. Gloucester Place is on Heriot land and George Heriot was jeweller to James VI; and when he succeeded Elizabeth and brought the Welsh dynasty to its end, while many Scottish nobles came south, a sufficiency remained to be the patrons of arts and letters to our own day—a tradition which the Scottish Arts Council has nobly inherited.

*

Edinburgh has been for us the centre of exploration: to the Lammermuirs and the Borders, to the strange sophistication of Glen Kiln in Galloway, with Henry Moore's 'King and Queen' presiding silently over their kingdom and above them, the 'Glenkiln Cross' in half-pagan benediction, with Epstein's 'John the Baptist' in gaunt rhetoric; to the Fife fishing villages, their beauty wholly derived from their resolute struggle with the Scottish seaways and beyond; to Crieff and the Sma' Glen; to Pitlochry and on to 'The Queen's View' with Schiehallion nobly dominant; to Sutherland and the gentle beauty of waterlilies on a lochan; and to Ullapool glowing in the falling light of sunset when first seen from the road to the south.

The most majestic of these explorations was, happily, the most recent. The road by way of Lochearnhead, Rannoch Moor and Glencoe was long familiar but this time it was to the land below Skye, the land we called 'Herman country', for here in 1942, Josef Herman had drawn and painted the fishermen of Arisaig and Mallaig and watched the Cuillins—as we did—form and transform themselves in the mist. Hence the Burkean sublime of the drive past the lost slate quarries of Ballachulish through Fort William and the dramatic road to Arisaig. Dawn saw Eigg in its cloud cover, and at the return journey, through Strontian to the pass of Glencoe again, a gap in the forest showed us on the far horizon, the heights of the Cuillins, their nobility undiminished by the distance.

Several years before, we had taken a long detour through Aviemore and then westward, to reach Skye and the home of Sorley

Maclean, gazing out to his birthplace on Raasay. There the soft English was overlaid with the sound of Gaelic and his wife Rene's gentle voice, and we heard the springs of his poetry as he recounted the annals of his childhood and his young manhood, as the Gaelic became more consciously cherished. It sent me back to my memories of Saunders Lewis, bitterly protecting his Welsh inheritance; and one honoured Scotland for its celebration into mature age of its Gaelic 'poet laureate'.

*

A meal at Gloucester Place brought Sorley's friend, Norman MacCaig, to give 'presence' to his poetry, which I already knew and admired. (It was a triumph later to be able to publish his 'manuscript poems' at the Rougemont Press). The ironic fastidious-ness of his talk of poetry was matched by the nice discrimination of his leading us into the secrets of 'the malts'; now a world of distinctions on the palate was opened to me; and as he talked one tasted the flavour of Glenfiddich and Glen Morangie and knew the under-tang of the peaty streams as we savoured in his words the flavour of Islay. There was the notable moment, as Eluned Brown gave us our wee drams, when, in reply to my question, "Should the drink always be neat?" Norman said—without a flicker of a smile—"Always; unless you're fortunate enough to be able to add one wee teaspoonful of the cool water from the burn that neighbours the making of the whisky." Since this would, in the nature of things, be a rare experience, I have been content as yet, not to have added it to the savour of Scotland and her noble malts.

*

Our search for Pictish inscribed stones became mingled in my mind with a search for Scottish stone suitable for my sculpture. A chance visit to a shop in Dunkeld showed me the glory of GlenTilt marble debased to the status of ash-trays and miniature versions of curling-stones. I wondered where I could see the real, the raw stone: "Try Watty Weir in his workshop at the end of the town." So began a happy friendship. Watty was a fine craftsman who knew every quirk of the Glen Tilt stone and he gave me a piece or two to try my hand. It was superb material, a fine, consistently-grained marble and of rich beauty in its bands of blue-green oxidising, which traversed the white crystalline structure; it demanded therefore the greatest of austere simplicity in the sculpting. I have before me as I write a small obelisk which takes me immediately back to the kindly skills of Watty Weir and his invitation to meet me in Glen Tilt itself.

It is a beautiful valley leading eastward from the road near Blair Atholl. There are very rough stretches of road which did the car no good and we somehow missed Watty. But he had left for me by the roadside a little heap of stones which his eye had told him were unsuitable for his lathe-turning but possibly attractive for my carving—as indeed they were —and a little further search showed as the 'quarry' which turned out to be bands of rock in the river bank. The little cache sufficed for at least ten pieces of sculpture, one of which I finished just last year, blessing Watty as I did so. On our return to Dunkeld this autumn, I found to my pleasure that Watty, whom we had visited once in his retirement, still lived below Birnam Wood. I hope we may meet again.

A little further afield was a stone as rich as Glen Tilt but so different in its beauty. Some miles above Aberdeen, on the Banffshire coast, is the town of Portsoy, where the 'marble' is found in great masses on the sea-shore. It is not in fact a marble but a variety of serpentine, less colour-textured than its Cornish cousin and marginally softer to carve. You can rarely bear down on it with chisels or claws but gently lead it into shape with rasp, riffler, file and the ball of your thumb for final polishing. Careful search among the rocks will reveal the two main colour textures, the rich and uniform ox-blood-red boulders and the mainly green variety, delicately flushed with red and veined with inclusions of white or creamy talc. These establish a pattern in some simple sculptures, the surface of which tend almost to an abstract painting. Again, like Glen Tilt marble, the Portsoy demands a simple dignity in the fashioning and I always remember with gratitude that it was a torso in this stone which gave me my first approving gesture from Barbara Hepworth: "Yes, that'll do"!

Inland from Portsoy are the Coreen Hills and here we found an abandoned quarry of Coreen 'marble', a patterned stone of light and dark greys, sometimes ranging from a clear white to a shining ebony-black. This is a harder stone than Portsoy but once more demands the same simplicity in the carving.

*

For many years I had admired and been bewildered by the texture and variety of the poems of Christopher Grieve ('Hugh MacDiarmid'), whom David Daiches has called "the most explosive force in Scottish literature" and who could fail to agree? The early lyrics and then 'The Drunk Man looks at the Thistle' and 'On a Raised Beach' had all captured my imagination, but there were cryptic areas. First, there was the varied learning, as great as Ezra Pound's, and all marshalled in the poetry with the uncompromising assumption that the reader shared this learned terrain and could move in it with the familiar ease of the poet—Basil Bunting showed the same disconcerting courtesy. And there was the language of at least half the poems, the Scots which was more available than Sorley Maclean's Gaelic but still demanding recourse to a word-list. Was it indeed a true language of poetry or a wilful invention of the poet to confound the reader—especially if he should be English? And there was the dour Southern-ness and the communist credo. And there were the photographs, the portraits and the cartoons: here was the image of a man, the mane of hair, the brilliant eyes and firm mouth; was he even approachable?

Yet it seemed a waste of opportunity, that here he was at 'Brownsbank by Biggar', just twenty miles from Edinburgh, and we had not met. Before I telephoned him I determined not to conceal my disqualifications: a manifestly *English* name, a professor of English and an Anglican priest—an English 'Piskie'! could there be a greater bar to friendship? I telephoned and a gently courteous voice invited us down for a visit to the Lanarkshire home. This was the final conundrum: whence the frequent poetic violence when this voice declared a total courtesy in the softest of Border tones?

We arrived at Brownsbank in time to take him and his wife, Valda Trevlyn out to a hotel in Biggar for lunch. Christopher Grieve had

333

already learned in our little talk on arrival that I was Welsh (as Valda Trevlyn was Cornish) and so I was at least absolved from the taint of English blood. They were both well-known at the Hartree Hotel and on that day we had the dining-room to ourselves, for the other guests were out shooting or fishing.

Christopher was relatively silent, for already he was beginning to feel the effects of the cancer which in a very few years was to cause his death. But Valda was in her most impish mood and it seems to me now that perhaps the three of us were on a kind of trial of friendship. As the food was served, Valda related an exceedingly bawdy incident from a holiday of theirs. It was a long narrative which would have given great pleasure to the Wife of Bath and as the suspiciously numerous succession of waitresses returned to the kitchen, peels of delighted laughter came through the opened door. Christopher watched us all, with a pleased smile at Valda's naughtiness, and with a twinkling exploration of our reactions. We evidently passed the test.

We returned to Brownsbank; Christopher came wholly to life, at once both our gentle and very courteous host and the 'Hugh MacDiarmid' of his writings, and the talk was animated: current poetry, Welsh and Scottish Nationalism, friends we had in common, their writings and aspirations, and especially Ezra Pound, whom he was to visit at Venice, where Valda took a remarkable photographic portrait of them, Pound, the frail and silent man of his last years and Christopher, alert and compassionate as he walked with E.P.'s arm held in his.

So it was at all subsequent meetings. Almost all visits to Scotland were the occasion for a meal at the Hartree and a further hour or so of splendid talk. At the heart of it was a new revelation of friendship. Here was I, a stranger, a clergyman of an alien church and clearly from my expressed attitudes, no left-wing believer. I was surely everything—but for my Welsh blood—that would alienate me from Christopher Grieve. True, he wholly accepted my claim that the greatest poem in early Welsh, *Y Gododdin*, was written within recital distance of Edinburgh (Caeredin to the Welsh). Indeed, in all the few years I was to enjoy his friendship, we were in accord. The moments with him in Brownsbank, sharing poetry, a dram apiece of malt at the hearth and a companionable silence if his troubled throat brought fatigue, were wholly and serenely happy.

At just that time (1975) I published my first book of poems, *Breaking the Code*. I had read the echoing phrase throughout his verse, "this is the kind of poetry I want", and I sent him a copy of the book with some trepidation. I knew that no poem of mine reached the quality of the verse that my son Paul was now writing (and some of which Christopher had seen and admired) but I felt that it did not befit our relationship that I should refrain from sending him the poems.

On 2 February 1976 I had my reply, in the longest letter I had received from him:

> I have read and re-read your poems with great interest. This is the kind of poetry I want—a poetry that, read between the lines, discloses a microstructure of learning and of knowledge of the various arts. I have little use for 'woodnotes wild'. A huge proportion of published verse today emanates from the illiterate or near-illiterate, and is characterised by emotion without intellect, fancy without imagination, and a determination to reduce the whole thing to a level of mere entertainment. Ex nihil, nihil fit.
>
> . . .Professor Fowler [Regius Professor in the University of Edinburgh] came here yesterday and we went to the Hartree Hotel for lunch. Like you, he is far too diffident about his own work and has only just published a first volume of his poems—at 45.
>
> That you should only now publish your first volume of poems gives me furiously to think. I have published so many. One of the advantages of publishing a selection so late in life must be that the whole landscape of one's output is there and one can choose only what seems the best—and they reinforce each other and make the book a real artistic unity. In your case this is further greatly strengthened by the illustrations. The whole is a very treasurable book indeed . . .

Professor Fowler is of course head of the Department and Miss Lynne Brown is one of its staff. Professor Fowler spoke very highly of her.

> All being well with my health ... I have accepted the invitation to read my poems at Warwick University ... Your son has been extremely kind in making the necessary arrangements ...
>
> Two of the other poets reading are old friends of mine—Basil Bunting and George MacBeth.

His reading was a great success and, as I expected, Paul and he got on extremely well together.

In 1958 Christopher Grieve had been presented with the Andrew Fletcher of Saltoun Medal, 'for services to Scotland'. He was intrigued to know that the name 'Andrew Fletcher' meant more to me than the renowned legal figure; for, some twelve generations on, his descendant, also Andrew Fletcher of Saltoun, had inherited from his aunt the Margam Estate and so had become my father's laird—a strange accident of time.

We met a few times again but he was now gravely ill and talk had to be sparing; in September 1978 he died; Valda still comes with us to the Hartree Hotel, a most valued and generous friend.

At one of our meals I asked Valda how she had come to write her own very fine poems—was it daunting to have his powerful presence? "I think they began precisely as a challenge and I believe he approved."

*

Now, some years later, as I revise these pages for publication, I have sadly to recall that Valda died on the day we had planned yet another meal together. As the three of us stood in the burial-ground above Langholm on 29 May, it was difficult to believe that two such vivid people were now silenced.

*

Duns Scotus teased our minds. Where *had* he been born? We had gone where all the guide-books had instructed us and in particular had looked hard at Maxton, so confidently declared his birthplace but without real satisfaction. And it mattered to me. This great

336

mind and imagination held all the subtlety of mediaeval thinking; for me he was a more significant figure even than those towering minds of the Scottish Enlightenment and I really wanted a quiet moment at the place of his origins.

Then why not do the obvious?—look at Duns, the natural place for his upbringing, even if scorned by the guide-books, and as was to be expected, there was the evidence. It was found in the least likely of places. Duns was proud of its most famous citizen, Jim Clark, the motor-racing driver, in whose honour there was a 'Jim Clark Memorial Room' to hold the phenomenal number of Grand Prix and other trophies he had won. There, apparently, was the place to inquire about the other notable child of Duns. We were successful. John Duns Scotus had been born at Duns Castle and if we went there we would see his memorial.

We drove the short distance through the comely town and into the grounds of the castle. There, on the well-kept lawn was a pillar built of local stone, with an inscription which read:

JOHN DUNS SCOTUS
The Subtle Doctor
And Member of the Franciscan Order
Was Born on this Site in 1266
Wherever his Distinguished Name is Uttered
He sheds lustre on Duns and Scotland
The Town and Land which Bore Him

———————

Erected by the Franciscan Order
On the Seventh Centenary of His Birth
September 1966

———————

This seemed validation enough and we left the place contented.

*

It was a natural transition from the Franciscan 'Subtle Doctor' to the Church of Old St Paul's in Jeffrey Street, Edinburgh. It is a church wholly after my heart, spacious, quiet and with varying patterns of light revealing a noble sanctuary, approached by four marble steps for the Gospels and then three for the Trinity. Discreet incense marks the high moments of the Eucharist and in every way it maintains its great tradition, sanctifying the cliff-like buildings of the Old Town.

The present building is modern (c. 1839—and progressively until 1905) and is built on the site of the wool-store occupied by the Non-Juror congregation expelled from the High Kirk of St Giles in 1689.

The Episcopal Church in Scotland shares with its sister Church in Wales, (and not with their other sister the Church of England) the advantages of Disestablishment. They have also (and again unlike England) the rich inheritance of the Celtic Church and its saints. I confess I cherish the moment in the Governing Body of the Church in Wales, when its Archbishop, Glyn Simon, welcomed a distinguished visitor, "our younger Brother of Canterbury."

So it was in Old St Paul's on the fourteenth Sunday after Pentecost that we knew the stately order of catholic liturgy with the witty freedom of the celebrant, Richard Holloway, Bishop of Edinburgh. His sermon—on the distinction between Order and Freedom and their necessary union—had wisdom and the power of a glancing wit which enabled him thus to characterise the Puritan's God: "The only thing that really gets up His nose is if we should be *enjoying* ourselves!" Immediately following his sermon he was commissioning twelve 'Pastoral Assistants' gravely greeting each one and presenting each with a silver pyx in which they would take the consecrated bread to the sick. When he had presented the last, he turned with an impish smile to the Rector at his side: "That must have been terribly expensive," he said and in one sentence at the heart of solemn worship he had reminded those of us who heard that the mundane had to be reckoned with and sanctified.

The service ('Jackson in G') was splendidly sung and the Communion hymn, 'Ubi Caritas' will remain in my ears:

> Ubi Caritas et Amor,
> Ubi Caritas, Deus ibi est

*

338

The abortive first search for Duns Scotus had taken us vainly to Maxton—and yet by no means wholly in vain. Peering down every opening, we saw at one of them a plain cross which seemed to call for investigation. As we approached it, a row of cottages seemed to end in a kind of studio and when I saw the massed variety of stone alongside, "a sculptor!" I said. "Of course," said Lynne with pleasure, "It *must* be Jake Harvey!" It was, with Penny his wife and the three engaging children, Arabella, Ewan and Charlotte. When we had last seen Valda Grieve we had spoken of Jake Harvey and his brilliantly imaginative memorial sculpture for Hugh MacDiarmid. Now we had the opportunity for talk and exploration.

Penny had been a professional singer, a fact reflected in Arabella's violin playing. Charlotte in a surprisingly short time, presented all three of us with crayon drawings, while Ewan shyly unwrapped his birthday gift for his mother—a wonderfully tranquil and happy family.

We were soon immersed in comparative sculpture techniques and Jake revealed an astonishing range both of subject and material. I had long admired the MacDiarmid Memorial sculpture—an open book with inset motifs derived from MacDiarmid poems. Yet, as the maquette and the small studies had shown when we first saw them at the Talbot Rice Gallery in the University, they are not 'literary' but a translation of Christopher Grieve's temper and range of reference into sculptural terms; and the lithograph derived from the finished work (Lynne has the first copy of the edition—a familiar object) has the same tough quality.

In the converted Maxton Cross Cottages in which they live there were sufficient pieces from the past to allow me to follow each step—a powerful head in cast iron, with polished planes telling against the rough textures of the cast; a portrait of Penny in forged metal and yet retaining all feminine grace and a 'Slumbering Head' in welded sheet steel and 'found objects'—largely derelict tools, spanners and the like—which again, with great wit, played off the starkness of metal against the drowsy repose of the head.

Current work in the studio, both stone and metal, showed these witty incongruities still further: a commission to celebrate Coal-Mining which now stands in Newcraighall precinct, in which suggestions of a miner's life, his labour and his recreation, all

339

peered from the surfaces of the massive pillar; at that moment it was a compassable maquette; finished, it stands nine feet high, in dark granite with the contrasting textures of rough-tooled and highly polished surfaces.

And there was the moving allegory of the bridge assailed by flood—but each piece demands the space that I hope future visits will spare me in time. We had said we would spend a half-hour with them, in order to conserve Jake's working time. We left after a generous two hours, with smiling farewells and Arabella's rendering of a Scottish dance to see us on our way, the bagpipe drone palpable in her playing.

We blessed the sainted Duns Scotus, that he had led us again to an unexpected and happy goal.

*

On this latest visit to Scotland, Duns Scotus would not leave us in peace. In order to recall the voice of Christopher Grieve I was re-reading his autobiography, *Lucky Poet* and should not have been surprised—though I was—to meet this passage:

> I am constantly on the *qui vive* for every trace of that individuality which Duns Scotus called *haecceitas* and the *distinctiu formalis a parte rei*, agreeable to his love of objects between which minute distinctions can be made—and, further, the concrete individuality of each object known in at least a confused way intuitively; every body having not merely a material form but also a vital form; a special element of it being in its activity and movement.

A reading of *On a Raised Beach* alone should have alerted me to the fact that Duns Scotus would have been the philosopher after Hugh MacDiarmid's heart and here was confirmation:

> I cannot get rid of a certain participation in—or no great interest in and sympathy with—such Scotist ideas, since I myself am always so intent on 'the slightest integrity'.

340

A very different poet, Gerard Manley Hopkins, was similarly drawn to Duns Scotus and for the same reason as MacDiarmid's, the intense *particularity*, the 'Thisness', the *haecceitas* of things. As Hopkins writes in his journal in July 1871:

> At this time I had first begun to get hold of the copy of Duns Scotus on the Sentences (of Peter Lombard) in the Baddeley library and was flush with a new stroke of enthusiasm. It may come to nothing or it may be a mercy from God. But just then when I took in any inscape of the sky or sea, I thought of Scotus.

Hopkins was to write to Bridges that "I care for him more even than Aristotle" and, meditating in a poem devoted to Scotus, he is for him the philosopher "who of all men most sways my spirits to peace." A remarkable conjunction, the rebel MacDiarmid and the Jesuit Hopkins at one in Scotism.

*

Most evenings in Gloucester Place end with at least one string quartet, Haydn, Mozart or Beethoven but the visit to Edinburgh which had united the searches for 'Herman's islands', the birthplace of Scotus and the inscribed Pictish stones, seemed to demand something of even greater sublimity. And so the *Missa Solemnis*, the bold affirmation of four-fold 'Credo, Credo; Credo, Credo', when even Bach had been willing to subject himself to the ageless plainchant melody, 'credo in unum Deum'; and the beseeching 'Dona nobis pacem' which Beethoven seems reluctant to leave, as 'Amen' is given all conceivable complexity. It seemed, somehow, 'satisfactory'.

*

Windsor and Eton carried the happiest memories for my family. When Cumberland'Lodge in Windsor Great Park was opened as a kind of Western European University centre under the brilliant direction of Sir Walter Moberly, I was fortunate to be one of the regular lecturers and to take young colleagues and undergraduates from Cardiff to the vacation courses; there we met our fellows from Germany and France and the best minds in this country—there was an especially moving discussion with the senior Eastern Orthodox Archbishop, Anthony Bloom who brought a depth of spirituality to the austere discussion of theology.

Where Walter Moberly sat at table there was always laughter. His wit had a sly incisiveness that cut deep into any pretentions. When he knew that I was going for a visit to the University of Chicago, he advised me: "You must go to the University Chapel, the Rockefeller Chapel. I was there at its opening and Mr Rockefeller made a stirring speech, with this peroration: 'I have intended this chapel as a counter-blast to twentieth-century materialism. In fact it is a six-million-dollar attack on twentieth-century materialism.'"

The whole atmosphere was that of a highly intelligent and articulate household and domestic occasions were never forgotten. One Easter party saw my daughter Christina's birthday and the formidable and kind-hearted Amy Buller set up a birthday-party which embraced the whole house. During these visits, when Sir Walter realised that Paul had a good singing voice, he suggested that he should enter for a scholarship at the Royal Chapel, St George's at Windsor. Paul and I stayed with the Moberlys in their home in the Castle and Paul was duly tested. At the end Sir William Harris who directed the music of the Chapel, told me that Paul had no scholarship that year, for there was only one vacancy, but we were to be sure to come up the following time, for he had been the 'runner-up'. And would we like to stay for Evensong? To my great pleasure Paul agreed eagerly and we went into the choir. The anthem was Byrd's 'Ave Verum Corpus' and when the glorious music was ended, Paul whispered to me, "Wasn't that wonderful? I'm not surprised I didn't get the scholarship." I determined that if that was his temper, we would certainly return and indeed he was successful. There followed four golden years in which I believe he learned about five hundred anthems, from Palestrina to Britten, a splendid musical education.

I was wandering down Eton High Street one Saturday, waiting to take Paul out to tea. I saw Sir William Harris and, introducing myself as Paul's father, asked if he were learning his music well. "Oh, no!" was his reply. "They don't *learn* music here; they catch it, like measles." I was so glad Paul had not been innoculated against it.

There were many royal occasions, Garter Ceremonies and the Queen's Christmas lunch for the choir, in the castle; Paul bit into a puff-pastry 'cornet', to find that the 'cream' was in fact horse-radish sauce. I can't believe Her Majesty intended this to happen.

The Garter Ceremonies were very fine but had their lighter aspects in Paul's opinion. "Poor Mr Churchill! He looked so tired and fell asleep in the anthem!" and of Anthony Eden, with a little acerbity: "I wish he wouldn't use Brylcream."

*

Many years later, in 1981, I was invited to address the Head-masters' Conference at Christchurch, Oxford. I was making my customary plea for fostering the fine arts in our community and especially the schools, and my talk was received courteously by the headmasters but caused not a tremor among the Press. Then, during the discussion, one of the headmasters asked me about banal and damaging influences in our culture and after some consideration and more questions, I concluded, in my intense dislike and indeed fear of our so-called 'Pop Culture', "The true pornographers are the disc-jockeys." The Press woke to action and demanded an interview which deprived me of my coffee and for the next thirty-six hours my telephone did not stop ringing. In answer to questions I explained that the banality of 'pop'-singing carried with it a devalution of words and emotions and in its slick response to mass emotion, deprived the adolescent of the means of true response at any level but the most shallow.

I then turned the attack and asked, "now, why, when I was talking of serious matters did you pay no attention, and then sprang to life when I mentioned pop-stars and disc-jockeys?" I was amazed when one of the most respected of the education correspondents replied: "We enjoyed your lecture very much but there was no story in it; we have to satisfy the editor and *this* has a story."

Indeed it had! *The Times* gave me, I seem to remember, two half-columns, and Herbert Kretzmer in *The Daily Mail* devoted three-quarters of a page, under the double heading:

343

and coming to the conclusion:

> Songs are mirrors. You cannot crack or break a mirror and then delude yourself that the nastiness that used to be reflected in it no longer exists.

All the papers, even in the United States, as my friends told me in amused alarm, carried some report—not all as thoughtful as Kretzmer—and I was telephoned by a B.B.C. disc-jockey with the plaintive question: "Do you *really* think we're pornographers?" and I took a little time to explain why I did. I also hinted at my fear of pop's connection with drugs and the 'hard sell' which produced so many hundreds of expensive hours of dreary music on radio and television. He must have taken me seriously, for a friend told me later (though I don't know why he should have been listening!) that every morning for quite a time afterwards this disc-jockey put on a record with the introduction: "This is specially for you, Professor Merchant." There are so many kinds of fame.

Out of the H.M.C. there came a large number of invitations, to speak at Radley, Malvern, Shrewsbury, Repton, and most movingly, for an old man like me, an invitation from Michael Mavor at Gordonstoun, to teach there for a whole year, with facilities for my writing and sculpting. I explained that this was difficult for a man then of nearly seventy but I must confess that after four days in the school I found his company so stimulating and perceptive that I wished I were a lot younger.

Happiest of all the invitations had come before this from Eric Anderson. I had preached and lectured for him at Shrewsbury and now that he was Head Master of Eton College, the invitation was equally warm and welcome. There followed many years of going quite frequently for a few days' teaching, preaching and hours of work and talk in the Drawing Schools. I was at first the guest of Eric and Poppy Anderson in the Head Master's house but one St David's Day, when some Welsh boys had been invited to breakfast to celebrate our Saint, I hurried too fast down the stairs, missed the bottom step and broke three ribs (as I found when I got to my Leamington G.P.) against the ancient door-jamb. Conversation at breakfast even with young Gladstone about the Church in Wales, was a little forced on my part. Eric thought it sensible after that not to subject me to the stairs and I became on subsequent visits the guest of John Booth, the head of Art and his wife Joan. In between seminars, usually on Shakespeare, I then spent full days in the Drawing Schools, with John Booth and Bob Catchpole (in charge of sculpture). This was a singular piece of good fortune on one of the visits. I had the commission to produce my 'Growing Form' in aluminium for Burton-on-Trent and I was talking over the problem of building the pattern for casting. My solution was wooden rods, balsa wood and plaster but Bob countered with "Why not welded rods as an armature?" I said that I knew nothing of welding. "It will take an hour or so for me to teach you" and so it came about that while I was able to go happily to my friends in Leamington to get the hard and tricky work done, I could still say the dinner-stopping line "Oh yes, I learnt my welding at Eton." It never fails.

In 1983 Eric Anderson invited me to give the Lyttelton Lectures. This was an excellent chance to pull my ideas together, those arguments which Chicago and Exeter had explored, in theology and literature. Now, with four lectures in conditions which allowed me to use music and projected slides, I was able to carry the argument much further. Two aspects of the lectures which I had not been able to explore in Exeter or Chicago, now gave me especial pleasure. I had been arguing, from my love of the string quartet, that (as in the last quartets of Beethoven) this spare but flexible form could pursue insights which words were inadequate to express. Beethoven's Opus 131 was an obvious, but daunting subject for this argument and in the event I played them Smetana's E minor quartet, written in December 1876 and called 'From my Life'. In this work Smetana is moving towards the tragic expression of his increasing deafness, and he himself described it as expressing "the whirlwind of music in the head of one who has lost his hearing. Nobody has a notion how musical ideas fly about in the brain of a deaf man." The first movement is turbulent and agonised, set against the bitterly jaunty dance of the second movement—which always seems to me to anticipate the sardonic wit of Kurt Weil. The meditative resignation of the third movement is only a pause before the fourth movement comes to its climax of suffering in the screaming harmonic of the first violin which echoes the intolerable sound in Smetana's ears at the onset of deafness. It is all so very poignantly different from the temper of *Ma Vlast* in which Smetana celebrates the glories of his Czech homeland and "everything is remembered in a hymn of praise."

In this last paragraph, words have tried to 'paraphrase' the music; it is a hard fact that "I gotta use words when I talk to you." But, if we know the one external fact that Smetana's deafness was the kind that involved agonising sounds in the ears, then the music speaks even more strongly than any paraphrase can approach.

A similar experience came with my exploration of one of Henry Moore's greatest works, *Nuclear Energy*, set in the University of Chicago on the site of the successful experiments with atomic fission. It was in my path each day as I went to and from my classes and after all the years it never ceased to confound me by its ambiguity. It is at first a forbidding work, its skull-form repelling the observer. Moreover the dome of the skull is very like the mushroom-cloud of atomic explosion and the entrances to its central cavity lead one back to Moore's *Helmet* sculptures. Yet in Moore's own analysis of its impulse and force, the sequence of ideas is subtly different. Commenting on the skull shape he says, "I meant the sculpture to suggest that it was man's cerebral activity that brought the nuclear energy discovery" and later he says, "The lower half of the sculpture has something architectural about it, like the arches of a cathedral . . . suggesting the valuable and helpful side the splitting of the atom could have for mankind." Then, as we reconcile our emotions to these ideas, he adds, almost as an aside, "It can also suggest the mushroom cloud, the destructive element of the atom bomb." This bleak conclusion to the sculptor's analysis adds the final ambiguity to this complex sculpture, a work which expresses—without words—the tragic dilemmas inherent in any revolutionary scientific discovery. Faustian curiosity is weighed against the fundamental demands of humane society.

These evenings were a rich experience for me and the courteously attentive responses of the large audience gave for me the assurance—I hope not too ill-judged—that this was perhaps the best and happiest teaching I had reached. It was so good, in the quiet little party in the Head Master's house to meet the current Lyttelton who has maintained the unbroken relation of his family with Eton and to be thankful for Humphrey Lyttelton, whose playing exorcises the unseemly noises of jazz's uncouth little sister, the sounds of 'pop'.

*

Eton College library has one of the richest collection of mediaeval and renaissance works in the country and it was an imaginative conception to begin building a collection of nineteenth- and twentieth-century works of comparable riches to stand alongside the earlier works. Eton was fortunate at the time of this iniative that the Head Master, Dr Eric Anderson is a specialist in the works of Walter Scott and that Michael Meredith, a seasoned bibliographer and chairman of the Browning Society should have been given charge of the new venture as its librarian.

There were already valuable materials from the Romantics and Victorians and, apart from rare books to be bought or received as gifts, it was determined that among the main additions to this School Library should be the manuscripts, typescripts and proofs of works by living writers. This has the manifest advantage of providing the possibility of consultation with the authors in setting up and cataloguing the papers and published books. I have to confess that great as has been my pleasure in the days of teaching there in the past dozen years and giving the Lyttelton Lectures, equally happy has been the sorting out with Michael Meredith of my own papers and books.

May 1990 sees the five hundred and fiftieth anniversary of the founding of Eton College by which time it is hoped that the School Library will be substantially in place.

*

The process of printing and publishing a novel sets a distance between the book and its author; *Jeshua* was finished in October 1985 and a re-reading recently brought into focus elements in it both of conscious study and borrowing over the years and of half-conscious echoes from experiences that were not in the fore-front of my mind during the writing. The novel itself, brooded over for some forty years, had a clear, personal purpose. I may put it obliquely: I have always enjoyed and admired the intellectual force of theological argument, whether in the sharp exchanges of Christological debate in the third century or in the equally sharp, frequently acrid debates in our own day, as theological truths are pursued in many different arenas. The related doctrines, of the Trinity and of the Incarnation, have the elegance and the persuasive power which I have always admired (if with incomprehension) as my colleagues in the Mathematics department at Exeter tried to argue for me the elements of topology. The gulf between admiration and whole-hearted acceptance was brought powerfully forward when I tried to unravel the Doctrine of the Incarnation to a Jewish friend of many years standing. He cut through my questions and expositions with characteristic clarity: "Are you telling me that if we were in Nazareth in the first century, you would take me by the arm and say, 'You see that young man—he's God you know'; is that what you're seriously saying?" It was, of course what I had long tried to say but the dilemma had been sharpened for me by his question. 'The Doctrine of the Incarnation' is an abstract enough phrase to be accepted or rejected in its own intellectual terms; 'that young man, he's God' has a wholly different resonance. Its purely intellectual content is the same as that of the theological doctrine but its demand upon our imagination and our emotional responses is wholly other.

How resolve the dilemma? The basic demand upon an orthodox Christian (as I am) is that 'Jesus of Nazareth', whether mirrored in poem, narrative, painting or sculpture shall be, in the words of the creed, 'Very God and Very Man'. The perception of this unity ('the Incarnation') will vary in its stress according to the quality and nature of the artist's belief. But however the element 'Very God' is conveyed, there cannot, if 'the Incarnation' is to have any meaning, be any dilution or avoidance of the second term, 'Very Man'. Somehow, in whatever medium, the total manhood, his actions and physical context, has to be realised—and this impelled me to the novel form. This, it seemed to me, gave the only full opportunity to

348

set Jesus within the living, breathing context of first-century Palestine, a turbulent occupied country, passionately concerned with the integrity of its faith and above all its commitment to *Torah*. In this quest I had determined on two constraints upon myself: that 'fiction' be kept to the minimum *dramatis personae* that would flesh out the day-to-day living of the Gospel characters (no illegitimate sonship of Herod, no marriage to Mary of Magdala!) and the use of as much of the material of the four Gospels as could be compassed within the bounds of the narrative.

*

Three of the biblical characters, the Capernaum centurion, Lazarus and Judas gave perhaps the greatest opportunity for narrative expansion—and incidentally provided me, in my recent re-reading, with some of the most surprising hints of both conscious and unconscious borrowing.

The centurion appears in the Gospels in a single incident, the sickness and cure of his batman from a serious illness, with the accompanying words of the synagogue elders: "he loves our people and built us our synagogue." This was confounding on close examination: a Roman centurion, wealthy and willing enough to build the Capernaum Jews their synagogue?—and if the ruins of the second-century synagogue, quarried from the first-century building were a reliable indication, he had expended a substantial fortune. An archaelogical note provides a clue. Two large blocks which appear to belong to the frieze above the door to the hall of worship have, carved on the one, a *menorah*, a seven-branched candlestick, and on the other a scallop-shell surrounded by a laurel wreath. The latter is the Roman decoration for outstanding bravery and in particular for saving the life of a superior officer.

The centurion now begins to be a tangible, a credible character in the story: a 'God-fearer'? of a wealthy family but exiled? It seemed to justify the creation of Justus who talks with Jeshua of the contrast between the *pax Romana* validated by force and *Torah*, that law, both divine and of the natural order, which carries a compulsion beyond the dictates of armed power.

"I think it is just possible I might learn to respect Rome." The young, so flexible mind was exploring strange waters—"but I wonder if I could ever love your 'Pax Romana' as I love 'Shalom'."

"And Torah?" . . .

"Torah! that is another matter, the voice of my Father, heard by my people throughout the long ages . . ."

*

Lazarus presented quite different problems. The main question had been posed for me many years before by Epstein. His sculpture in the ante-chapel of New College, Oxford sets both emotional and intellectual problems which seem to me to have been inadequately explored. Bound in the grave-wrappings, Lazarus appears, his head turned agonisingly back to the grave, to regret, even to resent his being drawn back to 'death's other Kingdom'. The family at Bethany is vividly drawn in the Gospel narrative, the characters nicely balanced against each other; the contemplative Mary, the hyper-active Martha and the silently brooding Lazarus. The return of Lazarus to his family from the grave would seem a merciful boon—but Epstein forbade me that resolution of the incident:

"After a long silence, Lazarus whispered, "Why? Why have you done this thing to me? . . . I have thought much about death and have feared the pain and the severing of bonds. I had never thought of death as tender and compassionate, a longed-for quiet . . .'"

*

Judas was quite another matter. He has always been viewed with peculiar horror, the two conclusions to his life, betrayal and suicide, arousing a dual revulsion, with (strangely to our minds, perhaps), the latter action consigning him, in mediaeval judgment, to the lowest hell. These centuries-old overtones made him a difficult subject for extended narration, though his character had teased my mind for over fifty years. I first wrote a one-act play—

350

now lost—for my Union Dramatic Society in 1934 and then recast it in Welsh for broadcasting on B.B.C. Wales. This version was based on a mediaeval Welsh manuscript and though I did not stress this aspect, the suggestion that Judas's evil nature was a consequence of his illegitimacy (a fictional supposition in the manuscript) caused some offence.

This time I treated the man more soberly. The first decision concerned the element of his name, 'Iscariot'; of the two derivations I chose 'Ish-Kerioth' ('Man of Kerioth' in the south) rather than the supposed link, through 'sicarius', with the 'dagger-people' or Zealots. This made him the one Judaean among a band of Galileans. Further, there were three 'theological' considerations to be coped with. The first was an aspect of the quality of Jeshua's knowledge as 'God Incarnate'—did he not know the nature of Judas when he joined the Twelve? The second has reverberations from the predestinarian doctrines through the centuries: was not Judas pre-ordained to betray the Son of God? The third contradicts or modifies both suppositions and explains the motive of the betrayal as Judas's attempt to force Jesus's hand, to declare himself the Messiah. I hope that my handling of his relationship with Jeshua may be assumed to be not mere evasion but an acceptance of the mysterious springs of motive which we share with the betrayer.

*

No man is without his preoccupation with death, its mystery and its permanent assault on his fragile security, and it assails even a child. 'Timor mortis conturbat me' is a realisation too precise, too negative for childhood but there comes the moment for most young people when the fact of death has to be faced. This was naturally in the life of Jeshua an important matter—after all the Incarnation was subject to the limitations of time.

Within the community of Nazareth the crafts would supply close and friendly relations and intimacies and I had early resolved that the Greek word *tekton*, usually translated 'carpenter', could legitimately be extended to embrace the other 'building trades'. To Joseph and Jeshua, therefore the related craft of the blacksmith would be significant. The death of Reuben the smith was Jeshua's first experience of this loss:

Rabbi Lazar was hurrying past the house and saw Jeshua in the doorway. 'Your friend Reuben has died . . .,' The women had been about their work and Reuben lay bound in his linen . . .

Jeshua approached the body and placed his palm on the forehead; it seemed for the briefest moment to stir but a cold inertness checked the caress of his fingers. 'This is not Reuben', he said and walked out into the sun, aware of his deprivation.

Now, at this point, I have to confess the insecurity of the writer's mind, that twilight between conscious and unconscious derivation. When I re-read that passage I realised its source in my own experience some seventy years before. This was its setting: my early home in Port Talbot was two doors away from that of Edward Howe (grandfather of Sir Geoffrey, our Foreign Secretary). Edward Howe was a powerful and highly respected trades-union leader, but it was a rare friendship that led to my frequent calls at 11 York Place to ask Miss Howe, his sister who kept house for him, "Can Mr Howe come out?" Solemnly and I believe almost wordlessly we walked around the block and I was then delivered to my home. But one morning Miss Howe replied to my question, "No, Mr Howe will never come out with you again. Would you like to see him?" I was led upstairs and looked long at the noble face but turned to Miss Howe and apparently said firmly, "That's not Mr Howe" and returned home to question my mother about death.

*

An element in the novel which some readers might find alien, ambiguous, is Jeshua's attitude to Roman power, a relationship muted and obscure in the Gospels. There, the main indications are in his requirement to 'render to Caesar' what is rightly his and in his confrontation with Pilate with its contrast between Roman and heavenly power—legions as against 'legions of angels'.

Jeshua's view of Rome must have been complex and perplexing and we can do no more than speculate on the social and political tensions in the early Christian community which led to the muted rendering of it in the Gospels. Some of the positive aspects of the relationship between the 'Word made flesh' and the greatest

352

contemporary secular power I tried to indicate in Jeshua's two dialogues with Justus the Capernaum centurion. The negative aspects, prefiguring the final conflict during the Passion, I placed early in the book, when Jeshua observed from a high crag the march of a century of soldiers from the coast to the Sea of Galilee:

> It was a sombre sight, the dark skins and darker accoutrements, the occasional gleam from spear-point or gladius-hilt, the uniformly blank gaze ahead and, as they passed close beneath the spur on which he sat, the regular tread of two hundred feet, a soul-less rhythm unlike anything in nature . . . Jeshua, who knew the broken scamper of sheep or goat-hoofs over stony uplands, the drumming of wild ponies in a panic surge or the clumping tread of yoked oxen at the plough, felt he had known nothing so inexorable, so dehumanising as this regular tread, unbroken, undeflected . . . He turned to the open hillside, grieving that something had been violated in his sense of man and of man's dignity.

*

'At the feet of Gamaliel' is a resonant phrase but it expresses a commonplace in the intellectual life of first-century Jewry. Gamaliel, Saul of Tarsus's personal tutor (*guru* would perhaps be a better term) was a remarkable man; grandson of the gentle Hillel, who was possibly one of the Temple elders astonished at Jesus's 'understanding and answers', Gamaliel exceeded even his grandparent's distinction, being one of a mere handful of doctors of the Law accorded the honourable title 'Rabban'. Saul of Tarsus, then, at that stressful and turbulent period of his young life when he was the leading enemy of the 'Nazarenes', had distinguished teaching in *Torah* in a compassionate tradition which must have accorded ill with his fiery temperament.

What, on the other hand, was the intellectual training and discipline of Jeshua? Brought up in the humble backwater of Nazareth, he would appear to be inevitably the social and intellectual inferior of Saul, a birthright-Roman, citizen of Tarsus, 'no mean city' as he himself boasted, and trained at the centre of

353

Jewry, in the Temple precincts. Yet at the age of twelve, Jeshua astonishes the learned of that Temple, not only by the quality of his answers but also in that more mature art of 'asking them questions'.

It is vain here to appeal to a peculiar "knowledge of Christ Incarnate", in Bishop Gore's phrase. We can accept no intellectual deceit in the Incarnation, a latent fund of divine knowledge on which Jesus of Nazareth could draw. Like the other inhabitants of Nazareth, he had to grow in knowledge, as, like them, he grew in stature.

There would be both synagogue and rabbi in Jeshua's Nazareth and from his earliest years until, at the age of twelve, he became an adult member of the *minyan*, the minimum number required to be present at an act of synagogue worship, he would be in the rabbi's mental and spiritual care. It is indeed difficult to overestimate the significance of the synagogue and the rabbinate in the moral life of the Jewish people and I hope that my portrait of Rabbi Lazar in *Jeshua* is not unfaithful to the nobility of this tradition, of devout worship and sound scholarship in the Law and the holy literature.

*

These scattered notes on my borrowings and imaginings have been only tangentially concerned with the over-riding problem of writing in extended narrative a life which has already been outlined in four of the most remarkable literary documents of the ancient world and been illuminated (and obscured) by nineteen centuries of theological speculation, centuries which have seen the formulation of creeds and the shaping of liturgies, the canonisation of learned saints and the condemnation of equally learned heretics.

It would seem at best a work of supererogation, at worst a shocking revelation of *hubris* to attempt such a narrative as *Jeshua*. And yet to-day would seem in many respects a peculiarly suitable time to attempt once more 'the quest of the historical Jesus'. On the one hand scholarship has explored the linguistics, the theology and the archaeology of the inter-testamentary years with especial penetration. Apart from the many acute commentaries on the Gospels that have appeared in our own day, books have appeared which have radically re-shaped our thinking; among many to which

I am indebted, I should single out three for my deepest gratitude: Geza Vermes, *Jesus the Jew* (1973) and the two magisterial works by Edward Schillebeeckx, *Jesus* (1974) and *Christ* (1975). This is scholarship become incandescent.

But there is another and sadder reason for venturing at this time. The gap between the reverent explorations of theologians and the perception of their significance by the 'man in the pew' is tragically wide—nor are their priests and pastors in much better case. To consider a blatant recent instance: one would have hoped that his remarkable Bampton Lectures, *The Glory of Man*, would have protected the present Bishop of Durham from the more crass attacks of those who should have read his expounding the mysteries of Christ's humanity and divinity. In his public utterances he assumed (unhappily wrongly) a sophisticated distinction, in the minds of his hearers, between metaphor, myth and historical fact in the expression of religious truth. Indeed, 'myth' has degenerated in the popular mind into the 'fanciful' or even the untrue, as though the Book of Job had humbler status than the Book of Judges, that *King Lear* was inferior in its truths to *King Henry the Sixth*, as though Homer and Virgil dealt in 'mere fiction'. Brought to the forefront of even naive minds, these would be seen as absurd propositions; yet the credal clauses, 'born of the Virgin Mary', 'on the right hand of God the Father' and indeed a host of other valid assumptions of belief, are regarded by many as assailed, devalued, if the appeal is made to metaphoric, mythic or analogic terms in their exposition. Faith must indeed be fragile to require such fortress defences.

But it is not the antipathies of theological minds, of heresy against orthodoxy, or even orthodoxy against orthodoxy, as the reasoning minds stress one aspect of revealed truth against another, that causes the greatest dislocation in contemporary belief. It is rather that since the seventeenth century, the status and content of the arts and the validity of revealed truth, both dependent on the 'creative imagination', have been subjected to exclusively analytic processes. Poets and articulate visual artists have attempted the rehabilitation of imagination; indeed, Wordsworth (in the thirteenth book of *The Prelude*) carried the attack into the opposing camp: for imagination, in his terms, is

Clearest insight, amplitude of mind,
And reason in her most exalted mood.

The church, however, for all its sporadic patronage of the arts, has seen them as almost entirely decorative or, at best, to be optional extensions of her worship. To put this at its most mundanely functional: the training of our parish priests almost wholly neglects the penetration of the mysteries by our poets, painters and sculptors; it would probably be a vain gesture to assert in this context that a single reading of *King Lear* would do more than a liturgical year of sermons to enable the worshipper to take upon himself 'the burden of the mysteries'.

This is, of course, special pleading on my part and it would be unseemly to claim that any writing of mine weighed substantially in the balance against the volumes of serious theology. But until we are prepared to admit the possibility that a play, a fresco, a volume of poetry, a symphony or a piece of sculpture, can lead us more nearly 'to see into the life of things' beyond the reasonings of the mind alone, then we shall be condemned to a perpetuation of our imaginative sterility.

*

Jeshua, a life of Christ, had led naturally to an exploration of St Paul's travels and thought until his death—and what better medium for that exploration than a collection of letters? (*A Bundle of Papyrus* is now published at the Gomer Press.) The next two themes to press upon me were the nature of prophecy and Israel's experiences of kingship; so, Elijah seemed to be the obvious subject to explore the power and the tribulation of prophecy (*Fire from the Heights* is now published) and the succession of Saul, David and Solomon gave to the regal theme a setting both noble and tragic; at its publication it will carry a title of some omen—*Upon the King*.

Three figures of even greater antiquity now demanded consideration, if my hope of examining the major biblical figures through the medium of the open and exploratory form of the novel or short story were to be fulfilled; these were Cain, Abraham and Joseph.

Cain had always seemed to me to be the most tragic figure in the story of the Fall of Man. Carrying upon his person the weight of

356

inherited guilt and its deep mystery, he carried also an almost equally crushing burden. For upon him fell the breaking of the soil, the claiming of land which would yield fruit when the perfection of Eden was denied. Cain was the tragic counterpart of his brother, Abel, who bore Israel's constant intuition that the shepherd was of more honour than the tiller of the soil.

And yet Cain seemed to me, in his toil at a thankless earth to be straining for a vision of an Eden re-inherited—hence this short narrative, of a man born to inherit his parents' guilt and to be the keeper of his brother's integrity.

Abraham enters a world of another dimension, crossing from the realm of myth into that of history. Essentially 'a wandering Aramean', his search is for a land to inherit and a God to worship and this dual search is ultimately a search for his own identity: who is Abram/Abraham? The land he finds and inherits; his God has a stature far exceeding the vision of his contemporaries.

Joseph's history gives him a startling relevance in our own day. He is the first great figure of the Jewish *diaspora*: sold into slavery in an alien land, he conquers the society of his exile but in inheriting the land of his Israelite alienation be is left with the search for his Israelite identity. The inheritance of all three figures, both tragic and noble, spans a history of more than five millenia. The reverberations of their struggle sound in the lands they inherited to this day.

These three narratives constitute one book, called *Inherit the Land* and at its completion I assumed I had finished the task. But once more Josef Herman entered my considerations: "Why not a book for the greatest of them all—Moses?" And so I am at work at the last of these 'biblical novels': *The Wilderness—Refining Fire.*

*

It was good to have returned to writing, when severe arthritis had made sculpting almost impossible and now that my five 'biblical novels' were almost completed, I felt the need to write 'secular novels'. Three of them are now finished, *Scale of Perfection*, three studies of the search for a perfect realisation of a dream; *Circlet of Gold*, a 'green' novel with North Welsh gold at its centre; and *The Inheritance*, a longer novel which explores the extension of

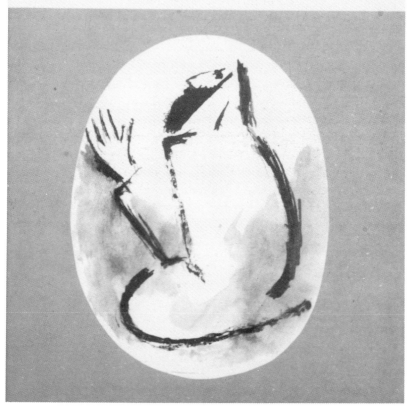

Joseph Herman's Jacket for *A Bundle of Papyrus*

358

inheriting a house and estate into the lives of three children; this gave me the opportunity of looking intently at two of my own particular obsessions, the theology of Duns Scotus and Spanish guitar music—yes, they do go quite happily together!

*

This has been a stimulating period of writing; the speculation now is the probability of my seeing all nine novels published.

Joseph Herman, Drawing for the Jacket of *Jeshua*

Colin Saxton, *Moelwyn Merchant* (pencil)

360

10

A KIND OF ENDING

Is this wise, this gazing into the mirrored pool? Narcissistic?—of course; we are all self-regarding but like Narcissus, not into a mirror but at a pool.

The pool is secret and remote, fringed and protected by willows; and the surface water, even to a little depth, is clear, appears sweet, unpolluted. But to write of the past involves not simply looking, but stepping into the pool, into the deeper water and stirring the silt. The sediment rises up into the clear water at the surface; the turbulence stirring about one's feet rises rapidly to cloud the clearer surface; the muddied ripples refract less light.

There are defences against recollection: one suppresses the bitterer memories but the scar-tissue remains. That child to whom (a child of five or six myself) I refused a sweet from the bag in my hand, a shameful betrayal; that manic schoolmaster for whom caning was the supreme pleasure—the memory still crawls.

The defences are defective. I can refrain from writing but during these weeks when I have recorded the surface memories, dreams have been troubling and the immediate waking moments have remained dark with the conflicts—the sediment denied.

No computer stores quite like this, nor retrieves without request.

*

As Macbeth comes to the end of his tragic course, he meditates on his premature disaster, the senescence of crime:

> My way of life
> Is fallen into the sere, the yellow leaf,
> And that which should accompany old age,
> As honour, love, obedience, troops of friends,
> I must not look to have.

361

Of these ultimate gifts, we probably treasure 'love' above the rest. 'Honour' and 'obedience' none of us may look to have as our right—looked for, they escape our grasp. But 'troops of friends'?

The sun is about to set as I write and in the increasing dusk as the clouds lower, they come crowding in, those friends: colleagues who understood the nature of learning and students who responded to their vision; craftsmen who retained their skills, sharply defined and wholly at their command; priests whose tranquil sanctity can be seen in the stillness of their eyes. Their presence, these friends, is not a presence 'over there', 'out there'; they are the texture of our lives, the substance that gives validity and power to what Thomas Hardy called "our tremulous stay".

*

Small memories come back, like the suckets and sorbets which punctuated the courses and refreshed the palate in an Elizabethan feast. One such brings Boston vividly to mind. A kindly librarian at the Folger Library, hearing that I needed to consult material at the Houghton Library in Harvard, commended me to a cousin, to stay for a night or two in Boston.

I arrived late and went soon to bed. The following morning at about seven, my bedroom door was opened and in danced a seven-year-old, whom I had missed the previous evening and she quickly leaped on the bed.

"Who are you?" was her question and I told her.

"Where do you come from?"

"From Wales."

There was a long pause and then comprehension:

"Do you know Moby Dick?"

*

One of the central instincts in ancient Hebrew belief is that of 'immortality' through the lives of children and grandchildren. Whatever agnosticism may be felt and expressed about personal life after death (and few people fail to share these moments of doubting with the Sadducees), the Jews and many others glory in the

362

extended immortality of one's heirs; the 'quiverfull', fruitfulness and multiplying express the riches of life to come.

This has been much in my mind in these last years. I believe that there will come a time out of time when I shall know even as I am known; but despite this faith, I am glad of the assurance that Christina and Paul and the three grandchildren extend my life with more grace and assurance than I have shown. And their skills and insights are so diverse: Helena, reading Mathematics in the University of Durham, is, so far as I can tell, the only truly numerate member of the family. She translates this skill (together with her elegant height) into her passion for campanology and I wonder if she will leave many bell-towers unvisited by the time she graduates.

Her even taller brother Owain runs truer to family form; a treble in the fine Leeds Parish Church choir, who needed only three weeks to return to the choir-stalls with a resonant bass voice. I sometimes wonder if his competence with the violin will similarly descend to the viola or 'cello. He is a member of both the National Youth Choir and the National Youth Theatre and threatens to become an actor.

Luke already shows American flairs and I envy him his explorations of primitive cultures, of archaeology and anthropology; I have no fears for him.

They are an exciting, competent lot and it would be good to share their next successes.

*

> Webster was much possessed by death
> And saw the skull beneath the skin . . .

Young Mr Eliot could afford such literary reminders of mortality, could even visit volumes more sanctified than Webster's:

> Donne I suppose was such another . . .
> He knew the anguish of the marrow,
> The ague of the skeleton.

Later in life we recognise the proposition that only a fool would not be 'much possessed by death', especially when he has spent his

363

capital, his seventy pieces of silver and is now moving into debt. 'Whispers of Immortality' have now an urgent sibilance and a fifteenth-century poet listened to the whisper at a deeper level of insight:

> Jesus Christ when he should die,
> To his father he gan say,
> 'Father' he said, 'in Trinity,
> *Timor mortis conturbat me.*'

Of what is this fear made and why are we all in some degree afraid of this last, this seemingly omnipotent enemy? One defence is evasion, never to say 'death', 'dead', 'die', 'He has passed away', we say; 'I have lost my husband.' At the most conscious level it is our permanent fear of deprivation, of the loneliness that besets every man. But there is anger too at the inequity of it all: that this child dies with almost all senses unawakened, all its experiences in the flesh denied; that man's inhumanity murders in war the young and vulnerable.

'What passing-bells for these who die as cattle?' Wilfred Owen's anger was to be silenced almost within sound of the bells of 'armistice', a silence which was to be nobly broken when Benjamin Britten joined his voice to Owen's in the *War Requiem* which prayed for all unjustly slaughtered.

We try so hard to mitigate the loneliness of death: that priest, a swift-spoken little Irishman in the old and notorious Bute Street district of Cardiff's dockland; a man had been fatally struck by a car and in his last moments had no breath for speech. The priest at his side held him securely: "If you're sorry for your sins, squeeze me hand"—and absolution was given and received.

And yet—the dread of loneliness or the anger we feel at the inequities of death leave unresolved the ultimate fear, *timor mortis*. Part of it, I feel sure, is our impatient bewilderment at the increasing joy we feel in everything about us, people, landscape, music, books and most of all, if we don't deceive ourselves, the increasing clarity of our minds, contrasted with the increasing decrepitude of what Hamlet calls 'this machine'. If only our bodies could have a garage servicing, a refit. Old age we feel should be a time of harvesting, of gathering the graces which life has so liberally given—and of course it is all that—but this machine?—sans this, that and the other, even 'sans everything'?

Hamlet leaves us in our familiar dilemma. In the nature of things death is an 'undiscovered country' and there is no way back, 'no traveller returns'. Perhaps the most fearful aspect of this knowledge is our assent to Hamlet's dying words, 'the rest is silence'. What will be 'speech' when the 'sharpness of death' is 'overcome'? Of one thing we can be sure; there is no more vain request than the Psalmist's:

> Lord, let me know mine end
> And the number of my days.

*

Is it some flaw in our nature that leads us so often to value the tentative, preliminary sketch more than the finished work? to cherish note-books, be they Turner's as he traced the evanescence of the clouds in his landscapes or the profound if fragmentary explorations of a Leonardo sketch-book? Is it a flaw, or a degree of humility, the recognition that fragments are all we merit?

It was a high moment of revelation—but so chastening—when I first saw Josef Herman's drawings of his 'Memory of Memories', gathering the fragments that remained of his Warsaw life. These fragments were all; no 'finished' work could emerge from them.

But a much later experience in that same studio was of another kind. Confronting us was a vision, beneficent but accusatory, which was a celebration of the women of Greenham Common and their protest at the obscenity of nuclear threats. The picture was massive, one of Josef's largest, and there were tragic contrasts within: to the left, a mother in a kind of protective ecstasy, holding a child in the air in front of her; balancing this figure and occupying the whole of the right-hand side of the picture, ranks of barbed wire, a fence to protect nuclear weapons that have the power to destroy the earth, against the depredations of unarmed women! There are depths in human stupidity that must surely arouse demonic laughter.

But if one took one's eyes from the large canvas one saw the preliminary studies: sketches that were not so much women as

365

'motherhood'; there were some lay-out designs and a gouache which defined most of the images in the finished picture. All these, Josef said, had preceded the preparation of the final version and gave a striking insight into the laboratory workings of an artist. I begged him to keep all these preliminary drawings together, partly because they were so fine in themselves, revealing the speed and sureness of the first insights and, perhaps even more important, as a 'running commentary' on the creative process itself, analogous to the successive drafts of a poem.

He threw this off with some laughter and deflected attention from his own painting with a characteristic dictum, the fruit of long and patient craft: "Do you know, a poor drawing can produce a fine painting but rarely does a fine drawing produce a fine painting—it often produces nothing at all but itself."

*

The storm has passed over the town and it is still clear enough daylight to give a brilliant translucence to my cloud-landscape. It is so tempting to put down the pen and say that this is the end of the story as I recollect it.

But I know that for the past two hours while the sun alternated with heavy storm and the clouds created continents and islands beyond the surrounding hills, I have been cheating—cheating you and myself. For in 'gathering the fragments' I have been postponing what is simply not there to be postponed. This book is not a novel to be tied up neatly in a final chapter; for no human being can there be the satisfactory cry, 'Consummatum est', for there is no completing, no finishing. I suppose it is arguable that the massive and complex creativity of Leonardo has a certain completeness, a fulfilment; that Picasso in our own day explored so many aspects of the human condition that his work has a kind of symmetry, a totality; and it would appear that Shakespeare, at the age of forty-eight, said to himself, "I have written what I wished to write" and retired for a very few last years to Stratford. But those final plays of 'losing and finding', of tragic loss and reconciliation, are perhaps themselves deceptive. For why had the reconciliation to be repeated? Why Leontes, Hermione and Perdita, 'the lost one' and

366

almost at the same time, Prospero and the marvelling Miranda? Would not either *A Winter's Tale* or *The Tempest*, each with its recovery of grace and joy after tragic loss, do for an ending? And why does Shakespeare so often hint that five acts were not enough to produce an ending; that we must leave the theatre and experience in our own imagining the sixth act beyond the play—as Malcolm has to restore Scotland, as England has to live, under reluctant rulers, after the deaths of Lear and Cordelia, as *Love's Labour's Lost* explicitly demands a return to the stage twelve months after the close of the fifth act and our departure from the theatre?

It seems we cannot end; we simply cease to speak as we recognise the vanity of our attempt to round off our life, to make of it a unity as valid as a work of art.